What Can I Write About?

7,000 Topics for High School Students

Second Edition

Revised and Updated

Based on the Original by David Powell

National Council of Teachers of English
1111 W. Kenyon Road, Urbana, Illinois 61801-1096

Staff Editors: Kurt Austin, Zarina Hock, Tom Tiller

Book Design: Tom Jaczak

NCTE Stock Number: 56541-3050

©2002 by the National Council of Teachers of English.

Library of Congress Cataloging in Publication Data
What can I write about? : 7,000 topics for high school students.— 2nd ed., rev. and updated.
    p. cm.
"Based on the original by David Powell."
Rev. ed. of: What can I write about? / David Powell. c1981.
  ISBN 0-8141-5654-1 (pbk.)
  1. English language—Composition and exercises. 2. Creative writing (Secondary education) I. National Council of Teachers of English. II. Powell, David, 1934- What can I write about?
  LB1631 .P66 2002
  808'.042'0712—dc21
                  2002015465

Contents

Acknowledgment

We are deeply grateful to David Powell for creating the first edition of this book more than two decades ago. Although we have brought the twenty-first century into the book, his framework and many of his original ideas remain. It is for this reason that we have retained David Powell's preface to the first edition and most of his introductory comments to individual chapters.

Preface to the First Edition

The question all composition students ask—"What can I write about?"—is answered more than 7,000 times in this volume. The teacher in search of assignments can simply glance down any page of a desired category of writing and see countless ideas spring forth. Appeals are made throughout the book to a comprehensive range of interests, knowledge, experience, feelings, and thoughts; there is an abundance of "something for everyone." Furthermore, mind being limitless, these topics passed on from teacher to students should suggest to all students (not just the inquisitive or imaginative ones) still other ideas they can identify with, many of which they may come up with on their own. Certainly one of the first aims of teaching is to bring students to self-discovery, and it is no small accomplishment if, by looking outside, students are brought to look within themselves.

Notes heading each of the chapters in *What Can I Write About?* briefly define the different kinds of writing, tell how to write them, and indicate how the book may be used to locate topics suited to them, leaving little need for formal classroom instruction. The best (and perhaps the happiest) teacher may be the one who has the least to say.

David Powell

Foreword

Revising and updating a successful book is no easy matter. In the first edition of this book, David Powell gave us a rich array of topics—some apparently simple but surprisingly complex and some so unusual as to make us sit up and think about a myriad of related subjects—topics so varied that it was difficult to know which ones to delete when the Acquisitions editors, Kurt Austin and Tom Tiller, and I began updating the book. We knew that teachers loved that first edition and used it enthusiastically. We also knew, however, that many dynamic changes had taken place in the United States since the book was written—that our classrooms, our demographics, and our universe are all radically different from what they were a few decades ago. Educational concepts of literacy, of inquiry, and of making meaning have also widened and shifted. Our challenge, then, of was to mirror here the diversity, the interests, the media, the technology, and the issues that so profoundly affect our students' lives today. We have captured these in some measure; indeed, in some cases a topic appears in more than one chapter, thus reminding the user that there are many ways to approach the same subject. Now it is for you, the teacher, and you, the student, to take these topics and genres as starting points and to go from there to discover and explore ideas that will intrigue you; that will fire your imagination; and that will help you write well because you are engaged in a meaningful enterprise.

Zarina M. Hock, Director of NCTE Book Publications & Senior Editor

1 DESCRIPTION

What Description Is

For our purposes here, we might say that to describe something—object, emotion, thought, event, and on over the horizon of human experience—is to surround it with words, much the way lines shape the subject of a drawing. The Greek root of the word "scribe" is instructive. It means to scratch, or sketch an outline. Often, in description, that implied lightness of touch can be important. We should seek to surround our subject—not so much to capture it (and least of all to annihilate it) as to liberate it, let it stand forth in a new fullness and freshness. Descriptive writing can free its subject from itself, from the obscurity of experience, and in the same stroke bear it to a life larger than the words surrounding it. The words should not draw attention to themselves; rather, they should scratch a descriptive network so tough and resilient it can spring the subject free of its own description. But description can also come from piling rich detail after detail, yet never getting so carried away that your description becomes what critics call "purple prose." However you paint your picture, the details make it come alive.

How to Write Description

Good descriptive writing is first of all concrete. Search out the telling detail, the essential characteristic, then nail it down. But the warning above applies here as well: the subject must be nailed down without stabbing it to death. We are not out to pin dead dry bugs to a board. Keep them alive. Keep them moving. This is best done with verbs and nouns. When we run on to a chasm between the verb and the noun, we can throw an adjective like a lifeline, or a bridge, between the two, always remembering, though, that such connections are seldom strong enough to support a sentence.

Look, for example, at N. Scott Momaday's opening description of a plain in Oklahoma, in "The Way to Rainy Mountain" (first published in *The Reporter*, 1967). His words vividly capture the landscape with its "brittle and brown grass," and "its writhing, steaming foliage." As he paints his picture, you become the observer in this landscape: "Your imagination comes to life," says Momaday even as he brings the scene to life. The topics offered below encourage the students to use their imaginations. Personal experience, books, videos, and the Internet are among the texts that students will look at as they explore a topic. Let the imagination run free; but finally mold it through carefully chosen words.

Locating Subjects for Description

Description is clearly one of the broadest kinds of writing. Just about any subject listed in this book could inspire a descriptive passage. Descriptive writing is, by way of example, sometimes fundamental to creative and narrative writing. This would, then, be an appropriate time to begin to regard this book as a whole and to move, by directing the assignments to students, freely from part to part. The subjects in the present chapter will be productive for descriptive writing exercises of all kinds, but the book strives to become, as a whole, a descriptive network not unlike the one we have described above, outlining, however lightly, the power and possibility of writing.

Nature and Natural Settings

Describe:

a morning rain

snow falling on a city street

a rainstorm over the ocean

sleeping in a tent in the woods

the desert by day

the desert by night

outer space

a fallen tree, dead or still growing

the wilderness next door

the wilderness in the garden

a blend of mist, geese, sky, and water

the spirit, atmosphere, and tone of a natural place

how the earth looks to someone from outer space

a sunflower

a muddy road

walking beans

detasseling

weeding a garden

gathering firewood

the center of a cyclone

a view of Mount Kilimanjaro or Mount Fuji

running rapids

an apple tree, a cherry tree, a chinaberry tree, a mul-
berry tree, a banyan tree

a mangrove swamp

a bamboo grove

a coral reef

the Everglades

April showers

March winds

the Grand Canyon, perhaps by concentrating on its
colors, the order of description determined by the
change of colors with the season

the natural scenes seen by Native Americans in North
America before the Pilgrims arrived (or before the
early explorers arrived)

some natural object that suggests something else or
someone else

"my territory"

something sight unseen

"under the sun"

a school walk in the mountains, slippery with rain

a part of (or something on) the Mississippi as Mark
Twain saw it

the landscape as seen from a descending parachute

a mountaintop as seen from it

a mountaintop as seen from the ground

a branch of madder

the "roof of the world"

a pre-dawn morning

"down-under" skies

fire on the water

a lonely mesa

a watering hole

a Peruvian landscape

a sunset on the river

a natural bridge

a dust storm

a tornado approaching

the dark side of the moon

the surface of Mars

ice thawing on a pond

sledding

a windstorm

a place named Windy

a sun-pounding day

the call of the Rocky Mountains

the lure of the sea

treacherous waters

a path off the trodden path

signs and seasons

the sun or moon as a rider of the sky

the beginning of the world

the world as split open and seen from the inside

shadowy, mysterious trails

an approaching storm

a rainbow of flowers

dandelion season

walking in the rain

a road not taken

catching the dawn

catching a falling star

"my woods"

a volcanic eruption

a wildfire

bringing the country to the city

the little picture in nature

the big picture in nature

a winter wonderland

redwood trees

infinity as evidenced in nature

color and light in nature

a snow in May

coming to life in the spring

sand castles

riding in mist

an early snow/a late snow

first monsoon rain

the desert after a rainstorm

a tropical storm

a sunny day

a smiling sky

winds that don't let up

tides

the "your land" part of "This Land Is Your Land"

the ending of the day

a catwalk over a rockwall canyon, over thundering water

an idyllic setting that conveys a certain mood

a setting with the title of a famous book (such as *A Tree Grows in Brooklyn*)

the quality of a natural setting by way of some aspect of it

unexplored territory that is terrifying

the outdoors taken inside

jogging on a beach

the most beautiful sunset you've ever seen

the view from atop Mount Rainier (or any other mountain)

the grandeur of Mount Everest

the Earth as "a little island of Creation amid the circumambient Void"

the Earth, as approached via spaceship by friendly extraterrestrials

vegetation growing through the cracks of an abandoned house

Iguazú Falls (bigger than Niagara Falls)

Where the Sidewalk Ends (name of children's book)

pleasure gardens

country roads

the view from a hilltop overlooking a great city

an artificial environment that intrudes on a natural setting

magnificent treasures or scenery available to the beachcomber

the same scene today contrasted with that seen by another writer years ago

snow in the forest (as if you are there in it)

a natural world "charged with the grandeur of God" (G. M. Hopkins)

a honeycomb (as seen scientifically and then as seen nonscientifically)

some natural object as for someone who has never seen one (say, a tree or a certain kind of cloud)

"the Pleiades in a silver row"

a natural setting *beyond* the commercial description of it

a natural setting as seen by a microscopic eye

the indifference of nature

an everyday occurrence in nature

Where the Wild Things Are (name of children's book)

a small island in a huge, rough sea

Creature Life

Describe:

a litter of newborn puppies

a slug moving on the sidewalk

an eel swimming

a shark eating

the biggest snake

spiders swinging from their threads

cockroaches scurrying for cover

a home where the buffalo roam

butterflies/fireflies by the thousands

mosquitoes in Paradise

circus animals

an ant with a grain of sugar

an animal that eats humans

a fox seeing a movement in the grass

a nest of field mice

a grouse running

a chicken coop

the caw of a crow

birds at a birdfeeder

a grizzly bear with its cubs

an ant colony

fish in an aquarium

a bloated tick

a bird feeding its young

a trick pony

otters playing on a riverbank

a water bird prying open a shell

a dragonfly

a grasshopper jumping a bumblebee gathering pollen

a gorilla eating a banana

a squirrel burying a nut

a family of chimpanzees grooming one another

geese in flight

a duck landing on a lake

two lion cubs playing

a bird building a nest

a house cat stalking a bird

a mother bird defending its nest

a hummingbird feeding from a flower

a cattle roundup

wild mustangs

animals fleeing from the enemy (man or beast)

the flight of an eagle

weightless birds resting on reeds

a homeless, hungry dog

Texas or Alaska mosquitoes

a snapshot of a beloved pet

insects seeking sanctuary from humans

a praying mantis praying

flamingos in flight

a whale leaping into the air

a bird colony

a civilization of insects in one room

the path of a turtle across the road

an endangered species

a walking fish

animals in battle to the death

animals fleeing from a fire

a Yellowstone bear hunting food

a dog that is the subject of a Beware-of-the-Dog sign

an animal (or an animal scene) in a medieval bestiary

the tiger as an image of awesomeness

a household dominated by pet cats or dogs

a civilized, almost-human, animal

gerbils jockeying for position in a revolving, circular cage

gorillas in the mist

the lamb as an image of innocence

the kestrel hawk (the windhover) as an image of something that does the difficult with great ease

scene at a dog obedience school

an animal adopted by one from another species

wildlife on the Serengeti Plain

Human Beings, Individuals

Describe someone:

who does as he/she pleases

who tells you more than you want to know about one subject or another

who is "chicken" about one thing or another

who delights in order

who delights in disorder

who wants a tourist to take his/her picture

who is homesick

who is superior to others but does not try to show it

who has an inferiority complex

who epitomizes dignity

whose fate is a far less happy one than predicted

who works just to be busy

who hates anyone who does not love him/her

who is a good-natured egotist

who is too hot, or too cold, to handle

who has, in character, many contradictions

who is an authority about something or someone he/she has no interest in or liking for

who is a seeker

who can't take criticism

who follows fads

who is double-jointed

who is a late bloomer

who opposes something without understanding it

who writes up the national psychological and vocational examinations

who is a "living legend"

who is oracle, sage, and know-it-all

who is the ultimate fan

who is left speechless

who has a short fuse

who "says little, thinks less, and does nothing at all" (quotation from George Farquhar)

who is trying to look sober but is not

who would rather give up life than material possessions

who has a mad impulse

who is a pragmatist

who is lonely

who is at a loss for words

who behaves like a deranged and frightened Ichabod Crane

who loves tattoos

who has only one idea, and that one a wrong one

who is a pebble on the beach, one of the crowd

who is in spirited conversation with himself/herself

who is a compulsive taker of notes

who tries to appeal to everyone

whose identity is revealed only at the end of your description

who is shrewd

who is one of those who will "inherit the earth"

who always says, "Let's get serious."

who is a saver or collector

who recycles compulsively

who is an unofficial psychoanalyst

who is expert at avoiding serious commitment

who has to settle for a second choice

who is just learning self-respect

who is on a soap box

who is "worth watching"

who is like his or her pet

who is in love with love

who has an unusual habit

who has an unusual interest

who is free again

who has gambling fever

who looks intelligent

who looks wealthy

who looks poor

who looks tragic

who looks self-pitying

who cuts into line

who takes herself too seriously

who should have quit while he was ahead

who is mean to animals

who lives underground

who lives in a tree

who rages at God whenever something goes wrong
(such as bad weather)

who is an actor without an audience

who has too little to do

who behaves characteristically

who is like Bartleby, a fictional character who says only,
"I would prefer not to."

who is a "roads" scholar, a wanderer

who is always "the one in charge"

who sings while at work

who is always first with the worst

who is shaped by experience

who is "crazy like a fox"

who is a pied piper

who succeeds exceptionally well in something he or she
does not seem suited for

who has no enemies

who has no friends

who is a "city-slicker" in the country

who behaves spontaneously

who is a quick study, a superb mimic

who suffers from the effects of someone else's trying to
break a bad habit

who is in heart but not in sight

who likes to dance

who is all business

who is dressed up to scare

who knows how to answer the question "How lazy can
you get?"

who learns everything without help

who has only initials as a name

who is a name-dropper

who is a troublemaker

who is a busybody

who is a heartbreaker

who is a daredevil

who is a class clown

who is a "dark horse"

who is without vices

who is without a single virtue

who appears, but is not, intelligent

who appears, but is not, ignorant

who is an advocate

who monopolizes conversations

who is one of a kind

who is his own man/her own woman

who is misguidedly zealous

who has a force or energy born of terror

who is like his or her residence

who is undeservedly famous

who is undeservedly infamous

who is pretending to like you

who is obsessed with you

who doesn't have a clue

who thinks he's/she's God's gift to women/men

who can't cope

who tries too hard

who wishes she could start all over

who is brave in spite of an obstacle to bravery

who is a freelancer at something

who is tight-lipped

who is a "wonder of wonders"

who is "programmed"

who is ageless

who is self-consciously middle-aged

who is a wayfaring stranger

who is poetry in motion

whose behavior is controlled by conditioning

who is responsible for having changed your life

who is a hermit in the city

who is outlandish

who is a great impostor

who tries to stay on a diet

who tries to give up smoking

who tries to give up drinking

who characteristically over-reacts

who is right off the comics page

whose main weakness is _____

whose main strength is _____

who is an angel

who has escaped from prison

who is a high-roller

who is flaky

who runs the wrong way

who is seeking the unattainable

who is a workaholic

who is "strange"

who is a born leader

who is a born follower

who is in a shaky position

who is prematurely old

who is cute (or "cutesy")

who is, though grown, a baby

who is godlike

who is a "good person"

who has the gift of gab

who never confesses to losing an argument

who has "coffee nerves"

who has "nicotine fits"

who delivers jeremiads

who is spoiled by success

whose name and personality match exactly

who can't tell the truth

who is at war with herself

who can't say "I'm sorry"

who can't stop talking

who can't stand to lose

who can't stand to be alone

who has a special gift

who is like a chameleon in personality

who is describing himself/herself only by what he/she sees in a mirror

who is a caricature

who feels discouraged because of having suffered in a natural disaster

who, even if not known, ought to be Man/Woman of the Year

who, even if not known, ought to be Student of the Year

who is confused by the world but not worried about it

who has a face and manner of authority

who wears "the smile of God"

who is a modern Sphinx

who has absolute confidence

who can see though blind

who is coming to terms with the fact of death

who is a double for someone else

who is an "All-American" type

who is obsessed by TV

who is tied up in knots

who is used up or burnt-out

who is blissfully unaware

who is austere

who is a scapegoat

who is "cool"

who is egotistical

who has a hidden talent

who is eccentric

who is a good judge, though without experience

who is a picture-straightener

who is a perfectionist

who is in need of special attention

who is "always around"

who is "never around"

who is a high-climber

who is just now finding a voice

who never gives in

who delivers tedious speeches or sermons

who is "asleep at the switch"

who is a "wolf in sheep's clothing"

who is an outsider or a pariah

who is a master fundraiser

who is utterly imperturbable

who is easily perturbed

who has a name that sometimes causes accidental humor

who is hopeful of catching a fish

who is hopeful of finding the right job

who has incorruptible scruples

who is in prison for political reasons

who is exhausted almost to the point of death

who has noble qualities

who knows what it's like to be alone

who doesn't know how to be happy

who loves the rain

who believes he was a dog in a past life

who has a lot to learn

who stops to smell the roses

who is compulsively clean

who is a non-heroic figure

who can be characterized by speech mannerisms

who has a voice "like a great bell swinging in a dome" (quotation from James Elroy Fletcher)

who is a scholar of esoteric subjects

who is a member or a joiner

who has (in the words of John Ford) "shaked hands with time"

who is nameless

who dares/who "dares not" do something

who is capable of inspiring confidence

who is exotic

who is a saint

who loves the stage (as observer, or as performer)

who has many kinds of deep troubles

who is a lover of the country

who is an audience of one

who speaks to one person as if to an audience

a relative or a close acquaintance

someone as the god or goddess of something

a pickpocket in action

a control freak

the child in you

someone you love to hate

someone with a "singing face" (quotation by John Fletcher)

a child in the White House

someone trying to sleep when it is impossible to sleep

a reluctant Santa Claus

someone who expresses an opinion without thinking

a great person known to you

a lunatic employer

a lunatic principal

someone surviving the winter

someone with a distinctive laugh

someone who is uncommonly shy . . . who laughs, for example, with great embarrassment at just about anything

someone surviving a great public embarrassment

someone who is ostracized

someone who is too conscious of his/her best profile

someone before and after

someone hard to catch, hard to conquer

an uninvited guest

someone who is lovable and loving

someone who is unorthodox

someone throwing a tantrum

someone who is an authority on a wide range of obscure subjects: for example, derbies, hieroglyphs, praying mantises

a first-time Broadway playwright awaiting first reviews

someone who is a "clear-cut choice"

someone who has the lowdown on someone

someone who has retained elegance and charm

the president as through the eyes of a child

what *your* inferiority complex is like

the child in someone

an heir

a wild public celebration

the unknown soldier/the unknown citizen

a bouncer

a broken individual

your interview with a famous person

someone in the moment before death

a veteran

someone shopping online

someone who lurks on the Internet

someone who gossips compulsively

someone who is self-consciously kind

a night security guard at work

someone who would like to harm you

someone watching something intently

an IRS official as seen by a reluctant taxpayer

a reluctant taxpayer as seen by an IRS official

the thing in you that others admire

someone who is unknowingly self-revealing

someone surviving the loss of the savings of a lifetime

someone surviving the failure of an important examination

someone rushing to catch a bus

someone suddenly realizing he or she is late

someone reacting to an unfunny joke

someone reacting to a speech

someone suddenly remembering something

yourself as you were at one time

someone, such as a small child, who can get dirty where no dirt is

someone who walks hundreds of miles to prove love to the one waiting at the destination

someone in despair

"someone I ought to know better"

someone who "wrote the book" on _____

the top-sergeant, still more active than the recruits after more than thirty years of military service

someone who has weathered *everything*

an underdog who likes the role of underdog

someone real or fictional who is a slumbering giant awakening

someone who is made up of many different parts, all of which are funny

someone who laughs at everything

someone who cries at everything

someone who needs a good talking to

someone who knows how to keep a secret

an unusual child whom you met on a trip

someone who disproves the following: "No one can read the comment behind an expression."

a petty bureaucrat

a painting—say, "The Blue Boy" or the "Mona Lisa"—come to life

a person who uses ceremonial language for any occasion

Hagar as a living type

Senator Dianne Feinstein

Muhammad Ali as a legend in his lifetime

Thomas Jefferson at home

a once-maligned person who is lauded now

a once-lauded person who is maligned now

a globe-trotter

a person described as though by William Faulkner

a thinker/dreamer

someone who is fascinated with the ordinary

a shallow person/a dull person

someone with a long comic history invented by you

someone who has beaten the odds

someone who was right there where it happened at the time it happened

yourself as others see you

someone who is politely, coolly efficient

someone who is shy only because of being too proud to risk being made a fool of

any famous modern person as a child

yourself as in the first moment of your birth

Bill Clinton

Senator Hillary Clinton

Tiger Woods

Madonna

a psychic

The Williams sisters (tennis champions)

Mephistopheles as a living type

someone made hesitant or too cautious by a bad experience

Human Beings, Groups

Describe:

world response to Princess Diana's death

the public's fascination with John Kennedy Jr.

autograph hunters

paparazzi

Pope John Paul II's appeal to the masses

Mother Teresa's impact

reverence for a local "saint"

soldiers in the face of battle

evangelical preachers

people celebrating a special occasion

soup kitchens

dj's

wanderers, wayfarers, nomadic peoples

snowboarders

skateboarders

ski bums

surf bums

people who go into the witness protection program

professional wrestlers

people who live in retirement

ranchers

bikers

game show hosts

houseguests

people who believe they have been abducted by aliens

people who follow fashion

people who ignore fashion

people who aren't aware of their surroundings

stock car drivers

Trekkers

Rocky Horror Picture Show fans

Star Wars fans

video game players

political demonstrators

soccer hooligans

Harley riders

beauty pageants

celebrities and the media

a daytime talk-show audience

a neighborhood (or a city, or a country) who has its own personality

a bullfight crowd

an enthusiastic opera crowd

everybody trying to get into the act

people with multiple tattoos/piercings

sightseers

a séance

a teenage dance

a political convention

a private club

a metropolitan bus station

people who carry their pasts around

people who leave their pasts behind

the early Vikings

listeners when a joke falls flat

rabid fans

prisoners

bored teens living in suburbia

people who help others

a retirement community

kids playing in a sandbox

an ethnic neighborhood

people who visit

lunch dates

a spring-break beach

an all-week party

people at Bingo Night

the rat race

an SRO crowd

pie-judging contest at the county fair

a POW camp in the United States

a Japanese internment camp in the U.S. during WW II

a slave auction

a citizen protest

an old-fashioned talent show

people who make every day a holiday

muscle flexers

sorority/fraternity party

an amusement-park crowd

a sidewalk sale/a fire sale/a rummage sale

a hog-calling contest

Londoners during wartime attack

American citizens immediately after the 9/11 terrorism

the gates of heaven

the gates of hell

much ado about something

much ado about nothing

the end of the world

a hometown celebration

a wedding party

the delivery room of a hospital

people in the streets of Paris during the French Revolution

people in the streets of Paris celebrating the end of World War II

group therapy

a concert

ice-hockey players

pop music concert audience

political activists

a snowed-in airport

people at the fall of the Berlin Wall

the crowds on Fifth Avenue or some other famous New York City thoroughfare

baseball announcers

the crowded stands at the Super Bowl

pedestrians, traffic, and the resulting confusion when all try to cross a small bridge at the same time

the Bolshoi Ballet

the ceremony at the beginning of a bullfight

a poor singer of the national anthem before a baseball game

the Gold Rush

Bohemians at home

a shantytown

the lost-luggage room of a major airline

an athletic team for which nothing goes right

a bilingual theater troupe

"just a big mess," anywhere

kids on the last day of school

teachers on the last day of school

the subway as hell

the firefighters'/police officers' ball

a "blended" family

a crowded beach

a sleepy village and its inhabitants

people saying goodbye

a "country on the brink of democracy"—riots, troops in the streets, etc.

the scene-behind-the-scenes for a certain film production

a big publishing house

newsroom of a major newspaper

a county fair

a demolition derby

a night club crowd as *you* see the people

"unpersons"

missing persons

people invisible to society

Places and Things

Describe:

your favorite museum

table scraps; leftovers

the packaging of your favorite CD

a burning barn

a ghost town

a favorite meal

the bottom of the Grand Canyon

a recycling center

a ski resort

a fully packed jumbo jet

a time capsule from today

a time capsule from 1980

a time capsule from 1990

a new hybrid fruit or vegetable (that you invent)

a food you hate

a food you love

a rusty fire escape

an overflowing dumpster

a barren landscape

a flooded basement

a dry riverbed

a desert in spring

the view from a train window

a hidden treasure

a public notice

a polling booth in Florida

a historical document

stained-glass windows

a particular painting

a "speakeasy" of Prohibition times

a roadside attraction

a box of rotting produce

a basket of laundry

a messy desk

a sink full of dishes

a cluttered basement

a misty morning

a long day

a favorite childhood toy

a dentist's office

a leather jacket

a rare gem
a fragile vase
a stolen moment
a swaying footbridge
your bedroom
your favorite place
view from the Sears Tower
view from the Empire State Building
on first seeing Ground Zero (New York City)
view from the Eiffel Tower
on first seeing the ruins of Machu Picchu
a condemned hotel
a lost-and-found office
Main Street
hand-me-downs
a bowl of cherries
a double-dip ice-cream cone
a locked box
a piece of ancient metalwork
a tapestry
an ancient book
a certain architectural style
a wrecking yard; a car dump
a deserted stage
the world in a grain of sand
a ferry boat carrying twice the number of passengers it
     should
a place named Easy Street
a ship passing by
something close-up and then faraway
the scene from the inside
the scene as viewed by the Statue of Liberty
the scene from a lighthouse
the view from the St. Louis Arch
the view from Seattle's Space Needle
something that is sterile in appearance
the lure of old almanacs and diaries
a book by its cover
a black book/an address book
the sense of being there where it happened—e.g., at
     Omaha Beach or Pompeii
an iconic image in a dorm poster
a mystical setting, using mystical terms
what's in a purse
what's in a backpack
what's in an old trunk in the attic
what's in a pirate's sea chest
what's inside a home on the Aegean Islands/Aran
     Islands
a pawn shop

a single-room schoolhouse
a sandbox
Air Force One
something without revealing what it is until the end
a quiet place
a shopping mall
bumper stickers
t-shirt messages
license plate messages
a campground
Woodstock (whichever one you choose)
graffiti
after the wrecking ball strikes
animal shelters
a sound bite
your grandmother's kitchen
a place that's mournful
an overgrown orchard
a weedy alley
a place that frightens children
a place that is too quiet
an empty city lot with a secret
a cheese shop that has run out of cheese
a library in the middle of the night
a shopping mall the day after Thanksgiving (or the day
     before Christmas)
an old-age home
an orphanage
the dust under the carpet
a medal
a reflection
a mirage
a cellar full of canned goods
a soup kitchen
a waterbed
a jewelry store
new sneakers
new braces
a gimmick
a city you consider to be cosmopolitan or glamorous,
     e.g., Las Vegas, Paris, New York
cereal-box surprises
The Book of _____
a work and hobby bench
something Byzantine
the inside of a doorknob
signs of the times—road signs, etc.
a golf course that has some unusual hazard
a *pentimento* painting
a palimpsest

what you see from the top of _____
the land passing by as you stand on a ship
the scene from the balcony
the scene from the back seat
the scene from the top of the Washington Monument
something that is dingy
something that glitters
Hell as if it were a certain city
items in a house abandoned years ago
the last book
an image from yesterday
velvet paintings
the view from the bottom of a swimming pool
an abandoned well
a rock quarry
a construction site
a house made of glass
a luxury doghouse
a costume shop
a king's palace
St. Augustine, Florida, the oldest city in the United States
Mesa Verde
Bath, England, as it was in the Middle Ages or before
a glass menagerie
a mystical setting, using concrete terms
what's in a medicine cabinet
a bell
a dilapidated boat
an unusual house
the local bookstore as a hangout
a single-room house
a soldier's home
a door
a map
a Viking ship
a shelter
an oil spill
your imaginings about a city you'd like to visit but never will
a future no one expects
a picnic
the scene after a parade
the scene after a party
a huge foreign city
a small efficiency apartment
the underside of a damp log
the contents of a buzzard's nest
your bare foot, as experienced by an ant
the inside of an old coat pocket

a piano abandoned at a junkyard
a bicycle left outside all winter in Minnesota
a vacant lot
a barn fallen into disrepair
Salvation Army shop window
what you imagine the _____s [decade] to have been like
deserted downtowns
a greasy-spoon cafe
a town dump
the last place on earth
old haunts
a city street at 5:00 a.m.
a crowded subway station
a cramped city bus
an empty church

Senses, Intangibles

Describe:

having an itch
sneezing
hiccupping
waking up
falling in love
falling asleep
getting dizzy
a bad headache
a paper cut
riding in a hot-air balloon
early-morning sounds
electronic music
Sunday smells
aromas on entering a coffee shop
smell of hops
smell of wet wool blankets
what you feel when you look into outer space
a certain musical style
the joy of playing a certain musical instrument
"a shining artistic achievement"
serenity
time/timelessness/eternity
sounds and sights in the moment between waking and sleeping (or between sleeping and waking)
your best friend's laugh
a pregnant pause
your dog's personality
the sound of a snowstorm
God
the Goddess

the "indescribable" by using unusual terms

the sixth sense

"more than a feeling"

nausea

physical manifestations of anxiety

springtime scents

"winter dreams"

the ever-changing flame of a candle

a dream house as a house that one has dreams in

an impulse or a compulsion

a situation that admits of ambiguity or ambivalence

the face of hope

the face of despair

the misery of _____

"sublime noise" (E. M. Forster's allusion to Beethoven's *Fifth Symphony*)

ominous silence

something "full of sound and fury"

a kind of hush

a "dirge without music" (Millay's term)

a pompous speech

being alone in outer space

Fourth of July spent in a foreign country

Christmas away from home

"shaking the spheres of the universe"

"the music of the spheres"

"the splendour of a sudden thought" (quotation from Robert Browning)

feeling free (in the sense of *unrestrained*)

a dream within a dream

flying in a dream

the dreamlike quality of something

the feeling you have when you dream you're awake

what it feels like to survive an accident or close call

the physical aspects of feeling furious

holding a purring cat

what gravity feels like

the intangible quality of something

surfing a wave

surfing the Web

virtual reality

déjà vu

a dream come true before the dream is dreamed

"a dream deferred" (Langston Hughes)

"I have a dream" (Martin Luther King Jr.)

the action and thought of an instant's time

it (*or* It)

a gesture which has deep meaning

a state of mind

"not with a bang but a whimper" (Eliot)

where _____ begins

listening in nature

the joy of solitude (as recorded in a diary)

"unbearable lightness"

terrible beauty

Actions/Miscellaneous

Describe:

a favorite kind of job

a bureaucratic operation

sticking together

mending a fence with someone

beaming signals

something comforting

the turn of the screw

breaking the glass ceiling

learning to ride a bike

rolling down a hill

teaching something to a child

how to blow a bubble with bubblegum

the steps involved in getting to know someone

how to play your favorite computer game

getting home after your curfew

arguing with a sibling

making up with a girlfriend or boyfriend

overhearing a conversation you weren't meant to hear

finding out a secret

stubbing your toe

dancing in public for the first time

a sneak preview

camera eye

the difficulty of sharing a secret

the interesting people you meet at _____

going home

undoing a great damage

biting the dust

bungee jumping

skydiving

a discus, javelin, or weight throw

the maneuvers of a non-glamorous position in football

flying off the handle

blocking the view

the last straw

hunting in a trash pile

_____'s Day

the center of attention

what there is to do in _____

a compromising position to be in

so as to answer the question, "What have we got here?"

on-the-job training
swapping roles
diversionary tactics
a showdown
a "smoke and mirrors" technique

Celebrations

bar mitzvah/bat mitzvah
Chinese New Year
Christmas Day
Diwali
Eid
Hanukkah
Iftaar
Kwanzaa
May Day
Native American festival specific to a particular nation
Seijin No Hi—Japanese Coming-of-Age Day
Thanksgiving
Whitsun
a celebration of your choice

2 COMPARISON/CONTRAST

What Comparison/Contrast Is

As a literary device, comparing and contrasting things to gain a heightened impression of them goes back in Western civilization as far back as Homer, in other cultures to an even earlier age. Here, abridged, is how James Joyce parodies one of those Homeric similes: "Clinging to the sides of the noble bark, they linked their shining forms as doth the cunning wheelwright when he fashions about the heart of his wheel the equidistant rays whereof each one is sister to another. . . . Even so did they come and set them, those willing nymphs, the undying sisters." Joyce would have us spoke our literary wheels with a craftsman's care and cunning. One of the handiest and most natural ways to do that is to compare two things that are somehow alike, or contrast one thing with something dissimilar in a certain telling way. Recall how the contrasting tones of a black-and-white photograph can cast a face into such compelling relief, or how Vermeer's colors beat so vividly in the dim lowland sun. That much and more comparison/contrast can do for language.

How to Write Comparison/Contrast

One way to use this device effectively is to make sure the things compared or contrasted fit. We might, for example, compare a redwood tree with a rosebush, but it probably would not gain us much beyond a laugh. If it is the skyscraping stature of the redwood we are after, we might compare it instead with the stalk that Jack climbed into the land of giants. The redwoods would be at home there.

Or we could compare a young guerrilla in an impoverished country, son or daughter of a peasant, with an American college student who goes to a business school, not because he or she feels impelled to work in business, or is even much interested in it, but because that is where the surest money is. The comparison might lead us to a study in irony, though probably there would be little room to sow much seed in the common ground between the two young people. This is possibly the place, then, where *contrast* might be more effective. Let us say that we contrast that same guerrilla with a young person from the revolutionary's own country: child of a wealthy landowner, graduate student in economics at the University of Chicago. The two threads of such a contrast could weave the social fabric of a nation and pattern the history of our time. One secret of comparison/contrast, then, is harmony.

Locating Subjects for Comparison/Contrast

Beyond the specific listings in this chapter, this book as a whole might itself become a study in comparison/contrast. It could certainly be readily used that way. Compare, for example, the chapter on description with the chapter on research-and-report writing. Contrast creative writing with process analysis writing, and so on. All the approaches to writing discussed here are spokes for the wheelwright's craft, all are sisters.

People

the real Pocahontas and media images of her

politician as candidate/politician as officeholder

shepherds/cattle drivers

actors off-screen/actors on-screen

a historical figure in two different periods of his/her life

cliff dwellers/New York apartment dwellers

fellow travelers/tourists traveling together

the nomad/the homebody

a certain person/the same person transformed

country person/city person

a "nobody"/a "somebody"

religious leaders of different religions

the adolescent as protester/the adult as protester

historian/dramatist

model of society/the average person

the just/the unjust

a gullible person/a stupid person

Nelson Mandela/Mahatma Gandhi

the same person in and out of uniform

one person in two roles

generals/privates

an alcoholic/a drinker

innocent today/guilty tomorrow

the right person/the wrong person

two all-time best athletes

person poor/same person rich

married person/single person

Baby Boom generation/Generation X

the mathematical mind/the mechanical mind

Spanish-speaking people in Europe/Spanish-speaking people in the Americas

the needy/the greedy

congress/parliament

blue-collar workers/white-collar workers

a past star now not a star

born to lose/born to win

Henry VIII/Ozymandias

fictional TV figure on camera/fictional TV figure off camera

a friend now an enemy

an enemy now a friend

the temperaments of _____ and _____

two faces of _____

Martin Luther King Jr. and Malcolm X

Dalai Lama/Pope John Paul II

Indira Gandhi/Golda Meir

Harriet Tubman/Sojourner Truth

child like an adult/adult like a child

the Stoic/the Epicurean

the lyricist/the composer

a real person/the depiction of him or her on television

Billy Budd/Claggart

revivalist/used-car salesperson

right brain/left brain

a person before and after winning the lottery

young Elvis/old Elvis

spouses/partners

defense attorney/prosecutor

a child before and after gaining a sibling

a person before and after acquiring a pet kitten or puppy

one rebel/people rising up as one

how one sees oneself/how others see one

the scholar/the untutored

different parts in same person ("Two souls, sadly, are in my breast."—Goethe)

two football players switching roles

the actor/the role the actor plays

amateur/professional

attorney/doctor

Captain Kirk/Captain Jean-Luc Picard

Data/Mr. Spock

Luke Skywalker/Darth Vader

person on offense/person on defense

original/imitation

two TV sitcoms

seeming free/not being free

ordinary person/uncommon person

the same person, tough and tender

citizen/noncitizen

the best/the worst

students in 1900/students in 2000

salesclerk/customer

hearts made of stone/hearts on fire

young college students/old college students

Albert Einstein/Stephen Hawking

compulsive reader/bookworm

pedestrian rights/driver rights

people modern and ancient in their view of the universe

folk rock singer/hard rock singer

the forever friend/the sometime friend

Benedict Arnold, before and after

the one blamed/the one who should be blamed

the powerful/the powerless

Shakespeare's Macbeth/a modern Macbeth

adolescents and their values/adults and their values

soccer mom/little league dad

Madonna/_____

William Jefferson Clinton/John F. Kennedy

George Herbert Walker Bush/George W. Bush

aristocracy/tyranny

student unrest/student apathy

scientist's view of the stars/poet's view of the stars

two major candidates for the same office

American opera stars/Italian opera stars

Harvard student/Berkeley student

John McEnroe/Pete Sampras

Pete Sampras/Andre Agassi

movie actor/television actor

movie actor/stage actor

ideal American/real American

oneself/old friend

oneself/new friend

swing dancer/step dancer

marching bands/orchestras

manic/depressive

Beatles/Rolling Stones

Massachusetts Colony as seen by a pilgrim/Massachusetts Colony as seen by a native person

baseball fan/football fan

yourself now/yourself 10 years ago

spending a night in your own bed/spending a night in a tent

learning something from a book/learning by doing

the person given the credit/the person who should have gotten credit

a famous person/someone who looks like the famous person

companionship/friendship

what I wanted/what I didn't want

life in a polygamous society/life in a monogamous one

"day people"/"night people"

Compare/contrast these opposing bases of marriage: In some cultures, it is said that "you don't marry the person you love; you love the person you marry."

Compare/contrast yourself with Thoreau as, for example, on the issue of imprisonment.

Compare/contrast opposing parts of your personality.

Compare/contrast short professional basketball players with tall ones.

Compare/contrast famous people with their children.

Compare/contrast famous people with their parents.

Compare/contrast in a theme, "Anything but What I Expected."

Compare/contrast the negative views of yourself against the positive ones.

Compare/contrast one person who has two occupations.

Compare/contrast the native of a country with a tourist to that country.

Compare/contrast tourists/explorers.

Compare/contrast the assassination of one president with that of another.

Compare/contrast yourself with someone like you.

Compare/contrast yourself with someone not like you.

Compare/contrast two people who are much alike in many ways.

Compare/contrast so as to show someone changing a role—Aladdin, for example, doing something for the genie.

Compare/contrast someone's bark and bite.

Compare/contrast the TV-watching habit with some other habit or obsession.

Compare/contrast newspaper and TV coverage of the same story.

Compare/contrast the Russians and the Americans of the Diomedes Islands.

Women spending time together/men spending time together

Write a comparison/contrast essay about a comic book hero as presented in the comic book versus as presented in a movie version.

Compare/contrast yourself with your best friend.

Compare/contrast a typical day for you during the school year versus a typical day during summer vacation.

Compare/contrast two different places you have lived.

Compare/contrast where you live with where you would like to live.

Use comparison/contrast to show whether a member of the clergy can be an entertainer.

Use comparison/contrast to show whether a teacher can be an entertainer.

Use comparison/contrast to show whether a politician can be an entertainer.

Use comparison/contrast to show which counts more in football: brawn or brain.

Use comparison/contrast to show which requires more work: casual dress or fancy dress.

Use comparison/contrast to relate the *beginnings* of the football careers of quarterbacks Johnny Unitas and Peyton Manning.

Use comparison/contrast to write on the subject, "If I can't have _____, I'll take _____."

Use comparison/contrast to show whether the choice at the polls is one more of comparison than of contrast.

Use comparison/contrast to show that people with disabilities are more like people without disabilities than different from them.

Use comparison/contrast to write of someone, unlike the average person, who would take the smallest piece of something good and give the best and largest piece to a neighbor.

Use comparison/contrast to show that, as William Cowper believed, God made the country and human beings made the town.

Use comparison/contrast to show how, according to Anna Barbauld, society is worse than solitude, and one human being with another is still the greatest curse.

Use comparison/contrast to show that, as Oliver Wendell Holmes argued, the world's great people have not commonly been great scholars, nor its great scholars great people.

Use comparison/contrast to show that, as William Lloyd Garrison believed, our country is the world and our citizens are all humanity.

Use comparison/contrast to show that it is reasonable that, as Madame Cornuel believed, great people are not great to their valets.

Use comparison/contrast to show that, as Oliver Goldsmith believed, little things are great to little people.

Use comparison/contrast to relate Richard Nixon and Shakespeare's Richard II.

Comparison/contrast topics about humanity may be drawn from the following:

"The hunger of love is much more difficult to remove than the hunger for bread." (Mother Teresa)

"It is not enough to prepare our children for the world; we must also prepare the world for our children." (Luis J. Rodríguez)

"If you find it in your heart to care for somebody else, you will have succeeded" (Maya Angelou). Compare and contrast different kinds of success on the basis of this comment.

"Religion without humanity is poor stuff." (Sojourner Truth)

"There are only two ways of spreading light—to be the candle or the mirror that reflects it." (Edith Wharton)

"I would have girls regard themselves not as adjectives but as nouns." (Elizabeth Cady Stanton)

Is "the face the index of a feeling mind"? (George Crabbe)

"Ask not what your country can do for you but what you can do for your country." (John F. Kennedy)

"When students get good grades they say Look what I got; when they get bad grades they say Look what the teacher gave me." (newspaper item)

"I describe not people, but manners; not an individual, but a species." (Henry Fielding)

"Be careful with him: He's going to be a father." (Ronald Colman, speaking of his dog, in a movie)

"There are two kinds of people here in Washington," says a cartoon—"those who know what's going on . . . and the rest of us."

"It is impossible to enjoy idling thoroughly unless one has plenty of work to do." (Jerome K. Jerome)

"Is a team better off resting for a week or staying sharp under game conditions?" an AP article asks regarding the NBA playoffs.

"Americans, of course, hold no monopoly on producing memoirs. The practice of celebrating the great leader's life by putting pen to paper (or hiring a ghost) dates back at least to Caesar's 'Commentaries.'" (re Nixon's memoirs, newspaper article dated May 29, 1977)

"It is easier to love humanity as a whole than to love one's neighbor." (Eric Hoffer)

"The real American is all right; it is the ideal American who is all wrong." (G. K. Chesterton)

"The people have little intelligence, the great no heart. If I had to choose I should have no hesitation in choosing the people." (Bruyer)

"They're only truly great who are truly good." (George Chapman)

"If youth but knew; if age but could." (Henri Estienne)

"Mediocrity knows nothing higher than itself, but talent instantly recognizes genius." (Arthur Conan Doyle's Sherlock Holmes)

"To be nameless in worthy deeds exceeds an infamous history." (Sir Thomas Browne)

"All the world over, I will back the masses against the classes." (William Gladstone)

"The living need charity more than the dead." (George Arnold)

"I have been a stranger in a strange land." (Bible)

"It is the province of knowledge to speak and it is the privilege of wisdom to listen." (Oliver Wendell Holmes)

"The love of liberty is the love of others; the love of power is the love of ourselves." (William Hazlitt)

"The most fluent talkers or most plausible reasoners are not always the justest thinkers." (William Hazlitt)

"In the depth of winter, I finally learned that within me there lay an invincible summer." (Albert Camus)

Human Conditions

dark days/happy days
choice between two roads
nearsighted, farsighted
style, comfort
discrimination/absence of discrimination
fasting/feasting
orthodox/unorthodox
two kinds of birth
dating in high school/dating in college
lazing/relaxing
despair/hope
meditation/daydreaming
assisted living/assisted dying
family dinners then/now
parents working/parents staying home

single-parent home/two-parent home

pleasure/duty

being alone/being lonely

controlling your life/letting your life control you

living deliberately/living accidentally

new look, new life

discrimination of one kind/another kind of discrimination

young Americans are healthier today than they were 20 years ago/health problems among young Americans have increased in the last 20 years

private things/public things

obligation/pleasure

families today/families 50 years ago

two kinds of death

different ways of mourning

different funeral customs

different marriage customs

body language/verbal language

different marriage customs

reading a printed book/reading online

mind/heart

mind/brain

overconfidence/insecurity

class clown/class bully

honor/fame

delusion vs. reality in sports

lean years/fat years

habit/disposition

God's gifts/human dreams

progress/improvement

apartment living/dormitory living

Compare/contrast two procedures at birth.

Compare/contrast the views two different cultures have of death.

Write a comparison/contrast essay on the subject, Things Gone Good.

Write a comparison/contrast essay showing that some things are common to us all.

Use comparison/contrast to show what the world would be like if millions of people exactly like you had controlled the progress over these past six million years.

Use comparison/contrast to show what it is besides courage that is opposed to cowardice.

Use comparison/contrast to show that blindness is, as has been said, "another way of seeing."

Show by comparison/contrast that, like a person, a neighborhood (or a class, or a country) has its own personality.

Show by comparison/contrast whether the big things, or the little ones, shape our lives.

Consider from the point of view both of individuals and of the United States government whether we know as much how to solve our own problems as those of others.

Compare/contrast on the basis of the title of an article in *International Wildlife,* "Animals Are Only Human."

"It has been claimed that war is the ultimate act of patriotism, yet war destroys the humanity in us." (Zarina Hock)

Compare and contrast traditional notions of war with feminist wars as described in this quotation: "Feminism has fought no wars. It has killed no opponents. It has set up no concentration camps, starved no enemies, practiced no cruelties. Its battles have been for education, for the vote, for better working conditions, . . . for safety on the streets, . . . for child care, for social welfare, . . . for rape crisis centers, women's refuges, reforms in the law." (Dale Spender)

Comparison/contrast topics about the human condition may be drawn from the following:

"Grow old along with me! The best is yet to be, the last of life, for which the first was made." (Rabbi Ben Ezra)

"Chains are worse than bayonets." (Douglas Jerrold)

"Dying is more terrible than death." (Henry Fielding)

"Wit has truth in it; wisecracking is simply calisthenics with words." (Dorothy Parker)

"I'm saddest when I sing." (Thomas Bayly)

"Into each life a little sun must fall." (L. E. Sissman)

"The heresy of one age becomes the orthodoxy of the next." (Helen Keller)

"Just remember one thing, son," says a cartoon father: "I know a lot more about being young than you know about being old."

"The act is all, the reputation for it nothing." (Goethe)

"Religion's in the heart, not in the knees." (Douglas Jerrold)

"Sometimes it's worse to win a fight than to lose." (Billie Holiday)

Science and Nature

prairie/mountain

drought/oasis

thorn/flower

plowing under/harvesting

bacteria/virus

toads/frogs

animals as humans/humans as animals

ethics of cloning sheep/humans

the mallard/the loon

green/ripe

the coral snake/the snake confused with it

life on earth/life in outer space

ice/dry ice

animal intelligence/human intelligence

two animals in intelligence

fingerprints/retinal scans

simple foods/fancy foods

natural gas/lignite

good things of spring/not-so-good things of spring

anthropology/sociology

science/art

domestic plant/wild plant

two sides of nature

typhoon/tornado

a doctor of medicine/a doctor of philosophy

hay fever/asthma

honey/bee

coldblooded/warmblooded

someone set in nature/nature itself

insect/another of its genera

science/science fiction

evolution/creation

Use comparison/contrast to show that nature has a way of keeping up its own beauty and humanity has not found a way to improve on natural beauty.

Distinguish between nothing on one hand and, on the other, coming into existence where there had not been anything before.

Compare/contrast the chestnut tree, the tulip, or the comet described by the scientist on the one hand, the non-scientific philosopher or poet on the other.

Compare/contrast someone who has an affiliation with nature with someone who does not. Show, for example, how the former can merge naturally with the landscape while the latter seems out of place.

Preparing and preserving foods then and now.

Carbon dating techniques in archaeology/another archaeological dating technique

Microwave cooking/crock-pot cooking.

Experiencing the news on the Internet/the news on television.

Two different ways of listening to music.

Language

old saying before/old saying now

oasis/watering hole

inhibition /restraint

known/renown

thing/thang

good conversation/ordinary conversation

thought/expression of thought

libel/slander

objectivity/subjectivity

radical left as political term/*radical right* as political term

bureaucratic language/clarity

introvert/extrovert

major speech/minor speech

re-creation /recreation

possibility/probability

something before being translated/something after being translated

Scriptures in one language/Scriptures in another

pessimism/optimism

thinking/writing

writing/speaking

denotation/connotation

what is said/how it is said

turned on by/turned off by

status quo/the norm

notoriety/fame

banter/teasing

first language/second language

scheming/planning

spin doctor/spokesperson

reactionary/revolutionary

spoken language/sign language

being direct/being rude

exchanging small talk in two different cultures

expressing courtesies in two different cultures

formal/informal language

speaking as people write/writing as people speak

induction/deduction

legalese/"legal-ease" (to quote *Time* magazine on improved legal terms)

English in England/English in America

Write a comparison/contrast essay in which you delineate a conventional truth using unconventional terms and ideas.

Use comparison/contrast to make a dull idea sound interesting.

Use comparison/contrast to make an interesting idea sound dull.

Compare/contrast the symbolic languages of music and mathematics.

Compare/contrast a headline and an article under its heading that does not match it in content.

Compare/contrast changing ideas of what "well-balanced" means to a psychoanalyst, a cook, or a coach.

Compare/contrast the views of language and thinking expressed in the following two quotations:

(1) "Language shapes the way we think, and determines what we can think about." (Benjamin Lee Whorf)

(2) "The words of language, as they are written or spoken, do not seem to play any role in my mechanism of thought." (Albert Einstein)

Dude, compare and contrast slang and scholarly language.

"Words differently arranged have a different meaning, and meanings differently arranged have a different effect." (Blaise Pascal)

Education, Knowledge

wisdom/knowledge

curiosity/inquisitiveness

innocence/experience

conventional teaching/Montessori teaching

traditional fairy tales/contemporary children's books

natural law/divine law

thinking/letting the mind wander

book learning/practical learning

homework time/television time

objectivity/subjectivity

philosophy/religion

conventional literacies/other literacies

learning/teaching

a book/another book of the same kind

opinion/belief

mental energy expended over a long time/mental energy expended over a short time

logic/instinct

knowledge in one situation/knowledge in another

what is right/what is taught as being right

in-person learning/distance learning

teacher's role 20 years ago/teacher's role today

rational argument/emotional appeal

ethics/morals

high school graduates then and now

virtual classroom/traditional classroom

learning by doing/learning by thinking

math as language/music as language

the teacher as coach/the teacher as *guru* (sage)

learning by observing/learning by doing

Compare/contrast the popular idea of what an educated person is with your own idea.

Compare/contrast a narrow professional area and a wide professional area: generalist teaching vs. specialist teaching, for example.

When do you think best, when you are sitting or when you are on the move?

Comparison/contrast topics about education and knowledge may be drawn from the following:

"Where ignorance is bliss, 'tis folly to be wise." (Thomas Gray)

"What I don't know isn't knowledge." (Henry Beeching)

"Knowing things is being them." (Ortega y Gasset)

"The unexamined life is not worth living." (Socrates)

"As light is greater than darkness so wisdom is greater than folly." (Bible)

"To learn something new, take the path you took yesterday." (proverb)

"Poetry is something more philosophical and of graver import than history." (Aristotle)

"There is no joy in smallness. Joy is in the infinite." (Chandogya Upanishad)

Places, Perspectives

up close/far away

clockwise/counterclockwise

NYC 1950/NYC today

Chinese communism/ Cuban communism

city alive with activity/large city deserted

coming/going

state/country

living on the margins/living at the center

space/the opposite of space

military bureaucracy/civilian bureaucracy

shopping mall/Main Street, USA

same solution, different results

bedroom community/suburb

Silicon Valley/Rust Belt

trip to Las Vegas/trip to the Grand Canyon

two different places of burial

forever-home/sometime-home

Alberta/Texas

Paris, Texas/Paris, France

Venice, California/Venice, Italy

Taj Mahal: monument to love/symbol of ego

South American gauchos/North American cowboys

up against the ceiling/up against the wall

Ground Zero on September 11, 2001/Ground Zero in 20__.

the view from outside/the view from inside

the view from below/view from above

the Great Wall of China/the Berlin Wall

your dream home/your real home

the underlying purpose of building the Suez Canal/the underlying purpose of building the Panama Canal

a village in the United States/a village in another country

a painting by Monet from far away and from up close

ups/downs

yin/yang

swamp/desert

cave/hilltop

Chicago/New York City

rural community 100 years ago/today

light penalty for something/heavy penalty for same thing

poor and rich at the same time

two kinds of hunger

youth culture of two kinds

kind cruelty

pyramids/Stonehenge

prairie sunsets/ocean sunsets

my house/your house

top half, bottom half, each making the other possible

two sides of a certain hotel, house, or town

Use comparison/contrast to show disparity in what free speech is and what it is not.

Use comparison/contrast to answer the question: What is happening in this very moment in another part of the world?

Use comparison/contrast to show that sometimes forward and backward, up and down, are all the same.

Write a comparison/contrast essay on a change of feeling, place, or situation.

Compare/contrast something other than in the conventional or popular way.

Compare/contrast different attitudes to aging in different cultures.

Write a comparison/contrast essay to show that nothing stays the same.

Write a comparison/contrast essay to show that (to translate from a French expression) the more things change, the more they remain the same.

Compare/contrast cloak-and-dagger conceptions with real espionage.

Write a comparison/contrast essay that answers the question, What is happening in this very moment in different parts of outer space?

Which is better, a harmless lie or a hurtful truth?

Compare/contrast the changing perspectives about scholarship, law, or machinery.

Use comparison/contrast to show a person before and after he or she is out of sight.

Compare/contrast the same kinds of orchards in different parts of the country.

Compare/contrast the Old South and the New South.

Compare who you think you are and who your parents think you are.

Compare who you think you are and who your teacher thinks you are.

Compare who you think you are and who your classmates think you are.

Compare/contrast two kinds of strategies for a campaign, a game, or a speech.

Use comparison/contrast to show the way a certain building dominates other buildings around it, even if the other buildings happen to be taller.

How does the average citizen of a country in Western Europe live differently from the average citizen of _____?

Compare/contrast a situation in the "Land where the light is darkness." (Bible)

Comparison/contrast topics about places and perspectives may be drawn from the following:

"Were Niagara but a cataract of sand, would you travel your thousand miles to see it?" wrote Herman Melville.

"They are ill discoverers that think there is no land, when they can see nothing but sea." (Sir Francis Bacon)

"It was the best of times; it was the worst of times." (Charles Dickens)

"It's always morning somewhere." (Richard Horne)

"It's morning in America." (Ronald Reagan)

Economy, Trade

browsing in online bookstores/in traditional bookstores

Compare/contrast ways of spending and misspending.

Write a comparison/contrast essay about old money vs. new money.

Write a comparison/contrast essay that distinguishes the dollar from the confederate note.

Compare/contrast spending in one part of the country with spending in another part.

Compare/contrast the dollar in the United States with the dollar in some other part of the world.

Compare/contrast two cars you would like to have.

Compare/contrast two jobs you know about.

Use comparison/contrast to distinguish between economy and economics.

Use comparison/contrast to distinguish between wet goods and dry goods.

Use comparison/contrast to distinguish between old values of farmland and modern values of farmland.

Compare/contrast the manufacture of something—candles or soap, for example—then and now.

Discuss by comparison/contrast: "In this economy average is below average," says a cartoon.

Compare/contrast authentic money and counterfeit money.

Compare/contrast stocks and bonds.

Compare/contrast online trading with trading through a broker.

Compare/contrast a global economy with a national economy.

Measurement

Compare/contrast the Arabic number system and the Roman number system.

Compare/contrast metric measurement with another principal kind of measurement.

Compare/contrast simplicity and precision.

Compare/contrast two things usually thought to be equally good.

Compare/contrast two things usually thought to be equally bad.

Compare/contrast something thought to be possible by one, impossible by another.

Compare/contrast statistics that mislead and "honest" statistics.

Compare/contrast a glass that's half empty with one that's half full.

Compare/contrast compliment and insult.

Write a comparison/contrast on the subject "Little but Important."

Write a comparison/contrast on the subject, "an eye for an eye makes the whole world blind" (Mohandas Gandhi).

Compare/contrast the degree of frightfulness in the realistic and the supernatural.

Compare/contrast musical and poetic meter.

Comparison/contrast topics about measurement may be drawn from the following:

"A minute's success pays the failure of years." (Robert Browning)

"Between good sense and good taste there is the same difference as between cause and effect." (Jean de la Bruyere)

"It is the nature of all greatness not to be exact." (Edmund Burke)

Art and Entertainment

this movie/that movie

television comedy/society

television shows past/television shows present

Oprah/Jerry Springer

"reality TV"/reality

circus from inside/circus from outside

wrestler as actor/actor as actor

two great architectural types

art criticism by self/art criticism by others

hit song/non-hit

movie acting/stage acting

American movie controversiality vs. foreign movie controversiality

background vs. foreground in painting or photography

humor/macabre humor

movie acting/TV acting

British TV ads and frankness/American TV ads and frankness

Seinfeld's world/the Simpsons' world

fictional character/same character given your name

Monet/Manet

Impressionism/Expressionism

watching something on TV/watching something on the Internet

U.S. news reportage of an event/another country's reportage of the same event

VCR versus DVD player

Past and Present

old city, new city side by side

word processor/pen and paper

film camera/digital camera

the scribe/photocopier

old demands, old conditions/new demands, new conditions

family farm/agribusiness

the generation gap then and now

old commandments/new commandments

cooking with a wood stove/cooking with a microwave

old views of divorce/new views of divorce

military training then and now

spanking/"time-out"

family reunions then and now

past danger/present danger

the same fable, old and new

the family unit, then and now

old and new dentistry

old-time religion/modern religion

Compare/contrast a situation in which something old has been added.

Compare/contrast what wildcatting was like in Alaska fifty years ago with what it is like today.

How did the treatment of children in 12th century Europe differ from that of today?

Compare/contrast Prohibition laws with today's marijuana laws.

Write a comparison/contrast essay to show that things are not that simple anymore.

Write a comparison/contrast essay to show that things (or, the times) are better, or worse, than they were before.

Compare/contrast old and new soap-opera scripts.

Compare/contrast a situation in which the modern and the traditional co-exist comfortably side by side.

Compare/contrast the before-and-after of an old picture or an old event.

Compare/contrast the American psyche before and after September 11, 2001.

Compare/contrast a situation in which something new has been added.

Compare/contrast politics (or some part of it such as language) before and after Watergate.

Compare/contrast medieval ways and modern ways.

A cartoon shows that a battering ram was the medieval equivalent of today's doorbell. Using comparison/contrast, draw other relationships of a humorous kind between medieval times and present ways.

See the opening paragraphs of Conrad's *Heart of Darkness,* where there is a description of England as it must have looked to the conquering Romans. Compare/contrast Conrad's description with a description of the modern scene of the same area (even if it is your own description rather than one you find).

Compare/contrast Dagwood's office and Dilbert's office.

Use comparison/contrast to discuss this quotation from Eisenhower: "Things are more like the way they are now than they ever were before."

Use comparison/contrast to discuss the import of the following: "In old time we had treen chalices and golden priests, but now we have treen priests and golden chalices." (Bishop John Jewel, 16th century)

Compare/contrast politics before and after the Berlin Wall came down.

Compare/contrast classic westerns with revisionist westerns.

Compare/contrast the attack on Pearl Harbor and the attack on the World Trade Center.

Analogy

the body/the body politic
a person's life/a book
river/mother
a person/a city
a person/a parade
professional football/warfare
an adult's home/a castle

eternity/moment
life/party
life/TV show
life/football game
camera/eye
writing/composing music
New York City street/battlefield
music/language
animals/United States presidents
marriage/driving
novice police officers conducting traffic/novice conductors conducting musicians
a hotel/an ocean liner
a blind date/_____
a child's room/a kingdom
a mind/a kingdom
an island/_____
eating with chopsticks/_____
mind/eye
the Irish Sea/_____
fame/river
dance hall/church
home/country
architecture/nature

Analogical subjects may be drawn from the following:

"Every drop of the Thames is liquid history." (John Burns)

Luther said that people stay busy as a factor making things to worship.

"Slavery is a weed that grows in every soil." (Edmund Burke)

In our destinies are we more like buses, free to move in any direction, or like trains, fixed in our tracks?

"Love is like linen often changed, the sweeter." (Phineas Fletcher)

"Reasons are not like garments, the worse for wearing." (Robert Devereux)

"Money speaks sense in a language all nations understand." (Aphra Behn)

"A good book is the purest essence of a human soul." (Thomas Carlyle)

"Justice is truth in action." (Benjamin Disraeli)

"It was my tongue, not my soul, that cursed." (Euripides)

"The leaves of life keep falling one by one." (Edward Fitzgerald, translation of a line in *Omar Khayyam)*

"The tree is known by his fruit." (Bible)

"Bad laws are the worst sort of tyranny." (Edmund Burke)

"The tongue has no bones," F. L. Lucas said, "but it can break millions of the bones of human beings."

"For how agree the kettle and the earthen pot together?" (Bible)

Show by analogy what sense some nonsense can make.

"Inflation is the neutron bomb of economics. It destroys everything in your bank account while leaving the figures intact." *(The Houston Chronicle)*

"Life is like a game of bridge. The players are dealt cards unknown to them. But they can play the game well or badly. A skillful player may have a bad deal and yet win the game, whereas a bad player may get a good and yet make a mess of it." (S. Radhakrishnan)

"There is no easy walk to freedom anywhere, and many of us will have to pass through the valley of the shadow of death again and again before we reach the mountaintop of our desires." (Nelson Mandela)

"There will always be some curveballs in your life. Teach your children to thrive in that adversity." (Jeanne Moutoussamy-Ashe)

"The human mind is not capable of grasping the Universe. We are like a little child entering a huge library. The walls are covered to the ceilings with books in many different tongues. The child knows that someone must have written these books. It does not know who or how. It does not understand the languages in which they are written. But the child notes a definite plan in the arrangement of the books—a mysterious order which it does not comprehend, but only dimly suspects." (Albert Einstein)

3 PROCESS

What Process Writing Is

Writing about a process generally tells the reader how to do something, or how something is done, by proceeding one step at a time. This procedure may be used in anything from a recipe to a repair manual to the complexities of a political movement. Process writing might best be understood as a particularly disciplined form of exposition. Writing about a process requires precise writing, often in linear order.

How to Write about a Process

As implied above, the central feature of process writing is that it proceeds from one point to another in whatever sequential order (logical, chronological, physical, mechanical, and so forth) the subject demands. The key to effective process writing is shaped to an orderly selection and presentation of the material. In that sense this form is usually more stringent than some of the other forms might be. The writer who breaks the sequence and disrupts the procedure risks jumbling the process and confusing the reader. But this does not mean we should use the key to process writing to lock the form in its tomb. Robust verbs and trenchant nouns will keep it alive.

This type of writing is especially useful for technical subjects. Here is a simple example from an article in the *Scientific American.* It has to do with a device that allowed Galileo to use his telescope as a measuring instrument: "There was a circular grid with a diameter of ten centimeters and a spacing between rulings of about two millimeters. The grid had a pin through its center by which it was attached to a rod ending in a ring that fitted snugly around the tube of the telescope. When Galileo looked through the telescope with his right eye, he looked with his left eye at the grid and optically superposed Jupiter on the central pin. The grid was then rotated to align a horizontal ruling with the plane of the satellites. . . ."

Locating Subjects for Process Writing

Process writing can become an important part of any other type of writing, including the most creative variety. Its relevance to the other parts of this book will be evident. But concentrating on some of the subjects listed in this chapter—ranging, as they do, from "how gravity works" to "how football drafts work"—and moving them step-by-step through a rigorous, concrete, and clear explanation would be a helpful exercise for anyone who wants to write anything at all. Process writing is that fundamental. The student who does it well will then be well into the process of learning the writer's craft.

Food and Drink

making sushi
making tandoori chicken
making baked Alaska
making earth bread
using the microwave
using an old-fashioned grill
cleaning a fish
making sausage
baking in a sand pit
making *arroz con pollo*
preparing fried rice
preparing refried beans
barbecuing
broiling
making ice cream
making candy
making tacos
making a combination pizza
making a flour tortilla
making a cake
making a spicy spaghetti sauce
presenting a recipe on TV
shopping for food in a foreign country
eating with chopsticks
brewing a cup of tea or coffee
how to sprout beans
eating a fruit from start to finish

Writing

creating a Web page
using endnotes
writing to _____
writing argumentation
writing more simply
using the pronoun "you"
writing pompously
writing an F paper
organizing a paper
saying nothing in many words
taking notes
proofreading
achieving clarity, brevity, correctness, simplicity, or
    thoroughness in writing
educating oneself to know genres one is writing in
writing a job application
writing a short story
writing an introduction to a composition
thinking creatively

sound writing or sound-writing
marking compositions
describing your personal writing process
creating an outline
writing an effective resume
writing a job description
how to prepare for a debate
grading or editing another's writing
revising one's writing
composing on a word processor
registering in writing a complaint about writing
getting down to the agony of writing

Education, Learning Processes

searching for a library book using an online catalog
using the *Reader's Guide to Periodical Literature*
reading a dictionary
researching a topic using a search engine
predicting success or failure
taking an advanced course
answering a question
wasting time effectively
meditating
using mnemonic devices
figuring by the Chisanbop method
learning through mistakes
teaching a language by a special method
saving public schools
getting or losing accreditation
communicating when you don't know the language
bringing out whatever talents you have
reading or teaching Braille
getting preliminary experience or education
learning how to read in an unfamiliar subject area
learning argumentation by practicing it or reading it
recording audiobooks
learning without taking notes
using the library card catalog
finding out information on _____
how to cut class
learning to ride a bicycle
using newspapers in the classroom
teaching a first reading lesson
choosing children's books
reading a map
learning how to ask the right question(s)
learning a second language
choosing a major
planning a degree

reading body language

planning a road trip using the Web

learning to like _____

telling an illustrative story

preparing an oral presentation

learning to balance school and extracurricular activities

being more observant

making drudgery exciting

learning how to put things off as long as possible

how children play

how parents can start a school of their own

how Alexander the Great was tutored

how television has changed learning

how computers have changed learning

how children were educated in England during the 19th century

how decisions are made in your school

how to be understood

how to solve discipline problems in elementary school or high school

how the Montessori method works

how playthings help a child grow

how a child (grows, learns, loves)

how to skim-read by skipping judiciously

how to experiment by the scientific method

critiquing World Wide Web pages and sources

how to write a précis

History

How were duties relegated in medieval abbeys and monasteries?

How are war criminals tracked down?

How was apartheid opposed and defeated?

How did a certain country put down a coup?

How is the past recaptured?

How did Napoleon plan the invasion of Russia?

By what process did the British colonies in America become independent?

By what process did Hawaii become a U.S. state?

How did Elizabeth I improve her navy?

What was it like to _____?

How can the forebears of a certain famous contemporary be traced?

How does a country surrender to another country in time of war?

How is wartime neutrality maintained?

How did De Valera rise to power in Ireland?

How did the draft system (conscription) come about? How did it first operate? What changes were made in the operation in subsequent years?

How is genealogical research conducted?

How is the coast defended?

How are votes from certain groups courted?

How did India achieve independence from Britain?

How did the "slavery triangle" work?

How does a presidential election work?

How did the Cold War end?

Trace the evolution of the Civil Rights movement.

What is the proper way to display the United States flag?

How did New York City physically rebuild after September 11, 2001?

How did the United States emotionally rebuild after September 11, 2001?

How can map-making be political?

Nature

how the earth is measured

how gravity works

how nature resolves overloading

how evaporation and condensation work

how an ox-bow lake is formed

how bees build hives

how ants construct colonies

how African termites build castles

how spiders spin webs (according to kinds of webs)

how the salmon goes upstream

how a wasp traps a spider

how the cuckoo nests its eggs

how to curb erosion

how a beaver builds a dam

how antlers are used

how fireflies can be used

how a bloodhound can follow a trail

how to conserve natural resources

how coffee is produced

how the weather is predicted

how infinity is measured

how *flora* and *fauna* are protected

how fruits and vegetables are inoculated

how insects, birds, reptiles, etc., live on their internal food reserves

how snails battle

how ants battle

how spontaneous combustion works

how creatures are protected from extinction

how the Grand Canyon was formed

how glaciers changed the landscape

how monarch butterflies migrate

how erosion creates certain geologic/geographic formations (choose a particular area)

Human-and-Creature Processes

how wildlife is photographed
how lakes are stocked with fish
how to fish in salt water
how to breed fish
how to tame a rabbit
how to crossbreed _____
how whale blubber was sliced in the 19th century
how to get rid of troublesome birds or animals without
    killing them
how to train an animal for a television commercial
how to talk with animals
how to milk by hand
how to rid a dog of fleas
how to bathe a dog
how to bathe a cat
how to set up a birdbath
how to breed a mule
how to shoe a horse
how to fish the old way
how to find the angle for angling
how to bird-watch
how to fish for halibut
how to share your backyard with wildlife
how to thwart squirrels from raiding bird feeders

Games, Sports, Outdoor Activities

how to judge a contest
how to skate using inline skates
how to use a sail bike
how to perform a certain figure in ice-skating
how to get lost in the wilderness
how to hunt for underwater treasure
how to hand-load a _____
how to load a blunderbuss
how to hit the bull's-eye
how to prepare for a hunting trip
how to buy the right tent
how to equip for a backpacking trip
how to practice falconry
how to trail-ride
how to pick a winner
how to warm up
how an umpire/referee makes a call
how to keep long-distance bicycling from becoming
    painful
how women have entered formerly all-male sports
how football drafts work

how to maneuver a sailboat
how to stay fit for _____
how to shoot a basketball
how to steal bases
how to make a certain tennis shot
how to get the hang of hang gliding
how to run the 100-meter dash
how to use strategy to win the race
how to use strategy rather than brute force in _____
how to play badminton
how to set up the football wishbone; how it works
how to challenge an umpire without being thrown out of
    the game
how to perform a certain kind of high jump
how to juggle
how to ride a unicycle
how to make a certain wrestling hold or movement
how to swim a certain stroke
how to train for a marathon
how to take an early-morning constitutional
how to get up again after falling down (in skating or
    skiing)
how to lift weights the wrong way
how to perform a certain judo hold or movement
how to roll a bowling ball
how to cut corners in skiing
how to deep-sea dive
how to ribbon-rope in a rodeo
how to bungee jump
how to blaze a trail
how to break a leg
how to play jacks
how to play checkers
how to play pool
how to juggle
how to dribble a ball
how to fly a kite
how to mountain-climb
how to perform a certain water-skiing maneuver
how to skateboard
how to teach visually impaired people to ski
how to ski cross-country
how not to win at _____
how to be disqualified in _____
how plays are called from the bench
how to shoot a certain kind of gun
how to set up a certain chess strategy
how a jockey is responsible for the success of his/her
    mount

how to hike with the family

how to walk a certain style

how to run a certain style

how to perform certain calisthenics

Religion

how someone converts to _____ (pick a religion)

how someone is exorcised

how one becomes canonized

how to enter the priesthood/ministry

how the Pope is chosen

what happens at a bar/bat mitzvah

what happens at a Hindu "thread" ceremony

rite of passage (or coming of age ceremony) in a particular religion

Airplanes, Air Travel

how flight accidents are investigated

how a "black box" works

how to fly a hot air balloon

how to pass time between airline flights

how to survive a plane crash

how to skywrite

how to fly over the Alps (or Andes)

how to dust crops

how to fly—as a bird, passenger, or pilot

how to barnstorm

how to land a plane where there is no airport

how a fire-engine airplane works

how to get through security smoothly

Cars, Road Travel

how to drive defensively

how to catch a car thief

how to put a car together from scrap

how to jump-start a car

how to ride a motorcycle

how to take a driver's test

how to control/minimize pollution

how recalls of cars are made

how to care for a car

how to get more miles out of a gallon of gas

how to change a tire

how to drive on icy roads

how to drive on rainy roads

how to change the oil in a car

how to detail a car

Travel, Travel Preparation

how to pack a suitcase

how to find the best fare online

how to get a visa

how to get a passport

how British soldiers crossed the Darien Gap of lower Panama

how to get medical help abroad

how to make reservations

how to travel light

how to protect your luggage—from loss, from theft

how to visit _____

how to travel in Europe

how to travel with a family

how to communicate when you don't know the language (e.g., how to order a meal)

Telecommunication and Audiovisual Processes

how cellular phones work

how telephone cables work

how to trace a telephone call

what a telephone operator does

how a pager works

how the Internet works

how a telecommunications satellite works

how to build a sound system

how to build a radio

how to install a hard drive

how to install a sound card

Grooming

how to use dental floss the right way

how to choose the right clothes for the time of year

how to cut hair

how to tie a shoe

how to look casually elegant

how to choose the right soap, shampoo, or other toilet article

how to sew on a button

how to care for shoes

how to launder clothes

how to fold your laundry

how to maintain a particular hairdo

how to look cool

how to color your hair

how to look shocking

Sleep/Sleep Processes

how to relax
how to go to sleep by not trying to go to sleep
how to wake up a little bit at a time
how to learn the fine art of napping
how to handle insomnia
how not to snore

Entertaining, Social Arrangements

how to run a restaurant
how to eat at _____
how to dj a party
how to be a bore at a party
how to have fun at a party
how to arrange a surprise party
how to arrange a Super Bowl party
how to plan a party
how to arrange a wedding
how to arrange a baby or wedding shower that includes
    both men and women
how to celebrate a special birthday

Safety

how to stay safe in a foreign country
how to put out an electrical fire
how to put out an oven fire
how to put out a grease fire
how to react if mugged
how to prevent electrocution
how to use a flak jacket
how to protect yourself in a natural disaster
how to have a contingency drill—for fire, attack,
    disaster, etc.
how to protect yourself on the street
how to guard against poisonous plants
how to prevent childhood accidents or diseases
how to make _____ safe
how to cycle safely
how to keep camp life safe
how to make roller-blading safe

Medicine, Physiology, Health

how to take blood from a donor at a blood drive
how to give birth at home
how the human embryo develops
how to trace the cause of a certain sickness
how Lincoln's medical history could be researched to
    speculate on his health during his second term

how to avoid unnecessary health-care and hospital
    expenses
how a bypass operation is performed
how to put in a contact lens
how to gather information on a certain medical topic
how to deal with jet lag
how doctors and nurses prep for an operation
how to treat oxygen lack
how to eliminate most deaths from _____
how scientists proved the link between smoking and
    cancer
how to save your teeth
how to conduct a medical appointment effectively when
    the doctor is rushing
how dialysis works
how laparoscopy works
how asthma is treated
how the root-canal is treated
how a face-lift is performed
how cryosurgery works
how polio was conquered
how a certain vaccine was discovered or developed
how breast cancer is detected and treated
how alcoholism is treated
how to test for allergies
how AIDS is prevented
how AIDS is treated
how to treat bee stings or insect bites
how to cure acne
how to deal with frostbite
how to stop hiccups
how the pacemaker works
how to use the Heimlich Maneuver to save a choking
    victim
how the heart works
how the brain works
how to improve your sleep
how to correct a "lazy eye"
how your body tells you you're cold or hot
how the human eye sees
how the human ear hears
how the sense of touch works
how to perform an ultrasound scan
how to test for twins in the last trimester of pregnancy
how to determine whether pain relievers advertised on
    TV are dependable or safe
how an MD makes a medical prognosis
how to cure infection of _____
how to fight against infection
how an organ is transplanted

how to still butterflies in the stomach

how to treat snakebite

how to perform a certain operation

how to take someone's blood pressure

how to treat poisoning from poison plants

how to give artificial respiration

how midwifery works

how to read temperatures

Constructions, Constructing

how the Pyramids were constructed

how sewage systems worked during the Victorian era in England

how dams are built

how windmills are constructed; how they work

how oil pipelines are constructed under water

how to make adobe bricks

how to lay the groundwork for a house

how to build a crib

how not to design an auditorium

how to build a sandbox

how to make a _____ chair

how to make a _____ table

how not to build a house

how to build a modular home

how to build a solar-powered house

how to build a personal solar collector for powering, say, your stereo

how to shingle a roof

how to build a sweat lodge

how to construct a model inside a bottle

how to perform a certain kind of carpentry

how to make a porcelain figure

how to build a dugout

how bridges are constructed for strength

how to make buildings earthquake-proof

how to build an inexpensive bookcase

Repairing, Cleaning, Inspecting

how to inspect a restaurant for cleanliness

how to window-clean tall buildings

how to clean up a town

how to repair potholes

how to mow a lawn or trim hedges

how to clean a chimney

how to proceed if a bat flies into your house through the chimney

how to install a doorknob

how to install a deadbolt lock

how to paint a _____

how to refinish a _____

how to repair a heater

how to repair a bicycle brake

how to service a DVD player

Art, Handicrafts, Domestic Arts

how early animation worked

how to animate

how computer animation works

how to foreshorten in drawing

how to contour-draw

how an artwork is preserved or repaired

how an artwork is examined for authenticity

how to fake a Jackson Pollock painting

how to fake an Andy Warhol painting

how to make a collograph print

how to draw with a pencil

how to draw with charcoal

how to create a chiaroscuro effect

how to create distressed furniture

how to arrange furniture according to principles of feng shui

how to fake a Renaissance painting

how to engrave

how to turn scraps into decor

how to hang wallpaper

how to decorate a room

how to quilt

how to sew by a pattern

how to make clothes better and more cheaply than you can buy them

how to display your collectibles

how to make fractal art

how to do origami

how to do macramé

how to do batik

how to make a sand sculpture

how to make an ice sculpture

how to make pottery

how to decorate a Christmas tree by theme or color

how to decorate for Halloween

Plant Life

how fruits and vegetables are picked, processed, packed, and sent to the consumer

how to plant grass

how to clone redwood trees

how to plan a spring garden

how a seed grows
how to protect trees
how to get an orchard on the way
how to control the growth of grass
how to grow house plants
how to grow a bonsai tree
how to create a "nature garden"
how to create a windowbox garden
how to mulch your garden
how to make compost for your garden
how to get your violets to bloom
how to make an herb garden
how to make a rock garden
how to make a rooftop garden
how to start your outdoor garden indoors
how to do Xeriscape landscaping

Money, Business, Saving, Theft, Economics

how a pyramid scheme works
how smuggling is done
how to prevent hotel thefts
how to make out an income-tax return
how to save money on a drug prescription
how to take measures against shoplifting
how bill collectors work
how to collect on your insurance
how to save money
how travel agencies operate
how the IRS catches tax-evaders
how to plan an economical trip
how the phone company is defrauded out of payment for long-distance calls
how customers rip-off the electric-power companies
how customers are ripped-off by public utilities companies
how the economy of a foreign country can be undermined
how to spot counterfeits
how to keep from being reckless with credit cards
how to live off the wilderness
how money is spent by charity organizations
how to live simply
how to boost tourism in _____
how to collect unemployment
how to conserve energy in the home
how to sell _____
how to have a garage sale
how to buy public land
how to end unemployment

how students can pay their own college costs
how millionaires spend their money
how money is "laundered"
how money is printed at the mint
how old money is discarded at the mint
how an ATM works
how to exchange money at borders
how countries that have disasters are helped financially
how dividends are determined and distributed
how a hospital is administered
how to live within a salary or an allowance
how charity organizations work
how to be a philanthropist
how returned goods are paid for in the long run
how a stock exchange works
how grocers stock a produce section
how to sell your own book
how to hunt for a bargain
how to buy at an auction
how a Dutch auction works
how a silent auction works
how to conduct a meeting
how the realtor works after an agreement has been reached to buy or sell a home
how to trade foreign money without getting taken
how ancient traders did without money
how to lose a job through incompetence
how to do comparative shopping
how to bargain with a car sales representative
how to save for college
how to travel in _____ on a shoestring budget

Film, Film Media, Photography

how music videos have changed advertising/filmmaking
how to use a camera in soft light
how to keep a camera clean
how to take a picture with an old camera (specify what kind)
how to pick out an inexpensive manual camera
how to post a photograph on the Web
how to develop films privately
how Hollywood screen extras work
how television ads are pre-screened for bloopers
how to set up a television translator station
how the laugh track on television works
how an actor or actress plays a double role (or more) in the same take
how early filmmakers showed the passing of time
how modern filmmakers show the passing of time
how early filmmakers moved from one scene to the next

how modern filmmakers move from one scene to the next
how a television producer works
how a movie producer works
how to program a VCR
how to use a digital camera
how to use a CD burner

Language, Information, Communication

how to break a code
how the Chinese calendar works
how the Aztec calendar works
how the _____ calendar works
how e-mail works
how to prepare for a job interview
how to behave in a job interview
how libraries have changed since early days
how to outline
how to understand HTML
how Hitler used propaganda
how the Associated Press works
how the news is written
how the English language developed from its beginnings
how a search engine works
how words change meanings
how Webster worked on his dictionary
how James Murray compiled the _Oxford English Dictionary_
how slang becomes acceptable
how to break the language barrier
how to set up a debate between presidential candidates
how to debate on TV as a presidential candidate
how to speak as an insider to be part of a particular group
how to cajole or persuade

Mechanical and Chemical Processes

how a home pregnancy test works
how to test a driver for alcohol
how to program a computer
how a rotary engine works
how to bug an office
how a new invention works
how an oil well works
how _____ can be kept afloat (or aloft)
how to build a better mousetrap
how the Hughes toolbit worked
how a ticker-tape works

how to use earphones
how the first liquid-fuel rocket worked
how to desalinate water
how to purify water
how to control a certain kind of pollution
how sugar is refined
how copper is refined
how sulfur is mined
how coal was first mined
how strip mining is done
how waste can be converted for use
how mummies were mummified
how bodies are embalmed

Psychology, Emotions, Social Actions

how to handle fear of failure
how to change jobs
how to prepare for job-hunting
how to pass driver's education without stress
how to check on one's own honesty
how to come to a family decision
how to make a Zen garden
how to bring out the best in _____
how a secretary handles the public
how to live with a two-year-old child
how to meditate
how to keep a poker face
how to manipulate someone
how the person under psychoanalysis can get along while the doctor is away
how to kick a habit
how to live with a Waterloo
how to heal emotional wounds
how to control the violence that exists in us all
how to make the mind wander effectively
how to relax
how to go beyond your endurance
how to end post-meal hunger
how to pull your own strings
how to get your first job
how to handle overworrying
how the human mindbody system works
how to manage kids at a summer camp
how to release a friend from an obligation
how to fire a friend
how to help employees work better
how the public is sometimes "emotionally blackmailed" by public servants
how to get along with an older (or a younger) brother or sister

how to get away from someone
how to deprogram a person
how to psych out your opponent
how to recover from an emotional blow
how to get back on the road to confidence
how to get over feelings of guilt
how to avoid a scene (or other unpleasantness)
how to adjust to the first year of high school
how to adjust to the last year of high school
how to prepare for the first year after high school
how thought worked before the evolution of language
how to become involved in a community project
how to organize a community effort
how to help a visitor to your community
how to help an exchange student from another country feel comfortable

Law

how to organize a boycott
how to profit from complaining legally
how to file a lawsuit
how to protect yourself legally from the landlord
how the taxpayer can legally revolt
how to make a class-action suit
how to settle an account without trouble
how to unload a lemon legally
how border officials crack down on narcotics
how aliens are registered in the United States
how to get a permit for _____
how whistle-blowers are protected from their superiors
how the small-claims court works
how police use computers in identifying, tracking, and apprehending suspects
how a court decision can be challenged
how to read fingerprints
how a police officer is trained
how to make up a legal petition
how lawyers are protected from those they help convict
how eminent domain works
how to fight a traffic ticket
how to let thieves know you are not at home
how to help police in their work
how to proceed if arrested
how those who await trial are handled
how judges perform their duties
how to make a citizen's arrest
what to do at the scene of a car accident
how to prevent a certain kind of crime

Government, Politics

how a grand jury operates
how a census works
how a "political machine" works
how the government protects historical sites
how a town council can bring about the resignation of a city official
how to lobby
how to burrow into office when another party comes into power
how to run a national campaign
how computerized voting works (or is supposed to work)
how political pressure is applied
how a government agent penetrated the intelligence apparatus of a foreign power
how to set up a wiretap
how to conduct a nonviolent protest
how sabotage was committed
how sabotage was discovered
how a press secretary operates
how a Senate committee investigates
how a president is elected
how the Supreme Court operates
how to ratify an amendment
how Russia chooses its top government official
how the American political process works
how the "loyal opposition" is supposed to exercise its duty
how majority rule operates
how national polls are taken
how a bill becomes a law
how to spin bad news
how to run for office in your school
how to run someone's campaign for office
how to petition for change in _____
how one registers people to vote

Miscellaneous Processes

how fakery works in _____
how to find the killer
how to speak out against abuses
how someone becomes thoroughly Americanized
how houses were built in early colonial America
how to scare a reader or a moviegoer
how accuracy is checked for world record claims
how to select the right sound system or computer
how to change a baby's diaper

how to feed a baby

how to bathe a baby

how the U.S. Geological Survey researches its map information

how to get tickets for a television show

how the Muppets work

how to live primitively

how to behave like a _____

how to shop at an antiques store

how to conduct a _____ contest

how to collect valuable stamps, coins, etc.

how applications for employment are verified for such things as education and work experience

how to expose a rip-off or a con job

how to see backwards into time

how to take _____ apart

how to meld or blend _____

how to shave comfortably

how to drift

how to chill out

how to break a routine

how to thwart

how words are added to a language

how to stop _____

how to keep going in _____

how to get started

how to perform a certain monumental task

how _____ (money, a ship, a grade) was raised (or can be raised)

how to stalk the wild _____

how _____ works

how to revamp _____

how to learn the ropes

how to make a practice run at _____

how to get along better with your _____

how to observe something

how to collect art

how to learn the music scales

how a fire crew responds to a call

how an advertising agency works

how to arrive at the same result by opposing means

how to paint what is not there

how to read music by sight

how to tune a sitar

how to conduct a symphony

how to undo something

how a major hotel operates

how forest lookouts work

how an airport control tower works

how the metric system was arrived at

how a system other than the metric system was arrived at

how to do a pedicure or manicure

how to make a miniature _____

how to audition

how hunger works

how to make a guitar

how to get from here to there

how sweat glands work

how to make radio contact

how to get rid of a cold

how to recharge a _____ (something other than a battery)

how missing persons are located

how to get a job as a forest ranger

how thinking can be made into a hobby

how art can enrich life

how impostors fake their qualifications

how Pulitzer Prize winners are chosen

how to support a really worthy cause

how to organize a float for a parade

4 NARRATIVE

What Narrative Writing Is

A narrative tells a story or gives an account of what happened. It is certainly one of the oldest forms of communication. One thinks of the ancient epics—the *Iliad* and the *Odyssey*, the *Ramayana* and the *Mahabharata*, the trickster tales of West Africa, Beowulf, Grimm's fairy tales, the epic of Gilgamesh, the *Cantar de Mio Cid*—ancient narratives from all parts of the world, capturing the history, the values, and the imagination of a people and transmitting them orally or in writing. Even the drawings in prehistoric caves tell their own stories. It's the power of story that keeps Scheherazade alive in the Arabic story within a story, *The Thousand and One Nights*. Life itself is a narrative, a history, a story (Latin, *historia*). Would anyone's deepest heart not recognize and respond to that truth? It seems fair to say that people everywhere have always looked with pleasure and a certain awe towards the one who could tell that story well.

How to Write Narrative

It is no accident that this chapter on narrative follows the section on writing about a process. There is no question here about how those two spokes in the rhetorical wheel relate. The "and then and then and then" of the narrative is close indeed to the sequential advance from point to point of process writing. A similar attempt at precision and clarity should be made, but at the same time the narrative form demands that the writer be allowed more freedom. A narrative line may often be kept straight and strong by twining process techniques through the core of it. But here the rope must be allowed to fray, to soak up the smells, the colors, the taste, and the touch of circumstance. A good storyteller knows how to draw a long bow, the better to whistle the arrow dead to the heart of the matter.

Of course there are other, far more radical, narrative liberties. Many contemporary novelists delight in them. Most beginning writers, however, would probably do well to learn how to spin a straight yarn before they tangle it, web intricate plots, and risk getting the narrative confounded.

Locating Narrative Subjects

Everyone has a story to tell, even students who insist they have nothing to tell because they think their lives are dull. There are stories everywhere, in just about anything, and this book offers no exception to that commonplace. Let's hope that the subjects in this chapter will goad memories, spark imaginations, in a special way. Close attention could as well be paid to the chapters on creative writing, critical writing, and description. There is surely something here that should arouse any student to relive, in writing, an experience (even if the "experience" originates in the imagination) that ought to be shared.

Domestic, Personal, and Autobiographical Narratives

sibling rivalry
in the middle
the coming fury
stuck with it
the most important
unopposed
the addict
revealing for the first time
secretest thoughts
five minutes more
gaffes and bloopers
talking it over
curiouser and curiouser
over the edge
over the top
under the radar
under the boardwalk
punning around
good news
seeking independence
seeking identity
in the back of my mind
not being predictable
ready for a new start
blowing dust
on the brink
a special sound
winter love
summer love
at the wrong hour
a personal message
being spurred on
skipping class to do something else
job for the inexperienced
peak experience
determined to be
the oldest of many
one example, repeated ad nauseam
plunder
unexplained act
ready for prime time
sky's the limit
convertible car
not ready yet
hot shot
do or die, now or never
in command

the first day
the last day
cramping my style
all at one time
advancing steadily
making up for lost time
your turn now
best offer
old catalogs
the long, hot summer
joining a family
a student-exchange program
dream vacation
pulling an all-nighter during finals week
walking in the rain
a secret vote
bird in the hand
a rolling stone
the last one
rising again
under dire circumstances
private word
working off a debt, moral or financial
a supernatural happening
disappearing
closing a chapter
leaving someone for the first time
cover girl or boy
on the take
topping this or that
a place of honor
with this ring
spiders and snakes
doubtful deeds
even now
vacancy/no vacancy
a week ago
the target of threats
being bitter/not being bitter
first visit
trouble with the manager
claiming to be someone else
meeting your double
home to stay
home alone
flirting
dirty work
more than the usual
hearing/listening

last-gasp effort
fleeing
precognition
short-changing
fighting the doldrums
signing on, signing off
self-righteousness
just looking on
outside looking in
inside looking out
making up
gone but not forgotten
some changes or else
show of good faith
look who's talking
two for the money
critic's choice
street corner preacher
alone in _____
when all is said and done
adopting a baby
adopting a pet
the day the terrorists attacked
Sunday afternoons
a tornado approaches
walking on the beach
the face of terror
rediscoveries
frivolity
check not in the mail
winning a prize
winning the lottery
losing your cool
under fire
hearts on fire
on the hot seat
nothing the same
doing it best
still up in the air
in distress
laughing/not laughing
being ready
World's Greatest
coming out
for seven years
after school
separate ways
every step of the way
learning to adapt

feeling no pressure, feeling no pain
Yuletide
getting the gold star
hoax
urban legends
somewhere between
a significant aside
a significant other
a power trip
in conquest of others
playing second fiddle
to go out, or to eat here
teacher outdone by pupil
*$#@!
something I can't put behind me
small change
getting down
foreign currency
one sour note
one small step
one giant leap for _____
day on the farm
the institution
"inmates running the asylum"
anything for a drink of water
the measure of _____
going ballistic
going Hollywood
going, going, gone
May/December marriage
broken promise(s)
not alone
sounds and silence
sounds of silence
end of a song
taking consolation
a roaring wind
once over lightly
clearing the air
passive resistance
the day _____ happened
fearing the "other"
understanding the "other"
unlearning a response
fin de siècle
a recycling adventure
pizza parties
my job as a telemarketer
my job as _____

walking a dog
walking a cat
bump in the road
bump on the head
bad hair day
bad day for a zit
shielding someone
following someone
the awful truth
the last laugh
a country kitchen
favorite child
little joys—snow days, flowers growing up through
    pavement
nearing the finish
in disgrace
asking for money/the car/permission
parental bond with child/children
a charmed life
a flash of insight
graveyard shift
daydream
the midnight hour
breaking curfew
breaking the ice
breaking away
story behind the story
not being afraid
they all laughed
discovery of my father/mother/sister/brother
revitalizing spirits
breathing new life
friendship with _____
homemaking
in traditional dress
nursing
separating
one step closer
wake-up call
making merry
watching with amazement and alarm
day or night
being a complete person
earning a living in an unusual way
eating your heart out
a serious mistake made in childhood
a shot in the arm
a funny kind of _____
    variety

not over yet
footing the bill
nerves on edge
a time and a place
shut away
last-minute change
bridal shower
a stillness
when my computer crashed
farmers' market
flea market
a Million _____ March
promises to keep
feeling good
doing good
waiting for the other shoe to drop
meditation
many happy returns
hanging on
hanging out
a word from home
a family affair
in the midst of life
a day spent with a living legend
being an army brat
winning in a bargain or barter with a shrewd individual
only recently
sleeping on it
breaking loose
entering the mainstream
rejecting the mainstream
spending time
coming home
first results
too much of a good thing
early responsibility
seeing the family only rarely
greatest personal success
caring
face to face
coming full circle
clearing the tracks
covering your tracks
owning up
lesson from the expert(s)
talking and thinking backward to remember the past
dogfight
a voice from the past
going through it like everyone else

being predictable
reminding of someone or something forgotten
much ado about nothing
almost alike
almost famous
unmoving minute hand
bearing the pain
taking the cake
someone following
only yesterday?
I made it!
freedom personified in action
favorite spot
one day at a time
reunion/uniting old pals
the last word(s)
honest mistake(s)
a worthy accomplishment
when I fall in love/when I feel in love
climbing through the window late at night
losing the key(s)
second helping
puppy love
love of puppies
on turning 18
on turning 21
getting my driver's license
slacking
the ultimate eccentric
tempest in a teapot
the long road ahead
a piercing experience
making ends meet
where the heart is
green, green grass of home
on the road
on the river
defender of the _____
the day of reckoning
Ozark living
stage fright
bad moment
an instant's lapse of attention
humbling experience
supplicating
suffocating
I can see clearly now
the beautiful today
the simple made hard

letting off steam
marching to the tune of a different drummer

Dreams, Fantasies, Make-Believe

a pot of gold
free as the birds
setting the world on fire
Bigfoot
glorifying _____
invincible
the first moments before Creation, when God, in
    Shelley's words, was "weary of vacancy"
windjammer
meeting an archetype
encounter with a snallygaster
dreams in technicolor
magic
end of the rainbow
if I were the opposite sex
if I were rich
if there were no rules
going home with an extraterrestrial
pantomime
nightmare(s)
till the end of time
back from heaven/hell
soapbox
with the original Berserkers
family dream(s)
terror from the sky
out of time
dream(s)
prophetic dreams
Nostradamus
rewriting history
maelstrom
supernova
living symbols and images
the last frontier
a space odyssey
alien abductions
"If I were queen/king for a day."
teacher for a day

Sports and Their Metaphors

interference
winning combination
tennis without a net
loser take all

crossing the line
leveling the playing field
landing some big ones
giving no quarter
reruns/repeats/playbacks
illegal procedure
good sporting behavior
no substitute for rules
showcase talent
back seat to no one
maximum performance
Olympic spirit
passing the torch
two out of three
watching _____ run
the winner explaining how it was done
target shooting
glider, gliding
down the homestretch
a game of inches
running neck and neck
loose ball
strategic error
making all the difference in the outcome
coming out swinging
overbearing
a lightweight
fast service
rained out
gone fishing
fishing as a "contest against nature" (Steinbeck)
a big sweep
crossing swords
throwing down the gauntlet
rolling with the punches
rope-a-dope
sparring
shadow boxing
blockbuster
horse race
over-confident
moving the goalposts
getting injured in the game
making the leap

Travel, Adventure

driving in a blizzard
O, Paris!
big move

and away we go
border crossing
climbing a mountain
slow, unanxious ride
meeting in _____
fugitive
muddy road
last journey
someone met on a trip
surviving a natural disaster
the first/last bus/train/plane home
ships passing in the night
on the loose
long way yet
westward ho!
living on the coast
a long day's journey into night
trekking in _____
seven years in _____
sailing away for a night and a day (or more)
the Great Wall
the _____ route
the yellow brick road
scuba diving
a rafting expedition
getting lost in canyon country
security checks
subway adventures
captains courageous
going where?
having been where?
roving
long and winding road
rocky road
the call of faraway places
hard traveling
bon voyage
taking chances
train adventure
driving
national parks
easy way back
hard way back
the nomad finding a home
asking for something in another language
fording a river
stopping by the wayside
adrift on the Amazon
drifting

international friendships
atop a double-decker bus
strange places
pickpocket
born to danger
stranded at the airport
waiting all night for a ferry
package tour
the cruise
booking online
going to Mexico
the love boat
tourist in space
celebrity astronaut
roughing it
a blowing nor'easter
the call of the wild
already there
taking the road less traveled
tunneling through
visiting the "Forbidden City"
going on pilgrimage to _____

Mystery

at a séance
the uninvited
unexplained incident
premonitions
psychics' predictions
psychological terror
a figure in the shadows
a trunkful of old letters
a lost key
a twin brother or sister that no one told you about
a scar
a raspy voice on the phone
accident, or homicide?
no stone unturned
black cat
looking for the one that got away
investigation
mystery behind reality
at random
first discovery of the strange
sabotage
proofs
suspicion
a voice of eternity
surprises galore

portent
undiscovered country
an abandoned house
the attic
rattle in the attic
"You gotta believe me!"
"I didn't do it!"
"I know what you did . . ."
left for dead
the evil car
twilight zone experience
nightmare on your street
in the cellar
ghost in the machine
ghostwriter
the woman in white
the man in black
the glass eyeball
the rustling behind the door
creaking stairs
illusion or reality?
echoes
waiting for what comes next
chasing down a stolen/missing item
strange doings
flickering lights
impending but unseen or unknown danger
reading tarot cards
my visit to the psychic

Miscellaneous

out of tune
in the long run
nose for news
threat becoming actuality
folk custom
tricky going
junk-food addiction
dealing with bureaucracy
people of leisure
keeping up with the _____
glad to be here
at home/not at home
always watching, always being watched
honor among thieves
jury of peers
threat
a lesson for all
the old boy network

swimming upstream (metaphorically)

sitting/standing on ceremony

knowing what to do

breach of faith

laughing at/being laughed at/laughing with

curiosity-seeking

supporting locals

maneuver, strategy

spitting venom

shootings

race with the devil

baring your claws

diplomacy

white-collar criminals

living à la Martha Stewart

chivalry becomes sexism

Miss Manners says _____

prom night

volunteering

neighborhood watch

keeping up appearances

secular saints

polite applause

a joke that fell flat

common-sense scorn, as for UFO sightings

a pledge of quality

setting an example

snubbing

covering for someone

dog-biting man

handling being famous

follies of the wise

choosing only one

"oops . . . !"

putting your foot in it

"Netiquette"

leaving someone out

ingroups and outgroups

online chat groups

Write a descriptive narrative in which you re-create in the mind of the reader an understanding of some unusual experience you have had (or have heard about from someone close to you).

Write a narrative essay entitled, "Someone for All Reasons," about a person who was everyone and everything—say, a college president or a high school principal or a mayor who tended not only to administrative matters but also swept the sidewalks.

Use the narrative style of one of these writers as a starting point for your autobiographical narrative: Maya Angelou, Margaret Atwood, James Baldwin, James Boswell, Charlotte Brontë, Sandra Cisneros, Charles Dickens, Frederick Douglass, Isak Dinesen, Madeleine L'Engle, Ralph Ellison, William Faulkner, Anne Frank, Benjamin Franklin, Ernest Hemingway, James Joyce, Jack Kerouac, Jamaica Kincaid, Stephen King, Jack London, Gabriel García Márquez, Herman Melville, Nathan McCall, Walter Dean Myers, V. S. Naipaul, George Orwell, Gary Paulsen, Plutarch, Katherine Anne Porter, Arundhati Roy, William Saroyan, Aleksandr Solzhenitsyn, Brent Staples, Amy Tan, Henry David Thoreau, Ngugi Wa Thiong'o, Mark Twain, Thomas Wolfe, Tom Wolfe, Tobias Wolff, William Wordsworth, Malcolm X, Laurence Yep, Paul Zindel.

Write a narrative essay entitled, "If Anything Good Can Happen, It Probably Will." A possible opening could be, "To tell the truth I am sickeningly optimistic."

Use one of the following as a beginning for a narrative essay:

Without even trying, I have come face to face with _____.

What I planned to say and what I did say in my first public address were not remotely similar.

Draw suitable narrative topics from the section of this book on creative writing.

5 CLASSIFICATION/DIVISION

What Classification/Division Writing Is

The most immediate example that can be offered of this kind of writing is the book itself, which at the very least is an extended exercise in classification/division. The material of the book is classified in terms of various types of writing and then divided into more specific categories. Classification, then, is the systematic arrangement of something into classes—groups usually founded upon some common ground. Those classified groups may then be divided into their separate parts. Strictly speaking, it is virtually impossible to classify without dividing, but for rhetorical purposes it might be helpful to think of division as tending to be more distinct, more particular. Language-family history provides an excellent example of classification: Linguists group languages into language *families* (Afro-Asiatic, Indo-European, Iroquoian, Niger-Congo, Sino-Tibetan, Uto-Aztec, to name a few). These in turn can be divided and subdivided into language *branches, languages, dialects, varieties,* and ultimately, *idiolects*—the last term being used to refer to one's own private variety of speech.

How to Write Classification/Division

As with process writing, the key here is order, the systematic arrangement of our material. An essay on types of pain, for instance, might begin with the classification of pain into its two general types, mental and physical. That general classification could then be divided into the almost innumerable kinds of mental and physical pain. Pain—physical, emotional, psychological—can range from a nagging discomfort to an agony so unbearable that the afflicted person prefers to die. It is easy to see, then, why the kind of writing this chapter is concerned with can be an effective method for exploring such a wide-ranging notion.

It is also worth noting that mental pain can be related to and can even cause physical pain, and vice versa. Thus this example also points up the fact that seemingly distinct categories can, upon closer examination, blur together—as well as the fact that, oftentimes, distinct categories are established not so much because they simply exist in the "real world" but because they are constructed to serve a human purpose. Another example, and one where the human purpose has sometimes been unfortunate, can be seen in the use of various notions of racial identity.

Locating Subjects for Classification/Division

As pointed out before, this book is a handy example of classification/division. It might be of help to browse through it to mark how thousands of diverse subjects can be classified and divided. Keep in mind that the same subject can be classified according to different principles, depending on the criteria or even the classifier. For example, you may classify people by their age, their ethnicity, their class, their education or any other criterion, depending on the nature of your inquiry. Of course you will be looking at lists for the most part. Once classification/division is taken beyond the list format, other writing types and techniques will come along quite naturally, such as description and characterization. For example, consider subgroups in the student body at your school, e.g., "nerds," "jocks," "brains," and so on.

Animal Life

endangered species

unique ways of trapping

ways of taking care of animals

kinds of unwanted animals

emotional problems of animals

food habits of animals

ways of training animals

hibernation

bears

metamorphic creatures

creatures that use camouflage

kinds of eyesight

kinds of hearing

rodents

birds

rare animals

animal variety on the Galápagos Islands

recognizing poisonous snakes

the smartest animals

the dumbest animals

common diseases of animals

selective breeding of dogs

animal communication

group behaviors of animals

vertebrates

Intellectual, Psychological, and Emotional Perceptions and Reactions

various ways to look at _____

ways of organizing thoughts for _____

kinds of nonphysical weapons

words as weapons

kinds of hints, innuendos, accusations

kinds of old ways to learn

ways of looking at trees

kinds of intellectual climate

different kinds of teasing

the dreadful, the bad, and the not-so-bad

kinds of epiphany that influence life

kinds of impressions teachers/students have of one another

kinds of response(s) to crises

kinds of time thieves

several ways the world reacted to _____

emotions involved in courage

kinds of logic or rationale

kinds of knowledge

kinds of perception

kinds of "erroneous zones"

ways of observing

kinds of madness

kinds of terror

kinds of symptoms of violent patients

behaviors deriving from id, ego, superego

kinds of conditions under which it is impossible to concentrate

kinds of ways of opening paths to reconciliation

kinds of emotional retreats

kinds of pain

kinds of psychological games

kinds of eating pleasures

kinds of stress relievers

ways to relieve depression

ways to cope with fear

ways to offer comfort

ways to get revenge

ways in which _____ is manifested

kinds of dilemmas

kinds of laughter

personality types

kinds of ignorance

new ways to learn

kinds of temptations

kinds of taste(s)

kinds of thinking

kinds of moral courage

moods according to season

moods according to days of the week

moods according to certain incidents

kinds of ways of looking at something (using "Thirteen Ways of Looking at a Blackbird," by Wallace Stevens, as a guide)

ways of reading the world

kinds of literacy

kinds of groups within a community

ways to let off steam without violence

kinds of flattery

ways to show appreciation

ways of showing respect

kinds of humor

kinds of love

kinds of possessiveness/territorial behavior

Law

kinds of law(s)

kinds of legal professionals

kinds of legal fields
kinds of procedure by the defense
kinds of indemnity
kinds of homicide
kinds of appeals
extortion, kidnapping, blackmail distinctions
kinds of "strange" laws
degrees of felony
kinds of procedure by the prosecution
kinds of jeopardy
kinds of evidence
kinds of British legal professionals (barrister, solicitor, and so forth)
kinds of summons
kinds of legal courts
kinds of waivers
kinds of fraud
kinds of conflict between civil and religious laws
kinds of licenses
kinds of punishment

Human-Made Structures

kinds of places of worship
kinds of living quarters
kinds of architecture of modern times
kinds of ancient architecture
kinds of toys that are harmful
kinds of harmless toys
kinds of canoes/boats
kinds of adobe bricks
kinds of cheap hotels
kinds of specialized hotels
kinds of bridges
kinds of clocks
kinds of train cars
kinds of furniture
kinds of television sets
kinds of beds that cause trouble in sleeping
kinds of towers
kinds of monuments for self-glorification
kinds of shopping malls
kinds of memorials
kinds of aircraft
kinds of baby strollers
kinds of playgrounds
sophisticated bicycles
kinds of automobiles
kinds of recreational vehicles
kinds of bridges
kinds of parks and monuments

Natural Phenomena

kinds of carnivorous plants
kinds of drinking water
kinds of snow
kinds of mind-affecting plants
Alexander Pope's classification, "The Great Chain of Being"
kinds of sunsets/sunrises
kinds of colors
bodies of water
celestial bodies
gross things in nature
beautiful things in nature
cool things in nature
kinds of teas
kinds of winged insects
kinds of Medieval classification of the elements
kinds of clouds
kinds of storms
kinds of sounds
kinds of order among natural things
kinds of group/pack behavior
kinds of chemical elements
kinds of poisons
kinds of rock formations
kinds of canyons
kinds of prairie grasses

Arts and Entertainment

kinds of crime novels
kinds of action heroes
types of drama
writers imprisoned for their principles
superheroines, real or fictional
ways horror movies scare or surprise us
kinds of popular music
kinds of art interpretation
kinds of literary schools
kinds of technique in art
kinds of style in literature
kinds of criticism of art
country music
humor on TV
junkyard art
found art
garden/yard art
types of TV detectives
kinds of video games
kinds of computer games

kinds of parades

kinds of Madonna's personae

types of sitcoms

types of game shows

kinds of pop art

kinds of literary expression (surrealism, expressionism, impressionism, etc.)

kinds of oral entertainment

kinds of art not requiring special training

kinds of art

kinds of vocal music

Jerome Kern, Cole Porter, Irving Berlin as signature styles

Duke Ellington, Louis Armstrong, John Coltrane, Miles Davis as signature styles

kinds of composers

kinds of musicians

kinds of British Invasion bands

kinds of musical ensembles

kinds of talk shows

different audiences as seen by actors

kinds of fictional works

kinds of poetry

kinds of literature

kinds of schools of art

kinds of views of humanity in art

kinds of racing

kinds of "whodunnits"

kinds of science fiction

kinds of fantasy literature

Sociopolitical Concerns

organization of the (local, state, federal) government

causes of homelessness

kinds of social status

kinds of city problems

divisions of Los Angeles or another city of your choice

kinds of slavery (not just physical slavery)

kinds of social units

kinds of discrimination

kinds of animal rights groups

kinds of activist groups

kinds of corporate pollution

types of women's groups

kinds of election conclusions

the boring 1950s, rebellious 1960s, selfish 1970s, greedy 1980s, the _____ 1990s, etc.

kinds of things seen as status symbols in society

types of popular fashion trends

kinds of mail service in different countries

kinds of war

kinds of governments

kinds of views of what obscenity, profanity, and pornography are

kinds of service learning

kinds of youth clubs

Saturday night activities

kinds of Web fun

kinds of "spam"

Religion, Myth, Worldviews

astrological groups

divisions of the Hindu caste system

ways the Medievals viewed the seven deadly sins

ways the ancient _____ honored their gods

types and sub-types of religion

major world religions

kinds of Judaism

kinds of Islam

various kinds of belief

kinds of prayer

kinds of paganism

kinds of Protestantism

kinds of spiritual experiences

kinds of Eastern religion

kinds of Western religion

cosmology of a particular religion

Native American ways of worship (choose a particular group)

kinds of supernatural figures in folklore

types of pilgrimages

religious rituals involving the use of food

types of religious apparel

types of religious training

kinds of sacrifices

kinds of agnosticism

kinds of atheistic worldviews

kinds of Buddhism

approaches to pleasure (e.g., hedonism, asceticism)

kinds of mourning

kinds of ecstasy

kinds of religious ceremonies connected with coming of age

kinds of feasting

kinds of fasting

Communication and Rhetoric

kinds of sentences

internal monologue, monologue, dialogue

kinds of insults

kinds of questions that children ask
kinds of language you use depending on your audience
kinds of television ads
kinds of titles for royalty
kinds of laughter
kinds of bumper stickers
ways of blowing the car horn to deliver a message to other drivers
body language
facial expressions
kinds of charisma
kinds of language within a single language
kinds of narrative
kinds of compliments
methods of news analysis
different levels of expression
kinds of funny things children say
kinds of roles you play depending on your audience
ways in which language is imperfect
kinds of rhetoric common to rebels of all time
kinds of language within a single group
kinds of comic-page devices for humor
kinds of testimonials
things done to poke fun at politicians
kinds of touch
ways to express the same thing
parts of a book
kinds of editing
kinds of occupational titles
kinds of city language
kinds of country language
ways in which new words come into use
kinds of advertising pitches
verbal techniques of telemarketers
kinds of obfuscation
kinds of "doublespeak"
kinds of language within a single country
kinds of letters
kinds of public speaking
ways to define what "is" is
kinds of written language
ways to communicate displeasure
ways to communicate "I told you so"
ways to apologize
different kinds of tales

Work, Customs, and Ways of People

ways to classify the books on your bookshelf
ways to be polite in different cultures
journalistic types

kinds of people I like
kinds of people I dislike
people in television ads
people in television shows
people at the stage theater
kinds of workers
kinds of bores
cool people
faces
cultures within your school or another community or population
doctors
lawyers
merchants
kinds of crowds
kinds of families
kinds of holidays
kinds of celebrations
kinds of frauds
kinds of city folk
kinds of country folk
types of factory work
types of farm work
types of coastal work
kinds of friends
movie audiences
kinds of TV hosts
kinds of workers in television
mental health professionals
small ambitions
kinds of companions
kinds of salespersons in different parts of the country
kinds of clowns
celebrity models
singing/courting customs in _____
the staff of the White House
types of martial arts
expeditions
kinds of racing
types of meditation
types of diets
types of volunteering
types of body alterations
types of hair styles
types of protests
types of extreme sports
types of festivals
types of wildlife enthusiasts
types of youth groups
nature lovers

types of groups to promote ethnic pride

drinkers

chewers

walkers

runners

conversationalists

jokes

kinds of pomposity

kinds of humility

Classification/Division items may be drawn from these quotations:

"In the language of screen comedians," said James Agee, "four of the main grades of laugh are the titter, the yowl, the belly laugh, and the boffo. The titter is just a titter. A yowl is a runaway titter. Anyone who has ever had the pleasure knows all about the belly laugh. The boffo is the laugh that kills."

"Broadly speaking," said Winston Churchill, "human beings may be divided into three classes: those who are toiled to death, those who are worried to death, and those who are bored to death."

"One religion is as true as another," said Robert Burton.

"To every thing there is a season," says Ecclesiastes.

"At twenty years of age," said Benjamin Franklin, "the will reigns; at thirty, the wit; and at forty, the judgment."

"Everybody has his own theatre, in which he is manager, actor, prompter, playwright, sceneshifter, boxkeeper, doorkeeper, all in one, and audience into the bargain," said Julius and Augustus Hare.

Philip James Bailey said: "America, thou half-brother of the world;/With something good and bad of every land."

Shakespeare says, "Some are born great, some achieve greatness, and some have greatness thrust upon 'em."

"Life is made up of sobs, sniffles, and smiles, with sniffles predominating," said O. Henry.

"Nations, like men, have their infancy," said Henry St. John, Viscount Bolingbroke.

Elizabeth Barrett Browning: "How do I love thee? Let me count the ways."

"If I were really asked to define myself, I wouldn't start with race; I wouldn't start with blackness; I wouldn't start with gender; I wouldn't start with feminism. I would start with stripping down to what fundamentally informs my life, which is that I'm a seeker on the path." (bell hooks)

6 CAUSE AND EFFECT

What Cause and Effect Writing Is

Cause and effect are correlative terms, and they are immensely useful as a rhetorical combination: if this and this and this happen the more or less natural result will be that (the effect). Or, to turn the technique on its deductive head, that happens because of this and this and this. Humankind has always looked for such connections, always wanted to know why. In fact, entire philosophical systems were developed out of cause and effect structures by ancient civilizations around the world, offering complex or simple cosmologies to explain the principle of causality, asking the same question in different ways that Stephen Hawking asks here: "Where do we come from? How did the universe begin? Why is the universe the way it is? How will it end? . . . If, like me, you have looked at the stars, and tried to make sense of what you see, you too have started to wonder what makes the universe exist."

How to Write Cause and Effect

Identify the fact, the person, thing or condition, describe how that circumstance brings about the more or less natural result, and you will find yourself in the midst of writing cause and effect. The method is orderly and, it would seem, obvious. And yet a caution is necessary at this point to guard against making too simplistic a connection between cause and effect. Twentieth-century physics, in fact, complicates causality, bringing the very notion into question—through the uncertainty principle as defined by Werner Heisenberg, founder of quantum mechanics, and through chaos theory, nonlinearity, and concepts such as the butterfly effect. At the rhetorical level, establishing cause and effect entails other perils: we need to make sure that the connections being made

are not just coincidental, that the argument does not fall into the logical fallacy *post hoc, ergo propter hoc*: "After this, therefore because of this." As Robert Todd Carroll says in *The Skeptic's Dictionary,* "Many events follow sequential patterns without being causally related. For example, you have a cold, so you drink fluids and two weeks later your cold goes away. You perform some task exceptionally well after forgetting to bathe, so the next time you have to perform the same task you don't bathe." Are the events connected by cause and effect? Examining the causal relationships, rejecting those that are coincidental, analyzing logical relationships, all help to clarify one's thinking, and more important, to theorize.

Despite the uncertainties and the perils, however, writing about cause and effect offers the opportunity to construct order from confusion when dealing with the unknown; in matters where a risk is involved, in confrontation with chaos, or when something personally vital is on the line, one can reach out to make sense out of the muddle.

Thus, though we know now more than ever that writing is more than explaining—that it is a way of exploring and even constructing reality—we can still value an orderly method of interrogating something and of making meaning. As far as humanly possible, given any individual's necessarily limited perspective, writing helps us to see what *is,* as we follow in its widest sense the imperative that E. M. Forster offers: "Only connect!"

Locating Subjects for Cause and Effect

This chapter is one of the most substantial in the book. Almost anything can be interrogated through cause and effect. The approach to this device can easily bring together process, research-and-report, argumentative, and expository writing. It can also be put to a more explicitly creative use, however. Consider a mystery story, for example, working its way backwards from the corpse to the first cause, the prime mover of the deed. Or, to turn the order around, consider a story tragic in a classical sense, where the inherent faults (causes) in a character of whatever nobility effect or at least affect his or her eventual downfall.

Clearly, cause and effect can be crafted in various ways, but we would do well *especially in this kind of writing* to let go of our opinion that everything is as ordered as it seems to be.

Art, Drama, Music, Graphics, Film, Etc.

Why is _____ considered such an accomplished artist?

What is the effect of experience on art?

What is the effect of art on experience?

What is the effect of war on art? On creativity?

What is the effect of the emotions on art? On creativity?

Why are some artists "discovered" only posthumously?

What would cause (or what *did* cause) a great producer, director, or actor to make a bad movie?

Discuss in cause-and-effect terms the moral dilemma of an actor who is asked to play the role of an evil person—say, of a Nazi war criminal.

Discuss in cause-and-effect terms the fact that in the movie world "you have to have talent, you have to work hard, and it is well to have a talent for luck."

Discuss in cause-and-effect terms the belief that we all have a little of the musician, the poet, and the crazy person in us.

Why is pottery a key to understanding past cultures?

What are the effects of a particular painting technique?

What effects can be achieved through special camera lenses?

Why do the works of a certain important artist affect you?

Assume that there is always an explanation for a like or a dislike, and tell why you like or dislike a certain work of art.

Through cause and effect, relate psychiatry (*not* psychodrama) to drama.

Where does the inspiration of a song come from? Which comes first, words or music? What things are there all around us that, not taken for granted, could supply us with material for songs?

As an exercise in sensuous description, listen to a favorite piece of music and write a description of the effects of the music on your senses. Obviously you will describe the sounds, but also bring your other senses into play: What visual images does the music cause (or create)? What smells, tastes, or textures? What particular details of the music cause these sensations and associations?

Pick a particular music group, e.g., Sweet Honey in the Rock. Why was the group created, and what has been its impact?

Is there a cause-and-effect relationship between listening to complex music and improving mental performance?

How does a particular piece of art reflect the artist's life?

Discuss in cause-and-effect terms whether jazz expresses a unique aspect of American culture.

How did Pablo Picasso's work change modern art?

How did surrealism in art become an expression of the times?

Is there a connection between great art and personal ethics?

What cause-and-effect lesson is there in the fact that Pandora opened the box?

Why is the art world usually considered as separate from the "real" world? What effects does this way of thinking have?

Why do we look up to the stars—that is, movie stars and singing stars?

Why do we spend time on art that might be spent more practically?

Why is a certain television show an unexpected success?

Why does something seen over and over still strike some people as funny?

What drains the life out of creativity?

Why would you want, or not want, to judge the work of your classmates or to have them judge your work?

Why do we value some artists' work more than others'?

Why do more women than men watch talk shows?

What makes something art?

Why are we so interested in child prodigies in music, art, etc.?

What theories have been posited to explain child prodigies? Which is the most convincing?

How does music create atmosphere in a film?

How do graphics influence how a message is received?

Choose a film-maker and describe his or her effect on the film-making industry.

How does a particular music group connect to popular culture?

Biological Sciences

What effects does oxygen or some other chemical element have on plants?

What effects do enzymes have on human physiology?

What causes food to spoil?

What damage does a certain non-human creature cause?

In what ways are animal instincts not always best for certain animals?

Explain the scientific observation that complex animals survive less well than simple animals do.

Why do jumping beans jump?

Why did the dinosaurs become extinct? Why have creatures in modern times become extinct?

Why do vines wind a certain way?

What effect does helium have on vocal cords?

Why is there no cure for a virus?

What enables diseases to become resistant to treatment?

How does introducing nonnative plants or animals change the ecosystem?

How does coloration benefit animals?

What causes bread to rise?

How do grapes become wine?

How do bacteria create edible food?

Why do mushrooms grow in the dark?

How do the rings of a tree tell time?

How is yogurt made?

How do seemingly unpleasant processes (fermentation, growing molds/bacteria) result in some tasty foods?

How do marinades work on foods?

How does composting work?

Business, Office, or Bureaucracy

What does industry do (or what can it do) to prevent routine from becoming depressing for its employees?

Show why, according to the Bible, "in all labor there is profit."

Why should one get a job?

Why can, according to Cervantes, "Many littles make one big"?

What factors cause airline prices to rise?

What factors cause airline prices to fall.

Why is time considered money? Why is money considered time? What would be the effect of your investing time?

How can complaints bring results?

Why does the "squeaky wheel get the grease?" Describe a situation where you've seen this phenomenon in action.

"A lot of determination is behind each little success." Explain.

Why has it been said that "losing a job can be the first step towards a new and better job"?

What comes of being in the right place at the right time?

Does avarice spur industry, as David Hume argued?

What would be the effect(s) of your putting off until tomorrow some important task that you have been advised to do today?

How does supply and demand affect the market for _____?

What factors affect consumer confidence in the stock market?

How does shoplifting affect the overall economy?

What are the causes of shoplifting?

What causes either the end of plenty or the end of a certain shortage?

What are the effects of inflation on people whose incomes are fixed?

Why do real estate prices rise and fall?

What effects did the New Deal have on the wealthy? On the poor?

Is turmoil the effect of progress? Or the price of progress?

Why are there restrictions on bringing plants and uncooked foods across national borders?

Why might Joseph Addison have said that "A good face is a letter of recommendation"?

What is the status of the solar-energy business? What is its status the effect of?

Why is it true that "all that glitters is not gold"?

Why do some businesses fail during hard times?

What factors make a small business succeed or fail?

What causes a decline in the quality of merchandise sold to a mass market?

Why has the reputation of the hamburger declined in recent years?

"A hungry rooster doesn't cackle when it finds a worm," said Joel Chandler Harris. Explain what effects "cackling" in the business world would have.

For what reasons can one be denied U.S. citizenship?

What are the effects on the individual of a bloated bureaucracy?

Give an example of how supply and demand works.

How can your body language help or hinder you in a job interview?

Children

Why do children run away from home?

What effects does television violence have on children?

Why is it assumed by some that an only child will be spoiled?

In what ways might it be true that "the child is father to the man"—or mother to the woman?

Why do siblings quarrel?

What is the effect on a girl who knows that the parent(s) wanted a boy, or vice versa?

Why do children need "quality time" with their parents?

How do children learn social behavior?

In the words of a song by Rodgers and Hammerstein, children "have to be carefully taught" to have prejudice. Is prejudice something that children learn? Can tolerance be learned?

Does television teach children (as it has been argued) bad grammar, bad language, bad manners, and bad diet?

Why do children learn languages more readily than adults?

"A child's best friend is _____." Why?

In what ways is the TV set a bad babysitter?

Why do more girls than boys go in for babysitting?

"One thing about raising children is that they grow in any soil." How can you justify this statement in terms of cause and effect.

Economics

"Money is the root of all evil." Show how this saying is true or false.

What effects does trucking have on the economy? What effects does the economy have on trucking?

What is behind the increase/decrease of _____ in the economy?

How does taxation contribute to a civil society?

What causes certain jobs to fail during hard times? What causes certain jobs to hold up during both good times and bad?

Is it so that, as Benjamin Franklin said, "Necessity never made a good bargain"?

Why did a certain economic measure fail?

In what ways can it be said that "poverty's catching" (Aphra Behn)?

"Change is not made without inconvenience, even from worse to better," said Richard Hooker. Apply this cause-and-effect argument to economics.

What were the causes and effects of the collapse of Enron?

Do inflated salaries cause inflation?

What is the prediction for the economy five years from now? Why?

What effects do natural conditions such as drought or heavy snow have on the economy?

How can "mom and pop" stores compete with superstores?

How would the world be different if its material stores were equally divided?

The family farm can no longer survive because_____.

Education

"Give a man a fish; you have fed him for today. Teach a man to fish and you feed him for a lifetime" (ascribed to Confucius). Apply this saying to any human being to show how he or she may be empowered.

What effects does a multicultural education have on you?

How can you promote multicultural awareness in your school?

How does diversity educate your community?

How might one's high school experience influence one's choice of a college?

What effects does education have on you?

Why can students in these times say after their education, All of that for *nothing?*

Why is it assumed that a university degree assures the graduate of a better life?

Why might students be bored in school?

How can extracurricular activities enhance a student's life?

What effects, if any, does knowledge of _____ have on us?

How might more reading make for more wisdom?

Why might criticism teach condemnation?

Why might hostility teach belligerence?

Why might fear teach apprehension?

Why might pity teach self-pity?

Why might encouragement teach confidence?

Why might differences teach tolerance?

Why might awareness of difference teach one to celebrate difference?

Why might tolerance teach respect?

Why might praise teach appreciation?

Why might approval teach self-respect?

Why might acceptance teach love?

Why might love teach acceptance?

Why might recognition teach goals?

Why might fairness teach justice?

Why might security teach faith in self?

Why might friendliness teach friendliness?

Why might learning often come from the strangest or least likely experience?

How can the truth make you free?

Why do some think that it pays to be ignorant?

Why might community colleges be more attractive options than traditional colleges?

Why, according to Sir Francis Bacon, is knowledge power?

How do low test scores among students of a certain area affect an industry's decision to move into the area?

What could cause us to love reading more? To hate it more?

What is the consequence of the fact that, as Heraclitus said, "All is flux, nothing is fixed"?

Does a learning problem necessarily cause a learning disability?

What effects do private schools have on public education?

Why did Blake think that "The road of excess leads to the palace of wisdom"?

Why is it considered that the one who knows much knowledge knows much sorrow?

What causes graduation depression?

What effect(s) did Socrates' ideas have on modern education?

What effect(s) did Aristotle's ideas have on modern education?

Why do some families/cultures put such a high priority on education?

What are the effects of learning in isolation rather than with others?

Discuss in terms of cause and effect the statement by Disraeli, "Experience is the child of Thought, and Thought is the child of Action."

Discuss in terms of cause and effect the statement by Johann Wolfgang von Goethe, "Treat people as if they were what they ought to be and you help them to become what they are capable of being."

Discuss: You have to carry knowledge with you if you want to bring knowledge home.

What effects did Maria Montessori's ideas have on modern education?

What effects did John Dewey's ideas have on modern education?

Why is it necessary to educate for democracy?

What comes of learning without preconceptions?

Why can learning be an effect of dialogue or conversation?

Why can learning be an effect of introspection?

What will be, or what would be, the effects of a nationwide "scientific illiteracy"?

What would be the effect of learning from a little bit of adversity at a time?

What would be the teaching effects if _____ (some public figure) were a teacher?

Knowledge helps us "escape the hell of subjectivity," said Samuel Johnson. Why should that be so?

What causes experience, and what does experience cause?

"Age teaches," says a Spanish proverb. What does age teach?

"No one is deafer than the one who does not choose to hear," says a Spanish proverb. Discuss this statement in terms of cause and effect.

"Wisdom denotes the pursuing of the best ends by the best means," said Francis Hutcheson. Discuss this statement in terms of cause and effect.

Discuss whether in education "better late than never" applies.

In what way will *society* be affected by *your* education?

What effects might a college education have on you as a person?

"You can't win unless you learn how to lose." (Kareem Abdul-Jabbar)

"A little learning is a dangerous thing." (Alexander Pope)

"Where ignorance is bliss, 'tis folly to be wise." (Thomas Gray)

"The education and empowerment of women throughout the world cannot fail to result in a more caring, tolerant, just and peaceful life for all." (Aung San Suu Kyi)

"Learning is a place where paradise can be created." (bell hooks)

Environment

What effects does building a dam have on animal, plant, and human life in the surrounding area?

What are the arguments for and against saving rain forests?

What are the arguments for and against drilling for oil in Alaska?

What are the causes and effects of having too much ozone in ground-level air we breathe and too little ozone in the atmosphere?

What are the causes of groundwater contamination? What are the effects on people or animals?

What are the arguments for and against storing the nation's nuclear waste in Yucca Mountain, Nevada?

How does studying ecology help us better our environment?

How does recycling a particular product have specific environmental effects?

Why is the ocean salty?

Why is the Dead Sea the saltiest?

Why do some creatures prey on their own species?

Discuss in terms of cause and effect the processes of natural selection and evolutionary change as Darwin explains them.

Discuss in terms of cause and effect: "The history of life tends to move in quick and quirky episodes, rather than by gradual improvement." (Stephen J. Gould on evolutionary change)

Ethics and Philosophy

Discuss from either side of the ambiguity/ambivalence the statement that nothing comes from nothing.

Is there ever "a victim of circumstance"?

Discuss whether or not ideas always have consequences.

Discuss whether it is possible for good to exist without evil or for evil to exist without good.

What is the effect of having someone else's thoughts in your mind?

Why can adversity be described as "bread"?

Discuss whether or not it is true that, according to Byron, the weak alone repent.

Explain in terms of cause and effect what Shakespeare meant by the comment that conscience makes cowards of us all.

Why do some people need keys to open doors that are already open?

Was Browning right in saying, "Truth never hurts the teller"?

Is humanity the sole mistake of Nature, as William Gilbert said?

Is it better to die on your feet than to live on your knees, as Dolores Ibarruri said?

Does virtue breed happiness, as Benjamin Franklin claimed?

Discuss mind over matter/matter over mind in terms of cause and effect.

Show whether it is true in life that when one door closes, others open.

Is it human nature to enjoy the struggle more than the achievement?

Discuss whether it is true that, as Thomas Hardy said, life offers, only to deny.

Is it better to lose with friends than to win with enemies?

Discuss a situation where cause *is* effect.

An idea from Edward Fitzgerald's translation of *Omar Khayyam* is that "the flower that once has blown for ever dies." Discuss in terms of cause and effect.

Is it better, as a Spanish proverb says, to be loved than not hated?

Is it so, as a Spanish proverb says, that one who walks from flower to flower will finally choose the worst?

Discuss Thomas Henry Huxley's position that "it is the customary fate of new truths to begin as heresies and to end as superstitions."

Does, as Mahatma Gandhi suggested, an eye for an eye leave the world blind?

What are the effects of the condition that, according to the Spanish proverb, the first one to get wet has more time to get dry?

Why do people seek success? Why do people fear success?

How is time an "effect" of life, or vice versa? Discuss Benjamin Franklin's comment: "If you love life, do not squander time, of which life is made."

Is life-after-life or death-after-life the effect of living? Why?

If you believe there is a next world, what is necessary in this world to enjoy the next?

What is the effect of the pursuit of perfection?

What is the effect of pursuing "sweetness and light," as Matthew Arnold used the term?

What effect does freedom have on human relationships?

What are effects of allowing or barring stem-cell research?

Discuss in cause-and-effect terms the observation by Emerson that "the reward of a thing well done, is to have done it."

Why would you be satisfied, or not be satisfied, with enough if others had more?

Trace the cause-and effect reasoning or the events behind a particular belief you hold.

Apply Huckleberry Finn's comment "All right, then, I'll go to hell . . ." to a real-life situation.

Why does our inability to conceive of the size of the universe lead us back to thinking about ourselves?

Do you control circumstance, or are you controlled *by* it?

How have attitudes about sex been affected by birth control?

Discuss in terms of cause and effect: "Youth is wasted on the young."

What effects does belonging to a group have on us?

If you help yourself, will heaven help you, as Jean de La Fontaine declared?

Discuss the proverb, "Man proposes, God disposes, and the devil discomposes."

What does it mean, in cause-and-effect terms, to "keep your mind level" when "life's path is steep"?

What makes people believe in, or want to believe in, immortality?

Why does tradition exercise such a powerful hold on us?

Link the following ideas through cause and effect: love, death, money, and life.

Why can intended good at times be harmful?

Do we try too hard to make it in the world and thus allow too much good to pass us by?

Why does Robert Frost's idea of "the road not taken" arouse such interest?

What are the consequences of bucking tradition?

Describe a personal encounter with the law of *karma*.

Address the following quotations in cause-and-effect terms:

"Voyager, there are no bridges, one builds them as one walks." (Gloria Anzaldúa)

"The mind is everything; what you think, you become." (Gautama Buddha)

"I think, therefore I am." (Descartes)

"Humankind cannot bear very much reality." (T. S. Eliot)

"If I enclosed truths with my hands, I would be wary not to open them." (Fontenelle)

"The unexamined life is not worth living." (Plato)

"The unlived life is not worth examining." (Tomás Shrink)

"The long habit of living indisposes us for dying." (Thomas Browne)

"The one who lives on hope dies fasting." (Benjamin Franklin)

"People who fight fire with fire usually end up with ashes." (Abigail Van Buren ["Dear Abby"])

"I make myself laugh at everything, for fear of having to weep." (Beaumarchais)

"Prosperity doth best discover vice, but adversity doth best discover virtue." (Sir Francis Bacon)

"What does it profit to know the world but not oneself?" (Jean de La Fontaine)

"Religion without humanity is very poor human stuff." (Sojourner Truth)

"I was raised to believe that excellence is the best deterrent to racism or sexism." (Oprah Winfrey)

"Those who are free of resentful thoughts surely find peace." (Gautama Buddha)

"As a person acts, so he [or she] becomes in life." (Kena Upanishad)

"Sometimes it's worse to win a fight than to lose." (Billie Holiday)

"We are shaped and fashioned by what we love." (Johann Wolfgang von Goethe)

"Who steals my purse steals trash; 't is something, nothing;
  'T was mine, 't is his, and has been slave to thousands;
  But he that filches from me my good name
  Robs me of that which not enriches him
  And makes me poor indeed." (William Shakespeare)

"Because our every action has a universal dimension, a potential impact on others' happiness, ethics are necessary as a means to ensure that we do not harm others." (Dalai Lama)

"Character cannot be developed in ease and quiet. Only through experience of trial and suffering can the soul be strengthened, ambition inspired, and success achieved." (Helen Keller)

"I am a part of all that I have met." (Alfred Tennyson)

"Everything you don't do has an effect." (Kurt Austin)

"Happiness is a butterfly, which, when pursued, is always just beyond your grasp, but which, if you will sit down quietly, may alight upon you." (Nathaniel Hawthorne)

"Knowledge and experience bring contentment." (Bhagavad Gita)

"Eternity is not something that begins after you are dead. It is going on all the time. We are in it now." (Charlotte Perkins Gilman)

"Hatred, which could destroy so much, never failed to destroy the man who hated, and this was an immutable law." (James Baldwin)

"Everything that lives, / Lives not alone, nor for itself." (William Blake)

"There never was a good war, or a bad peace." (Benjamin Franklin)

"Life demands to be lived." (H. L. Mencken)

"Lying is done with words and also with silence." (Adrienne Rich)

"To enjoy freedom we have to control ourselves." (Virginia Woolf)

"In adverse fortune the worst sting of misery is to have been happy." (Boethius)

"There are two ways of spreading light—to be the candle or the mirror that reflects it." (Edith Wharton)

Government, Politics

Dennis Brutus said, "Never take the students too lightly. Students have very often been the spearhead of the struggle in this [South Africa] and in other countries." Discuss the effect of student involvement in a specific political movement.

Why, in voting, is a political incumbent usually favored to win?

"What is past my help is past my care," said John Fletcher. Does this view explain why people take the attitude they take towards politics?

Why do friends (and relatives) in politics sometimes cause more trouble than enemies?

Will reforming a bureaucracy simply cause more bureaucracy?

What ails (now, or at any time) the American spirit?

What invigorates (now, or at any time) the American spirit?

Why is it so that, as Richard Hooker said, "One who goes about to persuade people that they are not as well-governed as they ought to be will always have listeners"?

What effect does bureaucracy have on idealism?

What effect does idealism have on bureaucracy?

What changes can student government make in your school?

In politics why is it so that (as James Anthony Froude said) "Experience teaches slowly, and at the cost of mistakes"?

In cause-and-effect terms, answer the question "What is happening to the American dream?"

Why does common interest not always determine what happens in a democracy?

Why do negative campaign ads sometimes succeed?

How does the media influence the results of political races?

Discuss Jeremy Bentham's statement, "The greatest happiness of the greatest number is the foundation of morals and legislation."

Tell what caused certain U.S. Congress members or Senators to leave office willingly rather than pursue other terms.

Discuss what makes stories of political chicanery so interesting.

What effects will government have on education in the near future?

How does personal charisma help build a political career?

Apply to politics the cause-and-effect Spanish proverb, "The one who walks with wolves will learn to howl."

How do regional backgrounds of certain presidents affect their presidential style?

Why is the government so often reactive rather than proactive?

What effects does being president have on the president? What does the presidency do to or for the moral stature of the person holding the office?

What has caused aristocracies to fail?

What brought about the downfall of _____?

Is it true in politics at any level that, as the Bible says, "A soft answer turns away wrath"?

Why does the government resort to doublespeak?

What does reason teach/not teach in government and politics?

What happens to military personnel who challenge the military?

What happens to government personnel who challenge the government?

Discuss in terms of government and politics the Biblical quotation, "One thousand shall flee at the rebuke of one."

Why did a certain government or country come into being?

In what ways did the end of apartheid affect the political balance in South Africa?

What factors contributed to the rise of terrorism in a particular country (such as Ireland, India, Germany, Japan, the United States)?

"Never doubt that a small group of thoughtful, committed citizens can change the world. Indeed, it's the only thing that ever has." (Margaret Mead)

"Feminism is the single most powerful social movement of our time, one that addresses every aspect of human and social life." (Richard Epstein)

"Power tends to corrupt, and absolute power corrupts absolutely." (Lord Acton)

"Children, who play life, discern its true law and relations more clearly than men, who fail to live it worthily, but who think that they are wiser by experience, that is, by failure." (Henry David Thoreau)

"Freedom never descends upon people; it is always bought with a price." (Harry T. Moore)

"This struggle [against slavery] may be a moral one; or it may be a physical one; or it may be both moral and physical; but it must be a struggle. Power concedes nothing without a demand. It never did and it never will." (Frederick Douglass on abolition)

Health

What are causes of acne?

Why is acne more than skin deep?

Why does caffeine affect you as it does?

What are the effects of rest and time off as remedies for health?

What are the effects of a smoker's stopping smoking?

How has the changing perception of HIV affected peoples' behavior?

Why do miscarriages happen?

What causes kitchen accidents? bathroom accidents?

What are the causes and effects of E. coli contamination?

What causes anorexia, snoring, depression, asthma, insomnia, ADHD, obesity?

What is a cure for each of the conditions noted just above? What unusual cure(s) do you know of?

Why is sound body related to sound mind?

What cause-and-effect relationship is there between exercise and mental health?

Why do people in Mediterranean countries have a low rate of heart problems?

Why is "happiness the sister of health"?

Why do eating habits affect health?

What are some of the different causes of heart disease?

Discuss these quotations from Sir Francis Bacon: "Cure the disease and kill the patient." "The remedy is worse than the disease."

Why was the frontal lobotomy outlawed?

What can be the bad effects of too much exercise?

How does pollution affect the health?

Why does one have to know the cause of something before suggesting its remedy?

What are the drawbacks of extending the human lifespan?

How might this statement be true or untrue: "Cheerfulness is the very flower of health." (Japanese proverb)

"Health is not a condition of matter, but of mind." (Mary Baker Eddy)

History

How have the definitions of "great men" and "great women" changed over time?

What makes immigration to the United States so attractive?

Why are civil liberties considered a mixed blessing?

Why will _____ be less visited than before?

What made the 1960s a decade of violence?

Discuss Malcolm X's quotation, "History is a people's memory, and without memory man is demoted to the lower animals."

What cause-and-effect connection was there between slavery and "Manifest Destiny"?

In history, has force been a remedy?

Discuss Thomas Jefferson's quotation, "The tree of liberty must be refreshed from time to time with the blood of patriots and tyrants. It is its natural manure."

Why was a certain city or a certain university founded?

Why was there such a delay in ending the Korean War?

What positive effects in human rights would we see today if slavery had really ended with the Civil War?

Why is the private life of the President of the United States expected to be impeccable?

Explain why Thomas Jefferson is so maligned.

Explain why Thomas Jefferson is so admired.

Explain why Franklin Delano Roosevelt (or John F. Kennedy, or Bill Clinton) is so maligned.

Explain why Franklin Delano Roosevelt (or John F. Kennedy, or Bill Clinton) is so admired.

What, specifically, do we gain from learning about history?

How have computers changed the lives of human beings?

Explain why a certain great historical event came about.

Does greatness result from intention, necessity, or accident?

Associate by cause and effect terrorism and _____ as it relates to September 11, 2001.

Point up some present influence from a past idea.

Discuss Edmund Burke's quotation, "You can never plan the future by the past."

Discuss John Lennon's quotation, "Life is what happens to you while you're busy making other plans."

Show what caused someone to be accidentally thrust into greatness.

Will there be a World War III? Why or why not? And if so, what effects will it have?

What were the causes and effects of the Persian Gulf War?

What were the causes and effects of the Spanish Civil War?

What is the effect of the war in Afghanistan?

What have been the effects of the Watergate scandal?

What is the effect of instantaneous telecommunications on our sense of history?

Why does bad news dominate the newspaper and TV newscasts?

Why might one think of history—as Daisy Ashford referred to it—as "piffle before the wind"?

What drives explorers to explore?

Discuss Thomas Paine's quotation, "Every quiet method for peace hath been ineffectual."

Discuss a large injustice in terms of cause and effect.

How has recent history given vindication for someone or something wronged in the past?

What is behind a prediction by a modern "prophet"?

Why should we view history with the phrase "truth or consequences" in mind?

What—considering recent history—are the future effects of tradition?

Why do other countries worry so much about U. S. policies?

In recent history, where have we come from and where are we going?

Discuss Thomas Henry Huxley's quotation, "Logical consequences are the scarecrows of fools and the beacons of [the] wise."

Why does each generation tend to view past generations nostalgically?

What are the effects of isolationism as a national policy?

Discuss with reference to history the quotation by William Norman Ewer, "I gave my life for freedom—This I know: / For those who bade me fight had told me so."

What has become of a celebrated figure among Americans during the last ten or fifteen years? What caused him or her to continue rising in esteem, or to fall?

What have been the effects, historically, of "gentle persuasion"?

Why are the United States and _____ wary of each other?

What has reason taught/not taught to history?

Discuss in historical cause-and-effect terms Chaucer's quotation, "It is not good a sleeping hound to wake."

Is custom, as David Hume said, the "great guide of human life"?

Why should Aristotle have considered poetry as "something more philosophic and of graver import than history"?

"History is the version of past events that people have decided to agree upon." (Napoleon Bonaparte)

Discuss Disraeli's quotation, "Assassination has never changed the history of the world."

Discuss Paula Gunn Allen's quotation, "I have noticed that as soon as you have soldiers the story is called history."

What recent event in the nation or the world will be considered significant _____ years from now?

Why might the following statement by Chinese prime minister, Zhu Rongji, be accurate? "History can never be covered up."

Language

Why did language begin?

Why do new times bring new language(s)?

How has the Internet (e-mail, the World Wide Web) influenced language?

What happens to babies who are not exposed to a rich variety of language?

Why are some languages valued more than others?

Why do we speak differently in different situations (for example, at home versus at school)?

Does language make its user, or does the user of it make language?

What makes a language fall out of use?

Discuss in terms of cause and effect: "Writing teaches us our mysteries." (Marie de l'Incarnation)

What social factors influence language change?

Explain why English was not replaced by French after the Norman Conquest of England in 1066.

Using cause and effect, outline the general path of the English language from its beginnings to the present.

Why does legal language read as it does?

How does body language speak for us?

Why does slang change so rapidly?

Why could someone who becomes fluent in a foreign language still have difficulty communicating with a native speaker?

To what extent and why does "inflammatory language" inflame?

How do some words or terms become value-laden?

What causes communication problems between generations?

What causes semantic changes?

What languages other than English are having an influence on world politics?

Aphra Behn said, "Money speaks sense in a language all nations understand." How can language be considered money and money be considered language?

How can learning another language change one's view of the world?

How can being bilingual help or hurt you?

Why do some immigrants give up their native languages when they come to the United States?

Why do some people drop their home dialect or language while others continue to value and use it?

Why is Yiddish not spoken as much as it used to be?

Why is one language or another gaining supremacy in the world ?

Why is one language or another gaining supremacy in world politics?

Why is English a world language?

Will English ever be replaced as the dominant language of the United States? What could cause such a change?

Describe the impact of an event or action that has been taken "in the name of God."

What would be the effect of legislation that makes English the official language of the United States?

"We write because we believe the human spirit cannot be tamed and should not be trained." (Nikki Giovanni)

"A riot is the language of the unheard." (Martin Luther King Jr.)

"Language is the roadmap of a culture." (Rita Mae Brown)

Law, Crime

"Civil disobedience becomes a sacred duty when the State becomes lawless or, which is the same thing, corrupt." (Mahatma Gandhi)

How was the Underground Railroad an act of civil disobedience?

Why is the crime rate higher in some areas than in others?

What would happen if everyone were a lawmaker?

What would happen if there were no laws, restrictions, or police?

What is the effect of law by vigilantes?

Discuss the result of a certain recent investigation (presidential conduct, a major bankruptcy, terrorism).

What accounts for the belief that "a police officer is never around when needed"?

How does upholding some laws have a negative effect on society?

Why does crime break out in the streets during a blackout of power in a major city?

What is gained, if anything, by punishing those who break the law?

What effects do parents who commit crimes have on their families?

Why are celebrities who break the law often treated differently than "regular" people?

Why do old statutes remain on the books?

Does a focus on "quality of life" crimes (littering, vandalism) help contribute to a lower rate of major crimes?

What causes police brutality (or what allows it to happen) where it occurs?

Discuss the probable result of dispensing justice according to "an eye for an eye."

Why are some drug crimes punished more harshly than others?

How does prison overcrowding affect punishment and parole decisions?

What is the effect on crime in states that support the death penalty?

Discuss the probable result of following the quotation by Edmund Burke, "Liberty must be limited in order to be possessed."

Why are all of us affected by major crimes?

What causes child abuse?

Why are there inequities in the law in the way the poor and the rich are treated?

Explain why a particular mystery remains unsolved.

What is the effect of enforcing personal safety laws (car seats for infants, bicycle and motorcycle helmets, drinking age)?

How does the Internet make some crimes easier to commit?

How does the Internet make some crimes easier to track?

Explore the cause and effect of speaking out or keeping silent about sexual harassment.

Literature, Writing

"The world I create in the writing compensates for what the real world does not give me." (Gloria Anzaldúa)

Show how fairy tales can condition our responses.

Why is the computer said to take over the writer's control?

Why do scholars of composition say that the computer can improve our writing skills?

Discuss how literature can manipulate others, for good or bad.

What makes a piece of writing "literature"? Who decides what is literature, and what criteria do they use?

What "causes" literature?

What are the effects of literature?

What benefits result from literature? Are people changed for the better by moral literature, that is, literature which demonstrates what ethical behavior ought to be?

What effect(s) can one word have in a sentence? In society?

What are the effects of a report that is easy to understand?

What are the effects of a report that is hard to understand?

Why do many people not like literature?

Why are Homer, Dante, Milton, and Shakespeare difficult to read?

Explain in cause-and-effect terms the quotation by Sir Arthur Helps, "Reading is sometimes an ingenious device for avoiding thought."

Why is it that some women and minority writers of the past are being "discovered" only now?

Is it true that, as Bacon said, writing makes one "exact"?

"Poets are the unacknowledged legislators of the world." (Percy Bysshe Shelley)

"Poetry makes nothing happen." (W. H. Auden)

"A poet's work is to name the unnameable, to point at frauds, to take sides, start arguments, shape the world, and stop it going to sleep." (Salman Rushdie)

"'And where is the use of a book,' thought Alice, 'without pictures or conversations?'" (Lewis Carroll)

Describe the effect of a piece of literature in terms of what Stephen King says here: "I don't want to just mess with your head. I want to mess with your life. I want you to miss appointments, burn dinner, skip your homework."

W. Ross Winterowd has said that "critical readers learn more and certainly enjoy their reading more than passive readers." Why might this be so?

"She is too fond of books, and it has turned her brain" (Louisa May Alcott). Show how this might apply to you.

"Books can be dangerous. The best ones should be labeled 'This could change your life.'" (Helen Exley)

"A book must be an ice-axe to break the seas frozen inside our soul." (Franz Kafka)

"The ability of writers to imagine what is not the self, to familiarize the strange and mystify the familiar, is the test of their power" (Toni Morrison). Use cause and effect to show how an author has familiarized and mystified something for you.

Media

What is lost or gained by watching a film instead of reading the original book?

How do Disney film versions of stories change the original source materials?

What has been the effect of cable networks on the television industry?

Why do networks play down certain world news?

What are the effects of advertising?

Why do advertisements often have such little connection with reality?

What are the effects of the "hidden persuaders" in the media?

Why might a newspaper lose its readership?

Why are people gullible about the news?

How does cigarette advertising make smokers out of nonsmokers?

Why do people smoke despite anti-smoking campaigns publicizing clear evidence that smoking is harmful to one's health?

How have advertisers responded to changing gender roles?

What effect do spin doctors have in politics?

What are the benefits and dangers of instantaneous telecommunications?

What impact has television had on education?

What impact has television had on thought?

Why is television called the opiate of the masses?

Why do magazines and newspapers collapse? What has caused the collapse of a particular magazine or newspaper that was very famous?

How are advertisers capable of manipulating people?

Why are certain facts released only gradually by the media?

Why is _____ a very popular magazine?

Why is _____ a very popular television program?

What is the influence of the media in national politics?

Discuss the causes and effects of the development of printing.

Discuss the effect of watching a sitcom that uses a laugh track versus one that does not.

What is the effect of selling reputations through the media?

Why do soap operas appeal to so many?

Why do game shows appeal to so many?

Why does "reality TV" appeal to so many?

Discuss the quotation by the television commentator Sander Vanocur, "How do you balance the necessity to be entertaining but at the same time informative?"

Discuss the quotation by Arnold Bennett, "Journalists say a thing that they know isn't true, in the hope that if they keep on saying it long enough it *will* be true."

How does "public service" advertising help big business?

How are contemporary beauty pageants trying to cope with feminist expectations?

Physical Science

"Landscape shapes culture." (Terry Tempest Williams)

What causes "acid rain"?

What are the causes of a certain weather condition?

What are the effects of a certain weather condition?

What are the causes and effects of "star death"?

What causes tornados?

What causes windows to steam up?

What is the value of studying astronomy?

What causes smog? What can prevent smog?

What are the positive effects of having been to the moon?

What causes static electricity?

Is there any effect in physical science for which there is no cause? Does everything in the world having to do with physical science have a cause?

Discuss Robert Ingersoll's quotation, "In nature there are neither rewards nor punishments—there are consequences."

Why is it, as Sherlock Holmes says, "a capital mistake to theorize before one has data"?

What scientific evidence, if any, exists to indicate the time and cause of the end of the world?

What effect has Rachel Carson's *Silent Spring* had on the world?

What was the cause behind a certain major power failure?

Thomas Henry Huxley said, "The great tragedy of Science—the slaying of a beautiful hypothesis by an ugly fact." Apply this quotation to a major scientific or medical discovery.

Discuss the quotation by Dr. George Polya, a mathematician, "What is the scientific method except Guess and Test?"

Drawing from the range of both superstition and fact, discuss some element of scientific revolution.

What causes global warming?

Why are coral reefs dying?

What caused a certain geological formation (such as natural bridges, the Grand Canyon)?

What are the consequences of relying upon a particular energy source?

What are the limits of recycling?

What have been the effects of the nuclear accidents at Three Mile Island and Chernobyl?

Read David Hernandez's poem "The Butterfly Effect." What does the poet say about causality?

Discuss El Niño in terms of cause and effect.

What effect has the Green Revolution had on developing countries?

Psychology

Why are stories of near-death experiences fascinating to most of us?

What motivates courage?

What motivates fear?

Why does losing breed losing?

Why does winning breed winning?

What are the possible effects of being "burned" emotionally?

Why might someone be made, in Thomas Hood's words, "Mad from life's history"?

Why is it, as Jean de La Fontaine says, "a double pleasure . . to deceive the deceiver"?

What caused _____ to come emotionally into her/his/their own?

Why do people behave as they do in elevators?

What purpose do emoticons serve in electronic communication?

What are the causes and effects of charisma?

Why do some psychiatrists say there is no such thing as an accident?

How can a single person's personality influence many others?

What psychological effect is there in standing over someone?

What are the effects of having a psychological edge on someone?

Why do we acquire habits? What causes habit to rule our lives?

What makes one method of persuasion more effective than another?

Why does the simple often become difficult?

What good results can we have by applying animal behavior to human behavior?

Why did a certain experiment with animals lead to a better understanding of them and/or of human behavior?

What is the reason behind a bully's behavior?

Why are "Some people . . . so fond of ill-luck that they run half-way to meet it," as Douglas Jerrold said?

Which makes the individual: heredity, or environment?

Why do wives/husbands/children run away?

What explains why some people choose one part of the room to sit in and other people choose another?

Why do smiles, winks, or sympathetic grunts affect us as they do?

Why do some people who have nothing to say talk anyhow?

What are the effects of a good/a bad sense of humor?

Explain what causes employers to react as they do to prospective employees who have a history of illness or who have been in prison.

What causes one phobia or another? What are its effects?

What causes one mania or another? What are its effects?

What causes an obsession? What are its effects?

Explain what psychological factors were responsible for

a good/a bad turnout for a recent event—an election, for example, or a major athletic event.

Why do we forget what we did?

Why do we deceive ourselves in thinking that time spent on an effort is all we need to accomplish it?

What causes stereotypes? What causes prejudice?

Why do popular superstitions persist?

Some people say they aren't "mechanically inclined." Why?

Why do we remember some things and not others?

What determines the physical distance one keeps from others in conversation?

What accounted for the fact that a certain day of yours went wrong/right?

Why do you feel/not feel at home at _____?

Why does love stoop in order to rise, as Robert Browning has said?

Why does love cease to be a pleasure, as Aphra Behn says, "when it ceases to be a secret"?

Why does the world have little to offer "where two fond hearts in equal love are joined," as Anna Barbauld said?

Discuss the opinion of Alfred Tennyson that "'Tis better to have loved and lost, than never to have loved at all."

Discuss this lyric by the rock group Yes: "Owner of a lonely heart, much better than owner of a broken heart."

Discuss in psychological cause-effect terms the quotation, "When the wine is in, the wit is out."

Why are happy surprises good for us?

Why do we need praise to do well?

Why do insignificant memories sometimes take precedence over important ones?

How does laughter help mental health?

Why do people lie about their ages?

What, psychologically, is behind our drive to "save time"?

Why do you and _____ not get along as well as you once did?

How is self-torture related to self-pity?

Discuss the causes for, and effects of, psychological crutches and psychological retreats.

Why is it accurate, or why is it not accurate, to say "What I'm to be I am now becoming"?

How can imagination or dreaming make us happy?

Why is there such an emphasis on youth in U.S. popular culture?

Might there be such a thing as reasonable paranoia?

What are the causes and effects of frustration?

What are the causes and effects of different methods of disciplining children?

What are the causes and effects of gossiping?

What are the causes and effects of venting?

Why are some shopping malls designed to mimic a small-town main street?

What are the psychological effects of urban sprawl?

Why are some people hypnotizable and others are not?

What are the causes and effects of deep despair?

What causes accident-proneness?

Why does staying bitter cause more pain?

What are the roots of, and causes of, embarrassment?

Why is one kind of death more terrifying than another?

Does television contribute to, or detract from, the thinking process?

What explains an individual's handwriting, especially the way we sign our names?

Discuss James Anthony Froude's statement, "Fear is the parent of cruelty."

Discuss Matthew Arnold's statement, "We forget because we must and not because we will."

Why does crying help us emotionally?

Discuss the relationship between the brain's biochemistry and mental illness.

Draw a cause-effect relationship between electricity and the brain.

Discuss a specific example of the relationship between bodily changes and emotions.

Why do those we love have the "most power to hurt us"?

How can a moral strength sometimes have negative consequences?

What are the causes and effects of anger?

Is cursing a sign of laziness, intelligence, vitality, or what?

Discuss the phenomenon of "behavior control."

Why do certain kinds of sounds or words convey certain feelings?

Discuss the proverb: "Tell me who your friends are and I will tell you who you are."

Apply this statement by Jean de La Fontaine to psychology: "I bend but do not break."

Discuss this cartoon caption: "I finally got rid of my inferiority complex, but it loosened my grip on reality."

What effects do feelings have on the facial expression?

What effects have advances in medicine had on our fear of (or lack of fear of) death?

What causes you to be who you are?

What are the effects of pain on the mind?

Discuss these lines from William Blake:

> I was angry with my friend:
> I told my wrath, my wrath did end.
> I was angry with my foe:
> I told it not, my wrath did grow.

Discuss a specific mind-body connection.

Discuss how belonging to a support group can have positive health benefits.

How does political satire benefit society?

What makes some people more likely to indulge in binge drinking?

Why does hazing continue to be popular?

What are the effects of making or not making eye contact with someone you are interacting with?

How does being online affect the persona you present to the world?

Why might different people remember the same event differently?

What could cause a person to "invent" childhood memories?

Why do they say opposites attract?

How can we learn from our dreams?

Why do we dream what we do?

How do "blind spots" affect human behavior?

What makes some people become quiet when they are angry and others become loud?

Why do people sometimes remain in destructive relationships?

Why might you act like one person with one friend and like a different person with another friend?

What makes you want to get to know someone?

Why do people sometimes confuse power with love?

Why do people sometimes confuse dependence with love?

What could cause someone to act against her or his individual principles when in a group?

What causes mob psychology?

What makes people want to be part of a group?

What are the effects of sleep deprivation?

What are the effects of falling in love?

What does it mean to "stoop to conquer"?

Describe the purpose of "tough love."

Why do we procrastinate?

"You lose a lot of time, hating people." (Marian Anderson)

Religion

Is morality an effect of religion?

Why do athletes—from opposing teams—pray for victory?

Why are there so many major similarities between major religions of the world?

What effect has religion had on a certain period of history?

Can good in the religious sense exercise influence on evil?

Can evil exercise influence on good in the religious sense?

What causes a religious believer to see the light? to be reborn?

What causes people to believe that they are doing the will of God ?

Do the religious convictions of persons determine how much help they are willing to give those in need?

Discuss this quotation from William Blake, "Love seeks not itself to please."

Why do people watch religious services on television?

What are the reasons for televangelism and what are its effects on society?

How did a particular religion shape the course of world events?

Has religion done more good or bad in the world? Why? Might this change?

How would the world be different if all people practiced the same religion, or if all people were atheists?

"True religion is real living; living with all one's soul, with all one's goodness and righteousness." (Albert Einstein)

How might religious conviction motivate you to do the right thing for the wrong reason?

How might religious conviction motivate you to do the wrong thing for the right reason?

Social Science
(Sociology, Social Theory, Etc.)

How do different cultures use shame to shape behavior?

"We all do 'do, re, mi,' but you have got to find the other notes yourself." (Louis Armstrong) What are the implications of this statement as a metaphor?

Why is it acceptable to be "classy" but unacceptable to be "classist"?

"There can be no deep disappointment where there is not deep love." (Martin Luther King Jr.)

Why were people so divided over the outcome of the O. J. Simpson trial?

Why do we vote as we do?

What causes giddiness? Why are laughter and yawning contagious?

Why do couples break up?

What makes a town begin in a place where there is "nothing"?

What causes people to engage in "ethnic cleansing"?

What is the current trend in marriage-divorce statistics? Why?

What effect did televising the Gulf War have on U. S. audiences' perception of the war ? Why?

In what ways can natural surroundings determine a people's practical and cultural ways of life?

What will people do, or not do, to gain fame, money, or public office?

Tell what would happen in your life if you lived with or without pets.

Why do some places have higher suicide rates than others?

Does custom reconcile us to everything, as Edmund Burke declared?

Why do people like cell phones?

Why do the works of certain authors come into, then fall out of, public favor?

Why are people fascinated with fire-eaters and other daredevils?

What effects does convention have on society?

Why do we lie? Why do we make excuses?

Why are beauty pageants popular?

What explains the compulsion we have to be with others? Why is the human being basically not a lone animal?

What are the first concerns and questions among family members united after an exceptionally long separation? Why?

What does its graffiti tell us about a community or about its individuals?

What social phenomena are revealed when there is a newly vacant seat on a crowded bus?

How does the definition of "society" vary from one person to the next?

What common values exist in society, and why?

What causes us to realize when we are most alone?

How does group behavior change in an electronic classroom? In a chat room?

What are the arguments for and against adopting a child from a different culture than the parents'?

How does the untimely death of a famous person affect that person's public image?

Why are societies so slow to correct pollution problems?

Explain the results of the 2000 presidential election in terms of cause and effect.

How does a victim's speaking out against wrongdoing affect an institution or society?

What is the effect of breaking a corporation's monopoly over certain products?

What are the arguments for and against legalizing same-sex marriages?

Is development of public land always in the best interests of society? Why or why not?

What questions does a poor person have who falls in love with a rich person? Why?

What questions does a rich person have who falls in love with a poor person? Why?

Discuss this quotation from Henry Fielding: "Some folks rail against other folks, because other folks have what some folks would be glad of."

What questions does a person who marries someone from another culture have?

Why do people appear as guests on tell-all talk shows? Why do people like to watch such shows?

Why does it become chic to have certain problems?

Discuss an example of the domino effect in society.

Apply to your life the metaphor of cause and effect described in this nursery rhyme:

> For want of a nail, the shoe was lost;
> For want of a shoe, the horse was lost;
> For want of a horse, the rider was lost;
> For want of a rider, a message was lost;
> For want of a message, the battle was lost;
> For want of a battle, the kingdom was lost!

Sports and Physical Activities

Discuss Bill Russell's argument that winning and losing depend more on "chemistry" than on skill or good players.

Why do people jog, or run?

Why do people who have no chance of winning a marathon still participate?

Why should a certain baseball player have felt obligated to give up part of his salary while he was in a slump?

Define sporting behavior in terms of cause and effect.

In what ways is sport some people's religion?

What do athletes think about while they are participating in their sports? Why?

Can nutrition and training make an athlete?

Why is winning so important to most athletes?

Why does one select one sport rather than another?

What aside from losing can break a team's morale?

Why are some mascots or team names considered offensive?

Why might an athlete prefer to set records rather than help the team win (or vice versa)?

What really constitutes or brings about "individual effort" in sports?

What accounted for the fact that a certain sports upset took place?

Are athletes controlled more by themselves, or by circumstances?

What, besides age, causes decline in an athlete?

Can one by intense exercise make up for years of leisure and physical non-activity?

Why don't more people exercise?

Why are some people obsessed with exercise?

How has the role of the coach changed in the era of big-money athletics?

What is the effect of trash talking in sports?

Is it more effective for a coach to be nice to players or mean to them?

Why are athletes called heroes when what they are doing is playing a game?

Why do some athletes use visualization techniques?

What cause-and-effect thinking underlay Muhammad Ali's rope-a-dope boxing strategy.

7 EXPOSITION

What Exposition Is

Exposition is the setting forth of purpose or meaning—not, in a strict sense at least, to criticize, argue, or develop a subject, but to open it up, lay its bones bare. A more literal image of the art might be described as moving the subject out of position, coaxing, jolting, or driving it into a fresh new perspective, so that it will stand more clearly forth and expose itself for what it is.

How to Write Exposition

Clarity is essential in exposition. Limit your subject. Keep it tight, unified, concrete. Do all that yet let the subject breathe and you will have turned the trick of exposition. Perhaps that can best be done by allowing the subject to explain itself, expose itself from within, from that depth where the bones are barest. Impose an explanation of your own and there is every chance you will violate that stricter sense of the form. Therefore, this form would probably be better used to explain a subject you know well, rather than to explore something you are only just discovering. In any case, effective exposition is good writing dis-cipline, useful in nearly any other kind of writing and fundamental to most.

Locating Subjects for Exposition

We have held to the stricter sense of exposition here partly because broader senses are more explicitly engaged in other sections of this book. Exposition shares a common root with the word "expound," which also describes a way of presenting a subject. But expounding on a subject will more likely lead beyond bare explanation into interpretation, argumentation, or other critical techniques best considered in their own right. Of course, almost any subject listed in those other chapters is open to an expository treatment in the stricter sense we are struggling to maintain here as well. (It might be helpful to recall that in certain musical forms the "exposition" refers to the first part in which the thematic material is straightforwardly presented. Later in the movement other techniques are used to shape, develop, and adorn that same material.)

An expository essay on *exposition* itself might toughen its *definition* by *contrasting* it with *narration*. It would take an excellent student essayist to explain a story without explaining it away.

Professions, Occupations

What jobs hold up best during both good times and bad times?

For what is Buckminster Fuller known?

For what is Bill Gates known?

For what is Mother Teresa known?

For what is Nelson Mandela known?

For what is Marie Curie known?

For what is Mother Jones known?

For what is Albert Einstein known?

How has prophecy become a profession?

What criteria qualify someone as an expert?

Describe the value of the _____ profession to society.

What factors have encouraged people to retire at a later age?

What new field creates many new professions?

Why are farmers sometimes paid *not* to grow crops?

Why are employees less likely to feel loyalty to a single company?

What must a poet laureate do to qualify for the title?

Describe Gloria Steinem's role in the women's movement.

What is a career politician?

Commerce, Finance, Economy, Economics

What were some common ways of making a living during the Depression?

What assumptions are implied by the statement "the customer is always right"?

Discuss the growth of multinational corporations.

Discuss how debts are paid.

Discuss whether the average person has the ability to make a lot of money.

What are some major financial frauds?

What will stores of the future be like?

Describe the history and current state of car pools.

Discuss Harry S. Truman's fight against hoarding.

Discuss government efforts to encourage consumer spending in times of economic crisis.

Discuss money devaluation.

Discuss the battle for control of a certain company.

What are alternate energy production incentives?

What tax breaks exist for individuals? For companies?

What are some calculated billing snares for credit-card holders?

Discuss government-supported student loan programs.

To what extent does customer protest affect the price of goods?

Discuss the abuse of expense accounts.

Discuss the estate tax.

What is a venture in which young people have become financially successful?

Describe the growth of the telemarketing industry and the backlash against it.

Discuss the increasing globalization of business.

Trace the increasing interconnections between educational institutions and big business.

How is Internet commerce changing the nature of buying and selling?

Why does one job pay more than another, even though both require specialized training?

Describe the shift from the family farm to agribusiness.

Why does economic trouble in one country cause problems in others?

What "extras" are offered by the telephone company but not generally known to the public?

_____ are not getting any cheaper/are not getting any easier to come by.

How accurately does Hollywood portray the financial world as it really is?

Why has social security lost its status?

Discuss the practice of giving children allowances.

Discuss owning a farm.

How has online shopping had an impact on department stores?

How are our tax dollars used?

Discuss television networks and money.

Write of an unusual entrepreneurial venture.

Are you, in these times, "what you own" or "what you owe"?

Write an extended example of how money makes money, or how money buys time.

Discuss insurance abuses, from both sides: the consumers and the businesses.

Discuss the growing divorce "business."

How independent is a salesperson?

What happens in an audit?

What employment prospects are there in the field of ecology?

How can one drive a hard bargain?

Discuss taxpayer revolts.

What caused an isolated (that is, not a national) labor-management dispute?

How does the stock market work?

Describe the problem of credit-card debt among students.

Describe the environmental impact of SUVs.

Describe the Enron debacle.

Describe the ongoing debate about affirmative action.

Discuss the ongoing debate on whether to privatize the social security system.

"From lemonade stand to _____." Describe the jobs you've held.

Describe barter as a means of commerce in a particular culture.

"America was built with small farms. They keep saying the farmer is the country's backbone. I never heard anything about agribusiness being the backbone of the country." Jessie Lopez De La Cruz. Describe how the farmer is the country's backbone.

Sports, Entertainment

Discuss the events that typify the Tour de France.

Discuss the set up of the winter Olympics.

Is there a way in sports in which both opponents can lose?

How accurately does Hollywood portray the sports world?

Discuss the phenomenon of a new craze or fad.

Discuss a certain sports scandal.

Discuss athletes and religion.

Discuss the fan phenomenon known as "the wave" and/or other sports crowd behavior(s) of your choosing.

Discuss rituals observed at sporting events.

Why do more and more fans stay home and watch sports on television?

Is it true that "there's no business like show business"?

Discuss the history of ratings systems for Hollywood films.

Discuss sports (radio, television) announcers.

Discuss free agents in sports.

Discuss a certain child superstar, such as Michael Jackson or Shirley Temple.

Discuss time as it applies to the athlete.

Trace an athlete's career from player to coach.

What do families do on weekends?

Do sports spectators like violence?

Why are stars (athletes, actors) paid so much?

Discuss drug abuse among Olympic athletes.

Describe how college coaches recruit future players.

Trace an athlete's career during and after the playing days.

Describe an athlete-recruiting incident that made headlines.

Discuss a favorite form of entertainment for you and your friends.

Education

Discuss the battle for control of a certain school or school system.

Discuss the idea that all teaching is political.

Be an expert in a specialized topic and, using the special language associated with it, explain it to someone who is unacquainted with it.

Give to a layperson some understanding of a difficult subject, such as a scientific law.

Discuss the rationale of organizing schools on the basis of grade level.

How is reading taught?

How is writing taught?

What do group homes offer people with disabilities?

What difficulties do public schools in urban areas have? In rural areas?

Is it possible not to think?

Explain a common logical fallacy.

Discuss self-education.

Discuss the challenge of balancing school security with student freedom.

At what age do we first become aware of ourselves and others?

Why do some high schools require proficiency tests for graduation? How do such tests work?

What is cultural literacy?

What purpose do college summer programs serve?

Write on the revival of _____.

Emerson said that life consists in what one is thinking all day. Discuss.

What new practices exist for grading papers?

What new teaching trends are there, either in methodology or subject matter?

What are the responsibilities of students in high school?

Develop the thesis: "_____ is an education."

What is "emotional intelligence"?

What does the term "multiple intelligences" mean?

What will your child's first teacher expect of him/her?

"He [or she] is wise who learns from everyone," says a proverb. Discuss.

Write on self-improvement.

John Donne said, "Go, and catch a falling star . . . ." How can you apply this to your life?

Why is the college presidency such a difficult profession?

What is service-learning?

Discuss opening up new worlds in education.

Discuss learning all the angles of _____.

Discuss a significant discovery about _____.

What did Helen Keller say she would concentrate on looking at if given only three days to see? Discuss her answer as it concerns you.

Judge the employment outlook over the next ten years in various areas of teaching (or in some other profession).

Many adults in the United States are functionally illiterate. Discuss this condition.

What is the role of an educator as defined in your community?

What role does the school board serve in your school district?

Discuss a key issue in university admissions policies.

What is a search engine, and how does it work?

Discuss how the human brain is—and is not—like a computer.

In some (few) schools, teachers do not assign grades. What are the potential pros and cons of this approach?

In many parts of the United States, some public schools are much better funded than other schools are. What is the history of this problem? What is being done (or suggested) to fix it?

What are "charter schools," and what debate has arisen over them?

Discuss the debate over whether evolution or creationism should be taught in public schools.

Cable television programming is piped into some classrooms. What arguments have been made for or against this practice? What may happen in the future regarding this practice?

Discuss the lunches provided in your school's cafeteria from a nutritional standpoint. Are they healthy or unhealthy? Who decides what will be on the menu?

Where does funding for your school come from? Has there been debate about whether to increase or cut funding to your school in recent years? If so, what were the arguments, and what happened?

What policy does your school (or school system) have about censorship? How was this policy developed?

Who decides which books you will read in your English class? What factors go into this decision?

In what ways is computer technology changing public school education? What debates exist over how to use the Internet in education?

Discuss censorship and freedom of expression as they relate to student publications (print and nonprint).

What is a "renaissance man"—or woman?

Law

Discuss legal proceedings on television.

Discuss first offenders and the law.

Discuss abuses in the armed forces.

Discuss illegal drugs in high school.

Discuss "the law's delay" (*Hamlet*).

Discuss how one can legally fight the boss.

Are there any uniform prison/jail standards?

How do natural-disaster victims appeal for government-assistance funds?

How is the legal system being called upon to judge mother against father, one lifestyle against another?

What are some unusual legal or insurance services?

What are labor unions? How do they affect the relationship between an employer and employees?

Discuss debate over cameras in courtrooms.

Discuss women in the military.

Discuss the issue of gays in the military.

Do research, and then write, on the question of who owns the mailbox legally. Does the government own it, or does the person whose mail is directed to it? What restrictions and so forth are there on and for mailboxes?

What was prison life like in the Gulag Archipelago?

What are some typical laws about posters—kinds of posters, kinds of display, and so forth?

How can one legally protect his or her job?

Where does the court stand on obscenity?

What ordinances about pornography exist at the small-town level?

Do military or political bodies in the United States have a record of "dealing with" people who threaten to blow the whistle on them?

Write about the pickpocket conditions of a certain area.

Discuss the law about racial-ethnic listings or identifications.

Discuss a loophole in the law.

Discuss personal property and the law.

Tell what it was like during the 1950s Red Scare in the United States.

Discuss violent encounters outside the law.

Discuss mail fraud.

Discuss counterfeit documents—passports, visas, recommendations, birth certificates, graduation certificates, university transcripts, and so forth.

Discuss the law and the right to protect news sources.

What does the law do about rape?

What does the law do about child abuse?

What happens in small claims court?

What are some legal abuses by the FBI? The CIA?

Discuss cracking down on _____.

Discuss the comeback(s) of "blacklisted" writers.

Discuss consumer protection and the law.

Discuss solitary confinement and the law.

Can students collect legal damages from their schools?

What are your rights concerning the pledge of allegiance?

Considered from the legal side, does our patent system work?

Discuss gang control of the law and government.

Discuss witness protection under the law. What does the law do about threats?

Discuss the law and bribery.

Discuss identity-theft crimes—telephone calls made free, misuse of bank credit cards, illegal bank withdrawals, and so forth.

Discuss Internet crimes.

What are "right to work" laws? How do they affect the relationship between an employer and an employee?

What is "welfare-to-work" legislation? How has it affected welfare recipients' lives in recent years?

Some courts now apply harsh drug laws that sentence relatively minor offenders to long prison terms. What are the arguments for and against this practice?

When and why did the practice of searching students' school lockers begin? What debate has arisen about it?

What new legal questions have arisen with the rapid development of the Internet? (Or pick one such question and lay out its dimensions and significance.)

Research and write about debate over "racial profiling"?

Some localities have enacted laws giving same-sex unions similar legal status to that of married couples. What arguments are made for and against such laws?

In many areas, eighteen-year-olds can be drafted into military service but cannot legally buy or consume alcoholic beverages. Why this difference?

Summarize the debate over whether it should be legal to smoke marijuana.

In response to the September 11 terror attacks, some lawmakers wanted to give more power to the authorities who fight terror while others wanted to ensure protection of the many freedoms that U.S. citizens enjoy. Summarize the resulting debate.

Discuss the Homeland Security Department created by President George W. Bush after the September 11 terror attacks.

Explain the ongoing debate about school prayer.

Discuss current issues relating to laws prohibiting sexual harassment.

Discuss lawsuits against tobacco makers.

Discuss educational programs in prisons.

Explore how white collar crime is treated differently from other crimes.

Travel, Transportation

Describe Route 66.

Discuss the rigors of traveling to remote places.

Write of a classic car.

Write about ways in which automakers put profits ahead of lives.

Discuss long-distance car travel.

Discuss modern ways of improving cars for luxury or comfort.

Discuss changes in air safety since 9/11/01.

Discuss modern ways of improving cars for safety.

Discuss driving in a foreign country.

Discuss bicycle speed barriers.

Discuss the popularity of SUVs.

Discuss road rage.

Discuss big-city driving.

Discuss Americans' attitudes toward their cars.

Discuss the development of airbags in cars.

Discuss child-safety features in cars.

Discuss the popularity of a certain vacation spot.

Discuss high-speed trains.

Discuss prospects for increased mass transportation.

Discuss the differences in pollution laws for cars vs. those for buses and trucks.

Discuss current work on cars using renewable energy sources.

Discuss "alternative spring breaks."

Discuss plans for a particular kind of expedition.

Animals, Plants, Natural Phenomena

Discuss the "animals nobody loves."

Discuss the illegal use of contaminated animals for food.

Discuss the abuse of animals.

Discuss the animal rights movement.

Discuss cat personality.

Discuss dog personality.

Discuss pet cemeteries.

Discuss the intelligence of animals.

Discuss the emotions of animals.

How do elephants establish graveyards?

How do animals demonstrate territoriality?

Discuss animals and language.

Discuss animals and neurosis.

Discuss the habits and characteristics of kangaroos.

What does it mean that the mother mink sets out five food settings for her five children?

How does the film *Jaws* differ from the reality of sharks?

Discuss ostrich ranching.

Do we have anything to fear from birds?

What is the truth about the black widow spider?

Discuss the spread of fire ants in the United States.

Discuss hunting for truffles.

Discuss the ecosphere, the area from which our natural resources (everything needed to support life, in this case) come.

Discuss the origin and/or control of forest fires.

What should plants be fed?

Discuss global warming.

Discuss the El Niño effect.

Discuss desert agriculture.

Discuss Siberian resources.

What is the value of a swamp?

Discuss the nature of electricity.

Discuss the "challenge of the deep."

Discuss current uses of the laser.

Consider the ramifications of the Law of Entropy—the theory that the universe has reached its peak and is winding down.

Discuss the Big Bang Theory.

Discuss String Theory.

Take a light-hearted look at Chaos Theory in your life.

Religion, Beliefs

What did early human beings believe about the natural world that we now do not believe?

What is involved in spiritual freedom?

What are some current religious problems?

What are some religious questions that are unsettled?

Discuss some intimations of mortality/immortality.

Discuss the belief that there are ghosts that don't know what happened to them, that don't know, for example, that they are ghosts or how they died.

Discuss the role of magic in ancient times.

Discuss the role of magic in modern times.

What is the role of the Bible in U.S. national life?

Write about snake handlers, an American religious sect.

Write about new religions.

Discuss Wicca as a recent popular religion.

Discuss Quakers and their beliefs.

Discuss the Amish and their beliefs.

Discuss Christian Scientists and their beliefs.

Write about the expansion of religion into television.

Write about the growing relationship between religion and politics.

Pick a belief system and explain its features.

Describe how Eastern religions/philosophies have influenced the West.

Discuss similarities/differences between various mythologies.

Discuss various beliefs about what happens after death.

How did the "founding fathers" view religion?

What role does religion play in the conflict in _____?

What do Hindus mean by "transmigration of souls"?

Discuss the Buddhist eightfold path as a code of conduct.

Discuss Yin and Yang as Taoist principles.

Discuss Islam's belief in a just God.

Discuss a basic teaching from Judaism.

The Media, Rhetoric, Communication

Discuss motivations for writing.

Discuss propaganda and elections.

Discuss the use of negative campaigning.

Do people really listen to the words of popular music?

Describe an instance of a song becoming popular despite widespread misunderstanding of its lyrics.

How do newspapers determine what is "news"?

How can the audience affect programming on television?

If people were taped so that they knew what they sound like, would they change in their speech habits or their behavior?

How has the development of cable and satellite television changed the media industry?

Discuss the appeal of African American rap music to White teenagers.

Discuss changing standards of what is acceptable on television.

Discuss the cult of personality in media.

What are some reasons movie producers have for delaying the release of their films?

Discuss a famous composer-lyricist team.

How is audio-visual technology used in the field of medicine?

How does TV present useful information in an interesting way?

What is a "real" person in fiction?

How is a symphony like a play?

Should news reporters be entertainers?

Write of a campaign waged against a certain advertisement or against certain kinds of advertisements.

Discuss how the reception of a given show/film has changed over time.

How might a writer's characters come to gain control of the writer?

Discuss the use of movie ratings.

What do we mean when we say that a certain TV show is "predictable"? Predictable why?

Discuss the changing content of television.

Discuss multiculturalism on television.

Write on legal language.

In what ways have certain futuristic novels (such as Huxley's *Brave New World* and Orwell's *1984*) proved themselves to have been accurate forecasts?

Write on the destruction of important records in a significant public event.

Write on "weasel words" used in advertising.

Write on TV and censorship.

Discuss how you can tell that a commercial is locally produced.

Discuss advertisements/commercials in which the product is hardly shown/discussed.

Tell what the Burma Shave commercials (or other past American folklore items in advertisements) were like.

Write about bumper stickers as American dialogue.

Describe an incident of censorship in schools.

Discuss the Harry Potter books and censorship.

Write on editorial cartoons.

Discuss reading trends among the American people.

How accurate are newspapers as keepers of history?

How accurate are historians as keepers of history?

"The strength of a community comes from the ability and desire of its people to communicate with one another," a newspaper item says. Discuss.

Write on propaganda in Soviet life in the 1960s.

Write on censorship in a foreign country.

Write on censorship in advertising.

What is the translator's greatest problem?

Write on the battle for possession of the mind—through radio, television, books, religion, and so forth.

Discuss the strengths and weaknesses of local reportage.

What role does public television have in United States society?

Write of a program in which business executives are learning how to communicate in other cultures.

Write about audio books.

Write on the decline of the LP.

Write an essay about the golden age of radio.

Write about how people adjust their speech to fit a given context.

Write on the growing importance of English as a political and commercial language of the world.

Write on the use of doublespeak.

What makes a commercial/advertisement effective?

How might the author of a classic from the last century react to today's analysis of the book?

Write on over-correctness or pseudo-correctness.

Write on the government and television.

Write on exchanges of favors among television networks.

Write on advertising in which there are direct attacks on opposing commercial products.

Write on what television advertisers and television producers do to avoid unfortunate juxtaposition between products and shows.

What are some important misconceptions about language?

Why do people write to the editor of the newspaper?

How can "plain talk" be used to manipulate an audience?

Do words often conceal more than they express?

How does slang/jargon mark a person as a member of a particular group?

Write about current technology used to make media accessible to people with sight or hearing impairments.

How has the Internet changed publishing?

How has the Internet changed reporting?

How are computers complicating the meaning of the "written word"?

Compare several news accounts of the same event. Draw out their differences, and explore how these differences present the event in a different light—or even as a different event altogether.

Compare several reviews of the same movie or book. Draw out their differences, and explore the assump-tions each makes about the work, about the process of watching or reading, or about readers of the review.

Describe some of the ways that women are "commodified" on television (shows or commercials).

Describe commercials that deconstruct conventional images and notions.

Health, Medicine

Write of someone who has regained eyesight after blindness.

Write about required drug warnings.

Write about healthy hobbies.

Write about the link between the mind and the body.

Write about schizophrenia.

Discuss the pros and cons of laser eye surgery.

Write about cellular phones and radiation fears.

Write about research into cures for HIV/AIDS.

Write about a high-functioning autistic person.

What are the newest medical developments regarding _____ (condition)?

Write on sexually transmitted diseases (STDs).

Write about food poisoning.

Write on the health problems caused by the Chernobyl disaster.

Write about research into cures for cancer.

Write about allergies in the home.

Write about the common cold.

Write about radioactive fallout and health.

Write about medical uses of plants and herbs.

Write about anthrax contamination.

Write about smallpox contamination.

Safe Nuclear Burial Unlikely: Geologists, says a headline. Discuss.

Write about intravenous feeding.

Write about emergency medical technicians (EMTs) .

Write about an emergency room.

Write about carbon monoxide poisoning.

What can be done to protect public water from being sabotaged?

What can be done to make drinking water safe?

Write about reconstructive surgery.

What are some complications of pregnancy?

What are operational problems of a veterans' hospital?

What new directions have been taken in epidemiology?

What does Aristotle observe about sleep and sleepless-ness?

Write on non-Western healing techniques.

Write on the use of stem cells in the treatment of genetic disorders.

Write about groundwater contamination.

Write about asbestos contamination.

Write on chiropractic care.

Write on prenatal technology.

Discuss recent medical breakthroughs in surgery.

Write about a sleep disorder such as sleep apnea.

Write about autism.

Discuss the rising level of obesity in the United States.

Write about organ donation.

Discuss race and the prevalence of a certain disease.

How much of one's health is determined by genetics?

Write on research studies on women's health.

Discuss the relative lack of insurance coverage for mental health care.

Discuss the problem of rising health care costs.

Discuss the advantages and disadvantages of HMOs.

Write about virus mutations.

Write on public health services.

Write on modern medical uses of the leech.

Write about the benefits of taking dogs to nursing homes.

Write about guide and care-giving dogs for people who live alone.

Describe vector-borne diseases.

Describe how you think a cold might spread in school.

What are the health hazards of asbestos?

What are the health hazards of radon?

Describe the health-giving properties of a particular food.

Describe "comfort" foods.

Politics, Government, History

What are some examples of intelligence failures by the FBI and CIA?

Write of someone who was immensely successful in a first venture at politics.

The personal is political. Discuss.

How does the Chinese government put down dissidents?

Write on the erosion of freedom in democratic states.

Can freedom be too much for many people to handle?

How is an aristocrat trained for rule?

Write of an attack that has been made on a certain political group.

How do intelligence agencies work to put down those against them?

Discuss the passing of the cavalry.

How accurately does Hollywood portray historical events?

Discuss immigration (or emigration) policies.

What goes on in the armed forces that the armed forces would prefer the public not know?

Write on political sloganry.

Write on the transition from one president to the next.

Write on the bureaucratic use of government vehicles and other items.

How popular is Britain's royal family?

Write on White House news conferences.

Summarize a certain public figure's position on a certain issue— terrorism, welfare, the environment, for example.

What are the vital functions of the United States Census Bureau?

Write on government in the former Soviet republics.

Write on island-hopping during World War II.

What crises play big parts in elections?

Write on prisoner exchanges or spy exchanges.

What determines who can run for political office?

Explain the Teapot Dome Scandal.

What was the last blow to the South in the American Civil War?

What was the Iran/Contra scandal?

What happened to the Watergate conspirators?

Write about a human rights watchdog group.

Write on White House media relations.

Write on fictionalized media portrayals of the White House/the presidency.

Write about an espionage case.

Write about Operation Desert Storm.

Write on the "Don't Ask Don't Tell" policy regarding gays in the U. S. military.

Discuss corporate welfare.

Write about impeachment.

Write about lobbying on Capitol Hill.

Write about efforts toward campaign finance reform.

Write about voting irregularities in the 2000 presidential election.

Write about redistricting.

What is pork in government?

Describe the structure of your local government.

Write on globalization.

What role has Nelson Mandela played in South African politics?

Write about the end of communism in eastern Europe.

Write about the reunification of Germany.

Write about the creation of Pakistan.

Write about Hong Kong returning to Chinese rule.

Write about a civil rights movement.

Write about parliamentary democracy.

What usually happens in off-year elections?

Write on the concept of global responsibility.

Write of minority representation in American government.

Write of foreign influence on American governmental decisions.

Why did a certain Japanese admiral say, "We have waked a sleeping giant"?

Why does the United States government not enforce the metric switch?

What part does celebrity status play in politics?

Write about living history in _____ (Williamsburg, St. Augustine, etc.).

Write of some issue having to do with territorial rights.

What happened at Babi Yar?

What procedure is behind a presidential decision?

Write of so-called "instant history"—bringing the pyramids, bridges, and so forth of the famous past to the United States.

Write on this quotation from Bill Moyers: "Most presidents don't rise above their times. They reflect their times."

Describe the different kinds of voting methods in the Florida presidential election of 2000.

Describe what experts claim that computers can do to count ballots. Describe why the claims may be untrue.

Describe the role of women voters in a particular election.

What is political asylum?

8 ARGUMENTATION

What Argumentation Is

In its root sense, argumentation musters proof and brings it forth in order to persuade, defend, or, at times, attack. In that stricter sense this process of writing is logical and formal. Let us free the term from its dictionary sense and let it come to grips with anything from a legal brief to a political showdown. Exposition strives to explain, argumentation strives to win.

How to Write Argumentation

Once again, clarity is essential as with any kind of writing. We emphasize it again here because argument so often tends to become melded with emotion. Even if argumentative material demands a certain degree of ambiguity or subjectiveness, the one who argues should be clear about it. The word "argue" is derived from the Latin *arguere*, which according to the *Oxford English Dictionary,* means "to demonstrate, make clear." As the OED tells us, the word is derived from the same root as that underlying *argentums,* meaning "silver," and originally referred to that which was "brightly shining," hence also "clear."

A balanced, reasonable approach is often most effective, and it is always better to gather more proof than opinion. Nothing is more likely to put people off than a hedgehog piece of writing bristling with opinions. Reason and logic are not the end-all of anything, however, though we sometimes find it comforting to believe they might be. Emotion is powerful; it has moved nations. But emotional appeals are skittish. They tend to bolt off the track. Riding them rhetorically is dangerous even for experienced writers. Anyone attempting to argue from emotion should remember that the faster the heart races, the tighter the rein.

It can be instructive simply to argue a position for the fun of it, to play the devil's advocate. But when you turn serious about it and are out to win the day, you had best believe in what you are doing. Be sincere. Sincerity convinces. It will help you see clearly through the thick of things. Anything else will work against you. Truth persists between the lines of a hypocritical page like checked light through a lattice.

Integrity, then, is the place where you make your stand. Imagination can broaden the field. Reason, logic, emotion, humor, irony, satire—any of these can be viable forms of argumentation. How you use them is another matter. You might find yourself brandishing a polemical club. Or is it an irenic olive branch you brush across the page? Then maybe you turn acrobat, tumble your argument on its grinning head, much as Swift did when he made his modest proposal. Circumstance will have its say. Only stand firmly in the integrity of your argument.

Locating Subjects for Argumentation

Argumentation is another substantial section of this book. Almost anything can become controversial, including most of the subjects listed in this book. A word of caution, though, before this chapter is crossed with other disciplines and techniques: It is best to keep forms and priorities straight. Although creative and imaginative thinking are necessary for a powerful argument, creative writing as such is, generally speaking, ill suited for the purpose of argumentation. Powerful arguments can be made creatively, but the difference between argumentation and art is definitive.

Education, Learning, Experience

Argue for or against: "Literature, whether handed down by word or mouth or in print, gives us a second handle on reality" (Chinua Achebe).

Should high school students be required to learn a foreign language?

Do Americans tend to undervalue intellectuals?

Why is it important to study history?

What educational philosophy of the past continues to influence education today?

Argue for/against school uniforms.

Should there be bilingual education in the United States?

Should we read "the classics"?

What should the university demand of its students?

Where should college and university costs be cut?

How should public funding for schools be determined?

Is there too much hair-splitting in education?

Which is it better to see: the forest, or the trees?

What is the place of, or what should be the place of, a public intellectual?

What are the most important factors to consider when choosing a college to attend?

What is the best way to prioritize your school activities?

Argue for/against standardized testing.

Argue for/against exit exams in high school.

Argue for/against travel as education.

Argue for/against grade inflation.

Argue for/against letter grades.

Argue for/against allowing students (especially young children) to choose for themselves among educational alternatives.

Agree/disagree: "A little learning is a dangerous thing" (Alexander Pope).

Agree/disagree with the argument that politicians and bureaucrats should be required to take literacy tests.

Agree/disagree with the practice of block scheduling.

Agree/disagree: The public education system is broken.

Agree/disagree: There are too many restrictions on teaching.

Agree/disagree: There are not enough restrictions on students.

Agree/disagree: There is too much time off among students for special activities.

Argue for/against school prayers.

Argue for/against sex education.

Argue for/against teacher strikes.

Argue for/against private schools.

Argue for/against a "value-added" approach versus a "weed them out" approach to education.

Agree/disagree with the practice of year-round schooling.

Agree/disagree: College entrance exams should be changed.

Argue for/against stricter college entrance requirements.

Argue for/against school vouchers.

Argue for/against textbooks.

Argue for/against censorship of certain kinds of books.

Argue for/against peer teaching.

Argue for/against public discipline by teachers.

Argue for/against a specific change in the curriculum.

Argue for/against a university education.

Argue for/against periodically evaluating teachers on their knowledge of the subjects they teach.

Argue for/against periodically evaluating teachers on their teaching ability.

Argue for/against fraternities/sororities.

Argue for/against student government.

Argue for/against strictness of form in schoolwork.

Argue for/against all-boys and all-girls schools.

Argue for/against busing of students to promote integration.

Argue for/against setting a life goal at an early age.

Argue for/against parents' determining their children's careers.

Argue for/against high registration fees.

Who ought to be permitted to serve on the school board?

Who ought to have the responsibility (and authority) for educational policy?

What should be the limit, if any, of academic freedom?

What measures of academic ability should be used in schools?

Agree/disagree: In the current age of specialization, it is impossible to be an expert in many things.

Argue with reference to your own experience: "The most interesting things are those that didn't occur."

Agree/disagree: Sometimes children misbehave because they want to be corrected.

Argue for/against the idea that youth is wasted on the young.

Argue for/against spanking.

Argue for/against curfews.

Agree/disagree: "Humankind cannot bear very much reality" (T. S. Eliot).

Whose history does American history as it is taught in your school represent?

Agree/disagree: "There's nothing wrong with sameness."

Agree/disagree: "It is easier to be reasonable than unreasonable."

Agree/disagree: Solitude is one of the happiest routes to happiness.

Agree/disagree: Solitude is one of our best teachers.

What opportunities should schools offer students to use what Howard Gardner calls "multiple intelligences"?

Argue for/against prayer in schools.

Agree/disagree with the opinion about experience that good is not always rewarded and evil is not always punished.

In growing up, *does* Hope reign supreme, or does it not even reign at all?

Agree/disagree, with regards to education and experience: "The road of excess leads to the palace of wisdom" (William Blake).

Does philosophy have a real place in the world?

Should everyone be admitted to the university? Should there be no restrictions on entry?

Agree/disagree: The Internet improves education.

Agree/disagree that students should be allowed to sue schools for wrongly educating them.

What should be taught?

What should not be taught?

Who should decide what curriculum is followed?

Argue for/against federal spending for education.

Argue for/against student employment as an educational or otherwise important experience.

Argue for/against viewing the university as a giver of moral education.

What modern songwriter's songs could be fruitfully studied in school?

Agree/disagree: "Education makes a people easy to lead, but difficult to drive; easy to govern, but impossible to enslave."

Should students be paid as an encouragement to make good grades?

Agree/disagree: Teachers should enliven their classes with entertainment.

Discuss argumentatively any book which educated and changed the world.

Argue for a particular way in which textbooks should be chosen.

Argue whether near-misses teach anything.

Argue what truth is and where to find it.

Agree/disagree with the opinion that knowledge can get in the way.

Does what we don't know hurt us?

Agree/disagree: The personal digital assistant in education is a fad.

Agree/disagree: Parents should be allowed to sue teachers for giving students poor grades.

Argue for/against gifted and remedial classes.

Argue for/against standardized testing.

Argue for/against tracking by ability.

Argue for/against athletic scholarships.

Argue for/against charter schools.

What, if anything, should be done about absenteeism in school?

Is it true that, as novelist John Gardner has said, our schools are "thrown up like barricades in the way of young minds"? Does school education thwart, or does it assist, life education?

Discuss argumentatively T. S. Eliot's poetic statement, "Teach us to care and not to care. / Teach us to sit still."

Discuss argumentatively Max Beerbohm's statement, "The Socratic manner is not a game at which two can play."

Discuss argumentatively Emerson's statement, "A foolish consistency is the hobgoblin of little minds."

Discuss argumentatively the statement popularized by Hillary Clinton, "It takes a village to raise a child."

Discuss argumentatively: "A worthy idea is one that withstands resistance."

Agree/disagree with Thoreau's argument that it is not necessary to travel in order to learn.

Discuss argumentatively: "Knowledge will forever govern ignorance, and a people who mean to be their own governors must arm themselves with the power which knowledge gives" (James Madison).

Discuss argumentatively Sir Francis Bacon's statement, "Silence is the virtue of fools."

Discuss argumentatively Sir Thomas Browne's statement, "We carry within us the wonders we seek without [outside of] us."

Discuss argumentatively Thomas Henry Huxley's statement, "Irrationally held truths may be more harmful than reasoned errors."

Argue for/against attending an Ivy League school.

Agree/disagree: "Still waters run deep."

Agree/disagree with the argument that grades indicate something about achievement.

How can it be that, as John Donne said, "affliction is a treasure"?

Argue a particular formula or standard for judging when a person is educated.

Argue whether it is fun to have to work in order to know.

Argue what is the best lesson that education gives.

Argue whether history is "bunk."

Argue for/against reading *only* for pleasure.

Argue for/against the opinion that there is too much learning and too little common sense.

Argue for/against the junior college or community college.

Argue for/against some procedure at a junior college or a community college.

How would you teach a particular class unit? Argue for this approach.

Agree/disagree: "A man's reach should exceed his grasp, / Or what's a heaven for?" (Robert Browning).

Agree/disagree: Education should be more connected to the real world.

Argue for/against the statement "Those who can, do; those who can't, teach."

Argue for/against Santayana's idea that those who forget the past are doomed to repeat it.

Argue for/against the idea that some questions might be asked but shouldn't be answered.

Argue for/against the opinion that teachers have enough time to teach.

Argue for/against the opinion that people are what they observe and absorb. Or think. Or do.

Argue for/against having security guards in schools.

What should be done to solve the problem of disparity in school funding?

Argue for/against home schooling.

"There is no true love without some sensuality. One is not happy in books unless one loves to caress them" (Anatole France). How would you argue for/against this statement in an age of electronic books?

Present an argument for or against this: "The function of education . . . is to teach one to think intensively and to think critically" (Martin Luther King Jr.).

"The media's the most powerful entity on earth. They have the power to make the innocent guilty and to make the guilty innocent, and that's power. Because they control the minds of the masses" (Malcolm X). Argue for or against this statement.

Law

Argue for/against closed meetings of governmental bodies.

Argue what should be done about spouse abuse.

Argue what should be done about child abuse.

Argue for/against noise ordinances.

Argue what should be done under the law to regulate charity organizations.

Argue for/against the decriminalization of marijuana.

Argue for/against lie-detector tests.

What should be done under the law about spam (junk e-mail)?

How do some people justify profiling by a given characteristic (race, age)? What is your view?

What law(s) should be created for certain new ways of life?

Argue for/against assisted suicide laws.

Argue for/against "privilege under law."

What old laws, if any, should be reinstituted?

Argue for/against some general position the law takes.

What can be done, or what should be done, to a biased or prejudiced judge?

How can public defenders' offices be made more effective?

Argue for/against raising the driving age to eighteen.

Argue for/against the existing high car insurance rates for male drivers under the age of 25.

Argue for/against laws against cellular phone use while driving.

Argue for/against vehicular speed limits.

Argue what ought to be done about hard drugs.

Argue what ought to be done about drug dealers.

If you want to effect change, is it better to fight the system or work within it?

What should the law be concerning censorship?

What should be done to protect patients in nursing homes?

What ought to be done under the law about stray animals?

Argue for/against capital punishment.

Argue for/against plea bargaining.

Argue for/against zero-tolerance policies/laws.

Argue for/against gun control.

Argue for/against "three strikes" laws.

Argue for/against abortion being legal.

Argue for/against parental notification laws covering abortion.

Argue for/against a certain hunting or fishing law.

Argue for/against acting as your own lawyer.

Argue for/against diplomatic immunity.

Argue for/against a world court.

Argue for/against unmarked police cars.

Argue for/against ambulance chasers.

Argue for/against minor offenses being legally treated as major ones.

Argue for/against major offenses being legally treated as minor ones.

Argue for/against stronger laws against corporate crime.

Argue for/against treating adolescents as adults are treated under the law.

Argue for/against a certain light sentence or heavy sentence handed down.

Argue what ought to be legally done to punish a foreign nation that has committed a crime against the United States.

Argue for/against questioning the judge.

Argue for/against televising court proceedings.

Argue for/against televising executions.

Argue for/against the jury system as it is.

Argue the point whether illegal acts by a president are ever excusable.

Argue what ought to be done with the accused who await trial.

Argue whether violent acts in self-defense are defensible.

Argue for/against certain parking laws.

Argue for/against FBI raids without recourse by the persons raided.

Argue for/against easing a certain ban.

Argue for/against being required to serve on a jury.

Argue whether or not jury verdicts should be unanimous.

Argue for/against oaths of loyalty.

Argue for/against subliminal advertising.

Argue for/against electronic eavesdropping.

Argue for/against allowing smoking in public places.

Argue for/against the conscience as law.

Argue for/against no-fault insurance.

Argue for/against change of venue (generally or in specific cases).

Argue for/against a catchall law—that is, one that covers many things at one time.

What ought to be done under the law about antitrust violations?

What standards ought there to be for medical lawsuits?

Argue for/against the practice of awarding monetary damages in wrongful death lawsuits.

What safety codes ought there to be for police chases, ambulances, and so forth?

Argue for/against cracking down on jaywalkers.

Should a lawyer seek the truth or pull out all the stops to free/convict a defendant?

Argue for/against attorney-client privilege.

Argue what should be the basis for deciding who gets custody of a child.

Argue what should be done about deadbeat parents.

Argue for/against public funding of political campaigns.

Argue for/against proportional government.

Argue for/against the right to die.

Argue whether or not needle-exchange programs should be legal.

Argue whether actors should be legally responsible for claims they make for the products they endorse.

Who ought to be responsible for paying for a window broken by a legal minor?

What should the penalty be for kidnapping?

What standards ought there to be for legal remunerative awards?

What laws should there be to protect innocent bystanders?

Discuss argumentatively Thomas Drummond's statement, "Property has its duties as well as its rights."

Argue whether drivers should be regularly retested.

Who, legally considered, should/should not be allowed to drive?

Argue whether there should be a maximum age for drivers.

Argue whether a stock market investor should be considered (for tax purposes, let us say) a legal gambler.

What laws ought there to be to protect privacy?

What laws ought there to be to protect confidentiality?

What laws ought there to be to protect workers from their bosses?

What laws ought there to be to protect bosses from their workers?

Discuss argumentatively Edmund Burke's statement, "There is a limit at which forbearance ceases to be a virtue."

Argue for/against capital punishment as seen *only* from the concept of justice.

Argue for/against presidential pardons.

Argue for/against a certain extradition.

Argue for/against minding your own business (as regards the law).

Argue for/against the nonenforcement of a certain law.

Argue what the rights of children ought to be under the law.

Argue for/against the stricter enforcement of speeding laws.

Should failure to honor campaign promises be considered a crime?

Argue for/against the measure-for-measure, eye-for-an-eye law.

Should those who make war be the only ones who have to fight it?

Argue whether or not the death penalty is a deterrent to crime.

Argue for/against using marijuana as a painkiller.

Argue for/against buying goods manufactured in sweatshops.

How should multinational corporations be regulated?

Argue for/against the United Nations.

What ought to be the laws regarding sexual harassment?

Argue for/against the position that the self is private property.

What ought to be the law for protecting private citizens against harassment by government officials?

Discuss John Locke's statement, "The end of the law is, not to abolish or restrain, but to preserve and enlarge freedom."

Argue for/against a law that restricts freedom.

Argue for/against absolute free speech.

Argue for/against the right of bigots to be heard, to be read, to march, to protest.

Argue for/against a specific legal position regarding athletics.

Agree/disagree: "No one has the right to destroy the land one owns."

Can (and should) punishment always "fit the crime"?

What ought to be done to protect people from being indiscriminately committed to mental health facilities?

How should property taxes be determined and used?

What should be the punishment for second offenders? for first offenders? (Choose a crime.)

What qualifications should a police chief have?

What qualifications should a trial judge have?

Argue for/against the statement: We reserve the right to _____.

What recourse under the law is there for _____? What recourse should there be?

Discuss argumentatively the right to remain silent and not reveal the source of certain information.

Discuss argumentatively the headline, Escapee Sues Jailers for Allowing Him to Break Out.

Interpret argumentatively a single passage of the United States Constitution regarding elections, immigration, personal rights, gun laws, or another issue.

Argue who ought to have immunity from prosecution in politics, medicine, law, religion.

Argue who owns space.

Argue who owns the seas.

Argue for/against increased security measures in airports.

Argue for/against increased security measures in schools.

Argue for/against state lotteries as a source of public revenue.

Argue for/against unionization.

Argue who owns Antarctica.

Should HMOs be able to determine what health care a policyholder receives?

Should students be required to recite the pledge of allegiance?

Argue for/against the concept of private property.

Argue what limits there should be on the right to litigate.

Argue for/against living wills.

Argue the point whether grand juries further justice or hinder it.

Argue whether there was obstruction of justice at Kent State.

Argue what should be done under the law with terrorists when they are captured.

Look into the local laws and see which of them ought to be obsolete.

Argue who can be legally excluded from receiving financial credit.

Argue for/against the position taken by Emperor Ferdinand I, "Let justice be done, though the world perish."

Argue for/against stricter DUI/DWI laws.

Argue for/against telecommunications deregulation.

Discuss the pros and cons of Blue Laws.

Write an argumentative essay entitled, "Which Is Better—Military Justice or Civilian Justice?"

How should police be involved during strikes?

Should flag burning be legal as a form of protest?

Argue for/against this statement: "The history of women's work in this country shows that legislation has been the only force which has improved the working conditions of any large number of women wage-earners" (Helen L. Summer).

Argue for/against this statement: "No written law has ever been more binding than unwritten custom supported by popular opinion" (Carrie Chapman Catt).

Government, Politics

Argue for/against this statement: "It is common knowledge among lenders—but a secret they keep from borrowers—that creditors are dependent on their major debtors for their own well-being" (Jeremy Brecher and Dennis Brutus).

Argue for/against this statement: "Africa doesn't need charity, Africa needs Liberation" (Ngugi Wa Thiong'o).

Argue for/against this statement: "The most powerful weapon in the hands of the oppressor is the mind of the oppressed" (Stephen Biko).

Should proceedings of office holders be televised?

Argue for/against MacArthur's firing by Truman.

Argue some point having to do with local or regional interests.

Argue for/against Clinton's impeachment.

Argue for/against legal rights for domestic partners.

Should publicly funded health care be provided for children of illegal immigrants?

Should the government provide universal health care?

Argue about some aspect of the 2000 presidential election.

Should electronic sharing of copyrighted music be legal?

Should tobacco companies be liable for damage to smokers' health?

Argue for/against campaign spending limits.

Argue for/against televising presidential debates.

Argue for/against reform of political lobbying laws.

Argue whether or not further limits should be imposed on immigration.

What should be the restrictions on public funds used by politicians?

Argue for/against Ayn Rand's position(s) as elaborated in her books.

Agree/disagree: "The world needs troublemakers."

Was Clarence Thomas treated unfairly in his confirmation hearing? Should he have been made a member of the Supreme Court?

Agree or disagree with the opinion that Sir Thomas More was the admirable person that popular history says he was.

Argue for/against a certain position taken by a president.

Argue what a recent poll proves/disproves.

Should the United States government make reparations to the descendants of slaves? To Native Americans?

Argue whether Puerto Rico should become a state in the United States.

Argue what the United States can do to control treatment of foreign peoples in their own countries.

Argue for/against isolationism.

Argue whether the United States is prepared for
_____.

Argue how the United States might prepare for
_____.

Argue for/against keeping things the way they are in
_____.

Argue for/against the premise of a certain movie on politics or government.

Argue for/against restraints on freedom of the press.

Argue for/against reform of voting methods.

Argue for/against voting via the Internet.

Argue for/against write-in ballots.

Argue for/against a political watchdog program.

Argue for/against warrantless activities by the government.

Argue for/against campaign finance reform.

Argue for/against young people in high political places.

Argue for/against very old people serving in high political places.

Argue for/against a larger role for the federal government.

Discuss Walt Whitman's statement, "The United States themselves are essentially the greatest poem."

Discuss whether our foreign policy is misguided.

Agree/disagree: "There are too many people—and consequently there is too much confusion—in Civil Service."

Agree/disagree: "Only in America do we pretend to worship the majority, reverently listening to the herd as it Gallups this way and that" (Gore Vidal).

Agree/disagree: "There's one sure way to tell when politicians aren't telling the truth—their lips move" (Felicity Kendall).

Argue for/against an independent Quebec.

Argue for/against executive privilege.

Argue for/against the use of Internet filters in public libraries.

What should be done about Internet spam?

Argue whether or not the United States should be the police officer for the world.

Argue for/against the creation of a Department of Homcland Defense.

Argue for/against the abolition of the Department of Education.

Argue for/against term limits for congresspeople.

Argue for/against military government.

Argue for/against: "The government should be responsible for toxic-waste problems."

Argue for/against a political individual who is generally considered radical.

Argue for/against the Peace Corps or AmeriCorps.

Argue for/against the opinion of Samuel Johnson, "Patriotism is the last refuge of a scoundrel."

Argue for/against revealing government secrets.

Argue for/against the opinion of John Dryden, "Better one suffer, than a nation grieve."

"The king never dies," said Sir William Blackstone. Argue whether the President of the United States ever dies.

Argue for/against parliamentary versus presidential democracy.

Argue for/against the Constitution.

Discuss argumentatively the contention by Charles James Fox that "the right of governing is a trust, not a property."

Discuss argumentatively the statement by Thomas Jefferson, "No duty the Executive had to perform was so trying as to put the right man in the right place."

Discuss argumentatively the opinion that those who are behind the president are the ones who really ought to be watched carefully.

Argue for/against appointing rather than electing people to certain political offices.

Why hasn't the United States had a woman president?

Just to sharpen your argumentative skills, argue *against* voting.

Argue a certain appointment that the president ought to make.

Argue what you can do when you disagree with the government.

Argue what the postal service can do to come out even, or perhaps even make money.

Agree/disagree with the opinion that we need political heroes today.

Discuss argumentatively this quotation from Thomas Jefferson: "When a man assumes a public trust, he should consider himself a public property."

Discuss argumentatively this quotation from Robert Frost: "Good fences make good neighbors."

Argue for/against the opinion that the state is the greatest danger to the well-being of humanity.

Argue for/against a constitutional amendment allowing prayer in schools.

Argue for/against a military draft.

Would you vote for a candidate you didn't like in order to elect the first woman or minority president?

Does polling have a good or bad effect on elections?

Argue whether or not power corrupts.

Argue for/against a public monument to a certain political figure.

Argue for/against an isolationist approach to foreign policy.

Argue for/against proportional government.

Discuss argumentatively how we can pay back the founders of the nation.

Discuss argumentatively what fight ought to be waged over America's future.

Discuss argumentatively what should be the prime target of government reform.

Discuss argumentatively whether nice guys finish last in politics.

Argue whether it is reasonable to think that people don't really want bureaucracies to end.

Discuss argumentatively the Spanish proverb, "The monkey dressed in silk is still a monkey."

Argue whether leaders are born great, or whether they rise to greatness.

Argue what the government can do to help those without food.

Argue whether government would protect freedom of speech where the people did not insist upon it.

What should be done about Social Security?

Argue for/against the value of having more than two political parties dominate government.

Argue what is an inescapable future for the United States.

Argue whether it is possible to be truly independent in politics.

Argue whether the American Civil War has been the worst internal event of the United States.

What should the government do to ensure that all citizens have health care?

Argue for/against televising presidential debates.

Argue for/against making it difficult to fire civil servants.

Take a stance on a local government issue.

What should be the limits of government surveillance?

Argue what the role of the president's spouse should be.

How does television influence the public's perception of candidates?

Argue for or against political figures making public confessions of personal indiscretions.

War and Peace, Strife, Violence

Discuss argumentatively Thomas Jefferson's saying, "A little rebellion now and then is a good thing."

Discuss argumentatively the quotation from Ibsen's dramatic work, "One shouldn't put on his best trousers to fight for what is right."

Argue for/against conscientious objectors.

Is it sometimes necessary to fight fire with fire?

Argue for/against the statement, "If you can't say anything good about somebody, don't say anything at all."

Argue for/against protesting the protester.

Argue for/against the contention that war is, according to Norman Angell, "the great illusion."

Argue which is more threatening to the human race: nuclear war or biological war.

Argue what is necessary for peace between Palestinians and Israelis.

Argue what is necessary to resolve the conflict over Kashmir.

Argue for/against developing the neutron bomb.

Argue for/against possessing weapons of mass destruction as a deterrent to war.

Argue where the moral responsibility lies for atrocities of war—whether with the political leaders, the military leaders, the enlisted soldiers, the munitions factory employees, the inventors or developers of weaponry, or the people as a whole.

Argue whether TV violence makes people more violent.

Which is worse, pornography or, to quote Tom Wolfe, "pornoviolence"?

Discuss argumentatively the Biblical statement, "The race is not to the swift, nor the battle to the strong."

Argue for/against the loving of one's enemies.

Argue for/against the opinion that the saying should be: "Speak loudly but carry a little stick."

Discuss argumentatively the violence in sports, to include violence in the grandstands among sports spectators.

Discuss argumentatively (but with reference to his obvious irony) George Orwell's statement in *1984*: "War is Peace, Freedom is Slavery, Ignorance is Strength."

Argue how much force is enough and how much force is too much.

Discuss argumentatively what can most assure national security. World security?

Discuss argumentatively Richard L. Tobin's statement about television violence: "There is little connection evinced between the use of violence and the suffering such acts [of violence] would inflict in real life."

Argue for/against allowing children to play violent video games.

Is there more violence today or merely more reporting of violence?

How did live coverage of the Gulf War affect the public's perception of it?

How would you define justifiable police violence?

What role does oil play in current global unrest?

What limits, if any, should there be on hate speech?

What is the best way to deal with hate groups?

What is the best way to minimize terrorism?

How are corporations involved in violent conflicts around the world?

Why did the September 11 terrorists do what they did?

Discuss argumentatively whether a person—say, a president—should be honored for having changed a position that had been harmful to humanity.

Argue what is the root of all evil.

Argue for a particular method of nonviolent activism.

Argue for or against going to war with a particular country.

Agree/disagree: "We have reached a place where it is not a question of 'can we live in the same world and cooperate' but 'we must live in the same world and learn to cooperate'" (Eleanor Roosevelt).

Argue for/against cooperation with a perceived enemy.

Athletics, Outdoor Activities

Argue for/against challenging the referee's decision.

Argue for/against a certain athlete's retirement.

Argue whether or not celebrity athletes are role models/heroes.

Argue for/against the calling of a certain play.

Argue for/against the pay of professional athletes.

Argue for/against paying college athletes.

Argue for/against social protest by way of athletic events.

Argue for/against the instant replay as arbitrator.

Agree/disagree: In working for perfection in their sports, many athletes practice the wrong things.

Argue for/against the contention that coaches should be given a certain time to produce winning teams.

Argue for/against the high or low rating of a certain athlete.

Argue for/against hunting or fishing—or the killing of a particular creature, such as the eagle.

Argue for/against fireworks.

Argue for/against stricter rules regarding steroid use.

Argue for/against giving student athletes special academic treatment.

Argue for/against a coach making more than the president of a university.

Argue for/against keeping a school mascot/team name even though some groups find it offensive.

Argue for/against boycotting the Olympics for political reasons.

Do the Olympics really promote international understanding and solidarity?

Argue for/against allowing professional athletes to compete in the Olympics.

Argue for/against reporting on the personal lives of athletes.

Argue for/against athletic scholarships.

Should physical education be mandatory at the K–12 level?

Do sports teach competition or cooperation?

Why are men's sports generally better attended than women's?

Should "recreational vehicles" be allowed in national parks?

Is golf a sport? Is bowling?

Freedom, Free Will

Agree or disagree with playwright Wole Soyinka: "The greatest threat to freedom is the absence of criticism."

Argue for/against standing alone for one's convictions.

Should one be required to stand during the national anthem?

Argue for/against "the right to die."

Discuss argumentatively: "Freedom of the press belongs to the one who owns the press."

Discuss argumentatively the opinion of Samuel Johnson, "The will is free, and that's that."

"Some say that free will does not exist, but I find it useful to say that it does." (Tom Tiller)

Agree/disagree: "Freedom is survival."

Agree/disagree: "All Americans are free."

Agree/disagree: "The worst frustration of all is getting what you want."

Agree/disagree: "All the world's a stage, / And all the men and women merely players." (Shakespeare)

Agree/disagree: Freedom depends on self-discipline.

Agree/disagree: You can't have a true democracy until everyone's stomach is full.

Do animals have free will? Do humans?

Your freedom to swing your arm ends at the tip of my nose. Agree or disagree.

Transportation

Argue whether or not the federal government should subsidize Amtrak.

Argue whether or not the federal government should subsidize the airline industry.

Argue whether a certain major roadway is correctly designed for smooth transit.

Argue whether Japanese cars are as good as they are said to be.

Argue for/against bicycles as replacements for cars in a certain locale.

Argue for/against using a car in New York City.

Argue for/against expanding train service.

Argue for/against seat belts.

Argue what the best outboard motor is.

Argue what the best transport for cargo by land is.

Argue whether public transportation servants are overworked.

Argue what the old _____ had that the new one does not.

Argue what the new _____ has that the old one did not.

Should commercial trucks be restricted to nighttime travel?

What role should public mass transit play in the United States?

Argue for/against carpooling.

How can cities be designed to make transportation easier?

Argue for/against subways in your city.

What should be done to reduce pollution from cars?

What should gas mileage requirements be for cars?

What should be done to improve air travel?

Eating, Drinking, Health

Argue for/against the supposed health benefits of garlic.

Argue for/against exercising.

Argue for/against fasting.

Argue for/against dieting.

Argue for/against a certain diet.

Argue for/against the latest health-food trend.

Argue for/against allowing fast-food companies to furnish school lunches.

Argue for/against the effectiveness of Vitamin C for controlling colds.

Argue for/against eating a vegetarian diet.

Argue for/against organic foods.

Argue for/against bioengineering foods.

Argue what the most useful food is.

Argue how you can get by in a drinking crowd without drinking but without making a big deal about it.

Argue whether there ought to be a law against television commercials that advertise foods children ought not to eat.

What is the best way to reduce smoking among teens?

What is the best way to reduce the tendency toward obesity among children?

Religion, Ethics

Argue whether or not confessions made to clergy should be confidential.

Star Trek's Mr. Spock once said, "The good of the many outweighs the good of the few." Argue for/against this idea.

Argue for/against doing the "wrong thing" for the right reason.

Argue for/against doubt, unbelief, or questioning.

Argue for/against the ethic of this ancient Sanskrit saying: "Be like the sandalwood tree that perfumes the very ax that cuts it."

Discuss argumentatively this quotation from novelist John Gardner: "Religion's chief value is its conservatism: It keeps us in touch with what at least one section of humanity has believed for centuries."

What, in religious terms, is the highest good? The lowest evil?

Is there ever a time, in ethical terms, when lying or even hypocrisy is better than truth?

Can science and religion be reconciled?

Should parents try to instill their beliefs about religion in their children or leave it up to them to decide?

What argumentative position does some sacred book (New Testament, Torah, or Koran, for example) take on a public question such as capital punishment, abortion, pacifism?

Discuss argumentatively this newspaper quotation: "A Roman Catholic bishop says restoration of the death penalty is 'counterproductive to the pro-life crusade of the church.'"

Argue for/against the Biblical injunction, "Judge not, that you be not judged."

Argue whether the content of holy scripture is the same in any language. Argue whether it is the same, consistently, even in a single language.

Argue for/against *in vitro* fertilization.

Argue for/against doing the right thing for the wrong reasons.

Argue for/against: the ends justify the means.

Can religion and culture be separated within an individual's life?

Should members of the clergy be held to a higher standard?

Should Catholic priests be allowed to marry?

Argue for/against posting the Ten Commandments in public places.

Should the phrase "In God We Trust" be removed from U. S. currency?

Should there be a Christmas tree on the White House lawn?

Is it ever all right to cheat? To lie?

Medicine, Psychology

Agree/disagree: Sometimes people don't feel well because they don't want to.

Argue what the obligation is of a medical doctor.

Argue for/against faith healing.

Argue for/against medical treatment.

Argue for/against treatment with herbs.

Argue for/against donation of human organs.

Argue for/against natural childbirth.

Argue for/against alternative medicine.

Argue for/against holistic medicine.

Argue for/against cosmetic surgery.

Argue for/against using organs form animals in humans.

Argue for/against the merits of biofeedback.

Argue the best way to break an unhealthy habit.

Argue for/against taking a certain injection or pill.

Argue for/against reducing the number of and power of X-rays.

Argue for/against stricter qualifications for medical doctors.

Discuss argumentatively, and in terms of psychology: "I love to keep work by me: the idea of getting rid of it nearly breaks my heart" (paraphrased from Jerome K. Jerome).

Discuss argumentatively, and in terms of psychology: "The existence of ESP cannot be proved."

Discuss argumentatively, and in terms of psychology: "'Deny yourself' is the never-ending song" (Johann Wolfgang von Goethe).

Discuss argumentatively, and in terms of psychology: Regarding change, "it is often a comfort to shift one's position and be bruised in a new place."

Argue for/against the use of fetal tissue for medical research and treatment.

Argue for/against animal experimentation.

Argue for/against international family planning programs.

What is the best way to improve nutrition in a developing country?

What should be done to respond to the AIDS crisis in developing countries?

Argue for/against human cloning.

What should be done to reduce the price of prescription drugs?

Science and Progress

Argue for/against the use of nuclear power.

Argue for/against the theory of _____.

Argue for/against recycling.

Argue for/against a new form of, or new source of, energy.

Agree/disagree: "In almost every case, progress takes back what it gives."

Agree/disagree: "Science is spoiling our way of life."

Agree/disagree: "Progress makes us lazy."

Argue for/against the contention that scientists are responsible for the destructive uses to which their discoveries are put.

Argue whether science cares about art.

Argue whether art cares about science.

Argue for/against the opinion that the moon has lost its poetic charm because human beings have walked on it.

Agree/disagree: "There is delight in simple things."

Agree/disagree: "Science is more moral than we usually give it credit for."

Argue for/against daylight saving time.

Argue for/against the contention that progress of a material kind holds back, or interferes with, spiritual progress.

Argue whether it is possible to argue with facts as posited by science.

Argue for/against the use of face-recognition technology in public places.

Argue for/against the growth of big-box chain stores.

Argue for/against hybrid cars.

Should national chain stores be required to blend in with existing local architecture?

Argue for/against investing money in space exploration.

Argue for/against the idea that there is alien life.

Argue for/against requiring Internet access in all public schools.

What should the international community do to respond to global warming?

Which is better: polyester fleece or wool?

Language and Communication

Argue for/against: "I like to tell the truth as I see it. That's why literature is so important. We cannot possibly leave it to history as a discipline nor to sociology nor science nor economics to tell the story of our people. It's not a ladder we are climbing, it's literature we're producing, and there will always be someone to read it" (Nikki Giovanni).

Argue for/against: "Music is the greatest communication in the world" (Lou Rawls).

Argue for/against practicing public speaking in front of a mirror.

Argue for/against observing the rules of "Netiquette."

Argue for/against requiring high school students to study a foreign language.

Argue for/against adopting a new trend in public language.

Argue for/against diagramming sentences.

Argue for/against a certain language usage.

Argue for/against the prohibition against using your first language when it is not the first language of the society.

Agree/disagree: "There is nothing sacred about words in print."

Agree/disagree: "One should fear silence."

Agree/disagree: "Silence is golden."

Agree/disagree: "All writing is persuasion."

Agree/disagree: "All language is persuasion."

Agree/disagree: "We speak even in our silences."

Agree/disagree: "Anyone can write, anyone can create."

Agree/disagree: "There is an immense amount of biased listening and inaccurate listening" (Eric Sevareid).

Agree/disagree on the point of whether language sets the tone of civilization.

Agree/disagree with the argument that language does not always mean what it says.

Discuss argumentatively the battle over the right to one's own language—Chicano Spanish, for example, or Quebec French.

Agree/disagree: "There are times when good language is bad sense."

Argue whether docudramas are distorted and therefore, as the writer Mark Harris has said, dangerous.

Argue for/against secrecy in a certain matter.

Want to Land a Job? You Might Try Lying, says a headline, with the idea that those who tell the truth, or too much of it, on job applications are often not hired. Discuss argumentatively.

Agree/disagree: "No people or group can be put under one heading."

Argue whether language is interpreted in different ways in a court of law depending on the persons being tried.

Argue for/against less formality in e-mail correspondence.

Argue the merits of a particular form of discourse in public speaking.

How do a contemporary culture's commercials comment on its values?

Is advertising more communicative or more manipulative?

Is surfing the Web an active or passive process?

Argue for/against commercial sponsorship of public broadcasting.

Argue for/against commercial sponsorship of scholarships.

Argue for/against keeping your variety of English, using this rationale from Chinua Achebe: "The African writer should aim to use English in a way that brings out his message best without altering the language to the extent that its value as a medium of international exchange will be lost. He should aim at fashioning out an English which is at once universal and able to carry his peculiar experience."

Argue who won a political debate based on your reading of the transcript.

Look at two newspapers and argue which is the best, and why.

Argue the strengths and weaknesses of a particular political candidate's communication style.

Society, Social Interaction

What is the most effective metaphor for American culture: melting pot, salad, mosaic?

Argue for/against Jesse Jackson's interpretation of the melting pot: "I hear that melting-pot stuff a lot, and all I can say is that we haven't melted."

Argue for/against "gated" communities.

Are you your brother's or your sister's keeper?

Each for oneself? All for one and one for all?

Argue for/against joining _____ .

Agree/disagree: To remake the world we have to start with ourselves as individuals.

Agree/disagree: Concern for others is concern for self.

Argue what the matter is with you/me/them.

Agree/disagree: Divorcing parents ought to think first of their children.

Agree/disagree: Apologies are usually better for those who do the apologizing than for those apologized to.

Argue for/against adoption by single parents.

Argue for/against adoption by same-sex parents.

Argue what should be parental responsibility under the law.

Argue whether it depends on the individual to say what is good and what is bad.

Discuss argumentatively Walter Van Tilburg Clark's statement, "A mob is no more intelligent than its least intelligent member."

Argue what our most worthy inheritance is as a society.

Explain argumentatively a certain shift of population that has occurred.

Argue for/against early marriage.

Argue for/against arranged marriages.

Argue for/against the "money dance" (in which those who attend a wedding reception pin money on the bride's dress).

Argue for/against birthright.

Argue what is reasonable adult or mature behavior in public.

Agree/disagree: "You can take a person out of _____ but you can't take _____ out of a person."

Agree/disagree: It is a stereotype that old people are conservative.

Argue for/against suburbia.

Argue for/against birth control.

Argue for/against being married.

Argue for/against being single.

Agree/disagree: Having biological offspring does not make one a parent.

Agree/disagree: Every child should be raised by his or her natural parents.

Argue what a particular society needs to cure its ills.

Agree/disagree: Tradition should be maintained at all costs.

What should be the roles for surrogate mothers?

Agree/disagree: A home without a pet is not complete.

Agree/disagree: "A person does not do enough merely to acknowledge equality."

Agree/disagree: "All of the nation suffers when one person suffers the loss of civil rights."

Agree/disagree: "So far is it from being true that people are naturally equal, that no two people can be half an hour together, but one shall acquire an evident superiority over the other."

Argue whether any individual is indispensable.

Argue whether neighbors are necessary.

Argue for/against giving up one's religion for someone.

Discuss argumentatively this quotation from Sir Thomas Browne: "Charity begins at home, is the voice of the world."

Argue when it is best not to be frank.

Argue whether the world, as Wordsworth says, "is too much with us."

Argue the redeeming qualities of someone or something not considered as having any.

Argue what psychiatry has done for society.

Argue some issue of feminism that until now has been completely ignored.

Argue for/against a universal definition of feminism.

Take a stance on a local feminist issue in your community.

Argue whether or not discretion is the better part of valor.

Argue whether there is any use in society for Mother's Day and Father's Day.

Discuss argumentatively the quotation from Hart Crane: "For we can still love the world, who find a famished kitten on the step."

Argue for/against labor unions.

Argue for/against your joining a union.

Argue for/against: "No people come into possession of a culture without having paid a heavy price for it" (James Baldwin).

Argue for/against: "We have become ninety-nine percent money mad. The method of living at home modestly and within our income, laying a little by systematically for the proverbial rainy day which is due to come, can almost be listed among the lost arts" (George Washington Carver).

Argue the worth of a certain city because of the things to do there.

Argue for/against putting the individual above the community.

Economy, Employment

Is anything ever "absolutely *free*"?

Argue for/against a certain boycott.

Argue whether it is true that two can live as cheaply as one.

Try to persuade your boss on a certain issue or plan at work.

Argue your worth to a certain employer.

Argue for/against gold, or silver, as the money standard.

Argue for/against a particular measure to reduce the energy crisis.

Argue what government spending should give priority to.

Argue for/against a national debt.

Argue what our assets are nationally.

Argue for/against subsidizing farms.

Argue for/against subsidizing corporations.

Argue for/against free bus travel for certain citizens over certain short routes.

Argue for/against a certain tax reform.

Argue what the best place is for inexpensive living for retired people.

Argue for/against parking meters.

Argue for/against tipping.

Argue for/against farming as a profession.

Argue whether one should be exempted from high payments of car insurance if proven accident-free.

Argue who should, or who should not, keep receiving financial support from the government.

Discuss argumentatively this quotation from Thomas Jefferson: "Never spend your money before you have it."

Argue for/against patronizing locally owned businesses instead of chain stores.

Argue for/against joining a food co-op.

Argue for/against "sin taxes" (such as on cigarettes).

Argue for/against the idea that the customer is always right.

What is the fairest way to determine who gets laid off?

Argue for/against investing in the stock market.

Should people not spend money on nonessentials?

Time and Eternity, Life Pursuits, Death and Life

Agree/disagree: "No man can serve two masters" (Bible).

Agree/disagree: "It is the best of all trades, to make songs, and the second best to sing them" (Hilaire Belloc).

"Desire for the fruit of one's actions is responsible for [a person's] bondage to the cycle of birth and death. [A person's] right is to work only, not to the fruit of his [or her] actions" (Bhagavad Gita). Argue for/against this position.

"All that we are is the result of what we have thought. We are formed and molded by our thoughts." (Gautama Buddha)

"What does it profit a man if he shall gain the whole world and lose his soul?" (Gospel according to Matthew). When have these words been relevant in your life?

Argue for/against "wasting" time.

Argue for a past custom that is worth bringing back.

Argue for/against the four-day work week.

Argue how one should spend time.

Argue for a particular pastime.

Agree/disagree: "There is nothing wrong with chasing rainbows."

Argue for/against the idea "carpe diem."

Agree/disagree: "In landlessness alone resides the highest truth" (Herman Melville).

Argue how our lives would be different if there were no recorded history.

Argue whether modern people are significantly different from people of ancient times or of medieval times.

Argue for/against age-defying drugs (such as hormones).

Agree/disagree: Humanity will not only endure; it will prevail (paraphrased from William Faulkner).

Agree/disagree: "Our life is frittered away by detail" (Henry David Thoreau).

Agree/disagree: "It's hell to be old in the United States."

Argue whether there is an age when a person can get by with just about anything.

Argue whether age is necessary for experience.

Argue whether you should buy life insurance.

Agree/disagree: "Why fear death? It is the most beautiful adventure in life" (Charles Frohman).

Argue whether life is a line, or a circle.

Argue what the milestones of life are.

Argue what the millstones of life are.

Argue for/against belief in life after life.

Agree/disagree: "It matters not how one dies, but how one lives."

Argue for/against cremation rather than burial.

Argue the point technically and spiritually: When is death, when is life?

Discuss argumentatively this quotation from John Donne: "Death be not proud."

Discuss argumentatively this quotation from the poet William Ernest Henley: "I am the master of my fate: I am the captain of my soul."

Agree/disagree: "Nature's Time should be left as it is."

Agree/disagree: "Time is your best ally."

Argue that time will show that _____.

Argue what in life, or in all eternity, is our greatest resource.

Agree/disagree: "Truly loving another means letting go of all expectations. It means full acceptance, even celebration of another's personhood" (Karen Casey).

Agree/disagree: "If you judge people, you have no time to love them" (Mother Teresa).

Agree/disagree: "Love without reason lasts the longest" (unknown).

Agree/disagree: "If I had to choose between betraying my country and betraying my friend, I hope I should have the guts to betray my country" (E. M. Forster).

Agree/disagree: "Friends are God's way of apologizing to us for our families" (unknown).

Agree/disagree: "It's no good trying to keep up old friendships. It's painful for both sides. The fact is, one grows out of people, and the only thing is to face it" (W. Somerset Maugham).

What benefits will come from extending the human lifespan?

What problems will come from extending the human lifespan?

Argue whether the arts are essential.

What is the best balance between a life of action and a life of contemplation?

Agree or disagree: the devil is in the details.

At what age does one handle success best?

Argue for/against keeping one's cultural identity rather than trying to assimilate.

Argue whether or not it is sometimes okay to "sweat the small stuff."

According to this saying, "We were given memories so we could have roses in winter." Argue for/against what memory affords us.

9 DEFINITION

What Definition Is

Definition seeks to establish the limits or boundaries of a word as it is used in any given context. This book offers only the most immediate example of the topic at hand. Each introduction attempts to define a particular kind of writing for the specific purposes of this volume. Many approaches are used. Some may appear almost to throw off the dictionary meanings as they wrestle with the demands of circumstances, but each definition is etymologically rooted. The etymology of *definition* itself has to do with "bringing to an end." But no dictionary definition is definitive—not in a living language. It may determine the meaning(s) of a word for the time being, settle the boundaries of a word, but not its hash.

Words are alive, and, like any other living thing, words grow and change. In fact, as linguists Hans Henrich Hock and Brian Joseph tell us, "Whole books are written—and indeed have been written for centuries—warning of impending doom, prophesying that our language will go to the dogs. . . . [However,] attempts at stemming the tide of change are ineffectual: Language changes inexorably" (*Language History, Language Change, and Language Relationship*). Nowhere is language change more visible than in slang, where, Hock and Joseph say, "the motivation for constant lexical renewal is similar to the motivation for constant change in dress fashion[s]. There is nothing more stale than outdated slang—or yesterday's fashion." Slang aside, however, even in more formal language you can trace how a word grows and changes in value and meaning. Take, for example, the word *black,* which has through the ages carried negative value in the English language. The civil rights movement of the mid–twentieth century, and especially the Black Power movement, redefined the word, imbuing it with a positive value, emphasizing that "black is beautiful."

It might be helpful to think of definition as a way of describing a word (in terms of our approach to description, say, which appeared earlier in this book). Here again our ultimate aim is not to capture our subject—and certainly not to bring it to a permanent end—but to set it free. Definition is one of the spokes in the rhetorical wheel we have been spinning through these pages and (to give the analogy one final turn) it is also part of the hub grease that keeps the wheel turning freely.

How to Write Definition

Definition is not only a way of explaining a word clearly, precisely, concretely; it is also a way of exploring both the word and how it relates to its private context. Sometimes it seems we do not really know what a word means—or what it means to us—until we attempt to describe it on paper. Definition, much like any other form of writing, is a way of thinking and of discovering what we know, of looking at all the many accretions of meaning that enrich it. An essay in definition could hardly avoid, nonetheless, digging into the roots of a subject, investigating its history. That kind of groundwork tends to deepen a word, build its muscle, give it centuries of room in which to swing its arms.

Surely the writer ought always to know the meaning of any word he or she uses. In the age of what Orwell called "doublethink," definition is not only imperative but crucial. Can there ever be a *holy* war? Are people oppressed to be free? Are countries destroyed to be saved? By all means, let us define our terms.

89

Locating Subjects for Definition

Many of the subjects listed in this chapter are quotations. Often they are aphoristic and their sense depends upon word definitions that are at once stringent and free. Wrestling with some of them will be vigorous exercise, both for the muscle-bound writer and the writer whose loose-limbed prose sprawls all over the page.

Definition rightly claims its own spoke on that rhetorical wheel. But the crafty wheelwright will shape it clear round the rim. Argumentation, exposition, research and report, critical writing—none of these will get very far without some solid element of definition.

Human Beings
and Human Types for Definition

A

Abelard, absent-minded professor, Chinua Achebe, acrobat, activist, actuary, adolescence, African, agnostic, airline pilot, air-traffic controller, Lewis Carroll's Alice, alpha male, amateur/professional, Amazon, the American people, Anasazi, Andromeda, anonymous, army brat, Asian, astronaut, atheist, athlete, auctioneer, Australian, auto mechanic, average citizen

What are the criteria for judging a great actor?

What are the criteria for judging a great athlete?

Athlete-recruitment programs—define ethical or unethical recruitment.

How would you define the "earliest American"?

"We are all Armenians," said William Saroyan. What did he mean, in terms of definition?

Define someone with "attitude."

B

Babbitt, Bach, backpacker, backwoods people, bad/good neighbor, Bilbo Baggins, Pearl Bailey, James Baldwin, top banana, barnstormer, Dave Barry, bartender, Count Basie, Batman, Mr. Bean, the Beatles, Harry Belafonte, Beltway bureaucrats, best friend (or dog's best friend), Benazir Bhutto, Big Brother as created by George Orwell, Larry Bird, the Black Panthers, blusterer, James Bond, bookworm, bouncer, "boy band," braggart, Brahmin, Brand X, brat, Eva Braun, breadwinner, brother, Charlie Brown, the Brownings, bullies, bumpkin, George Burns, George W. Bush

Discuss in terms of definition the fact that Mel Blanc created his voices from the beginning—before the cartoons.

Benevolent despot.

How would you define a Boston Brahmin?

What stereotype definition is understood in this cartoon item?—"He doesn't know the meaning of the word fear, or anything else for that matter," a manager says of his boxer.

Bristly personality.

Discuss Jack Anderson's saying, "All the world's a stage and bureaucrats play it."

Define the British sense of humor.

Is a bookish person different from a bookworm?

C

Cadillac, Cajun, Calamity Jane, Caliban, Canadians as seen by the Japanese, Captain Kirk, cardiologist, Andrew Carnegie, Lewis Carroll, Kit Carson, Enrico Caruso, Casanova, Casaubon, cavalier, cavalry, celebrity, Wilt Chamberlain, chameleon personality, Charlie Chaplin, charlatan, Cesar Chavez, Chief of Protocol, the child inside, Christ as portrayed on television and in movies, Cleopatra, Bill and Hillary Clinton, Kurt Cobain, Joe College of the '50s, "cop," Joseph Cornell, Crazy Jane as created by William Butler Yeats, Creole, Davy Crockett, Walter Cronkite, crusader, Marie Curie

What does the following poetical definition by John Collins Bossidy tell you about the Cabots, the Lowells, and other Bostonians high and low?

> And this is good old Boston,
> The home of the bean and the cod.
> Where the Lowells talk to the Cabots,
> And the Cabots talk only to God.

How would you define Calvin (of "Calvin and Hobbes") or some other famous cartoon character?

Explain how this is possible: "Character is destiny."

"The Child is father of the Man," said William Wordsworth. What special definition of the child is Wordsworth using?

The Children's Crusade is a book about a real movement by 50,000 children in 1212 to stop war. What characteristics of this movement can be defined in terms of what has happened in recent history?

The Chinese have stopped using the term *Mandarin* because it is too class-conscious. Define some class-conscious term formerly used in the United States.

Shirley Chisholm of the U.S. House of Representatives wants to be remembered, she says, for what she is able to do to help her constituents. What does her statement have to do with definition of the politician?

Explain the definition implied in the fact that certain churchgoers were reprimanded by the courts for making their "joyful noise unto the Lord" too loud.

Distinguish between a Christian Scientist and a Christian scientist.

A headline reads, Citizen Catches Police. Even if you do not know the subject of the article that follows, what fixed definitions come to your mind immediately?

A certain coach says that his team is number 2, not number 1. Another coach, referring to his playing a team now that formerly trounced his team, says that revenge does not fit into his vocabulary. Discuss both these coaches in terms of definition.

According to current world conditions, what is a communist?

George Eliot said that conceited people carry their comfort around with them. How would you define a conceited person?

What do conservatives usually denounce about society?

What stereotypes of Asians are encouraged by the Charlie Chan movies?

Is there any difference between a moral coward and a physical coward? Can a coward be brave and moral? Define in your own terms what a coward is.

"Thus conscience doth make cowards of us all" (Shakespeare, *Hamlet*). Define how this can happen.

Why does Curious George have so much appeal to children?

D

The Dalai Lama, Salvador Dali, a dangerous liaison, daredevil, Darth Vader, daughter, "Deadhead," James Dean, Agnes de Mille, Cecil B. De Mille, Democrat/Republican, deus ex machina, devil's advocate, Princess Diana, Dickensian, dictator, dilettante, Dionysian, the dispossessed, diva, do-gooder, Donald Duck, dot-com millionaire, Doubting Thomas, Frederick Douglass, down-home person, dowser, Dr. Dolittle, dreamer, drone, Isadora Duncan, dunce

How does the biblical character Delilah become a symbol that feminists reject?

Define what a doctor is in light of the following: Is a PhD, a Doctor of Philosophy, a doctor?

"Over-Doctor" is the Japanese term for an overeducated, unplaced, unemployable PhD.

"Every physician almost hath his favourite disease," Henry Fielding wrote in the eighteenth century. Does his statement still define the doctor, in part?

"Anger makes dull men witty," said the first Queen Elizabeth. How do you define a dull person?

E

Each and every one, early riser, Clint Eastwood, easy rider, eccentric, egghead, egotist, Elvis, emigrant/immigrant, Eminem, worst enemy, proponents of the English-Only movement, evangelist, Everyman or Everywoman, everyone a stranger

A certain entertainer's talent is that he can make himself look like any make of car. What other entertainer do you know who is defined by an unusual talent?

Everyone has some kind of handicap, it has been said. In what important ways can everyone be defined as being like everyone else?

How did Elvis redefine his image throughout his career?

"Evita—she has been called whore, feminist, tyrant, and saint. Evita was the beautiful, legendary woman who rose from poverty to become the hypnotically powerful First Lady of Argentina." What definitions of Evita emerge in the film, in the musical, and in historical accounts?

How did Elizabeth I, queen of England, define her nation and her era?

How does Elizabeth II, queen of England, define her nation and her era?

F

Face in the crowd, fair-weather friend, fakir, Falstaff, the American family, the "blended" family, the "extended" family, fanatic, farrier, Fascist, father, Father, faun, Fenian, Millard Fillmore, firefighter, firestarter, flower child, football widow, fox in the henhouse, Frankenstein, freedom fighters, friend, fundamentalist

What face is on a certain coin or bill? Why that face on that item rather than another face?

What can one do to determine human definition when the following is true?—"It is the common wonder of all men, how among so many millions of faces, there should be none alike" (Sir Thomas Browne).

"The family that prays together stays together." Discuss this slogan, or another that it reminds you of, so as to indicate that slogans do not define particularly but only generally. (One example of this fact: The Manson group called itself a family and had its own kind of prayers.)

How do movies about the famous portray them?

To what extent has the attitude expressed in the following statement (by H. L. Mencken, the famous journalist) become a stereotyped definition of farmers: "The only political idea he can grasp is one which promises him a direct profit."

If you are on file somewhere, are you therefore defined as no more than the file says you are? Are you merely the sum of the personal items mentioned there?

W. C. Fields was democratic: he hated everyone equally. What playful, complete definition do we have of W. C. Fields on the basis of his movies and popular image?

The Bible says "A fool utters all his mind" and "Answer a fool according to his folly." What, by your definition, is a fool?

How do descriptions of us sometimes limit or confound what we are? Note that sometimes people get swallowed up by name and town descriptions of them: "With him is his wife the former Mary Smith of Johnsonville." Does the word *former* mean that Mary no longer exists? Is Johnsonville where she lives *now* or where she used to live?

What, in definition, is behind the fact that Franklin is the name most used in naming American towns?

"Heaven has no rage like love to hatred turned, / Nor hell a fury like a woman scorned" (William Congreve). How would you define a woman's fury in feminist terms?

G

Clark Gable, gadfly, a gallant man in today's context, Mohandas Gandhi, Bill Gates, geek, geisha, Generation X, Mirza Ghalib, gift horse, God, God as defined by a child, Goddess, Goethe, Katharine Graham, a great person, Che Guevara, Lady Jane Grey (The Nine Days' Queen), guru, Gutenberg

How would you define a genius? Does a genius have time for the ordinary world? Is everyone a genius? Does genius require only a high IQ? Is a genius very much different from you and me? "To know what a genius is," says a GE advertisement, "ask a genius." "Genius is of no country," said Charles Churchill.

What can "godfather" imply?

Define a gospel singer as someone who does more than make "a joyful noise unto the Lord."

What stereotypes are suggested by the word "grandparent"?

Define a grave (serious) person after consulting this quotation from G. K. Chesterton: "It is really a natural trend to lapse into taking oneself gravely, because it is the easiest thing to do; for solemnity flows out of men naturally, but laughter is a leap. It is easy to be heavy; hard to be light. Satan fell by force of gravity."

What defines a great person? Is it misleading to call persons the "all-time greatest" in their fields? What definition enters into the idea in this quotation from Robinson Jeffers?—"Greatness is but less little; and death's changed life."

"Be not afraid of greatness: some are born great, some achieve greatness and some have greatness thrust upon 'em" (Shakespeare, *Twelfth Night*). How would you define greatness?

Some views of God for definition:

"And God said unto Moses: 'I AM THAT I AM'; and He said: 'Thus shalt thou say unto the children of Israel: I AM hath sent me unto you.'" (Torah, Exodus 3)

"An honest God is the noblest work of man." (Robert Ingersoll)

"In the beginning was the Word, and the Word was with God, and the Word was God. The same was in the beginning with God. All things were made by him; and without him was not any thing made that was made. In him was life; and the life was the light of men. And the light shineth in darkness; and the darkness comprehended it not." (Gospel according to John)

"It is God's trade to pardon." (paraphrased from Heinrich Heine)

"If God really existed, it would be necessary to abolish him." (Mikhail Bakunin)

"The nature of God is a circle of which the center is everywhere and the circumference is nowhere." (Anonymous)

God is the oldest of poets. (proverb)

God is _____.

"The groves were God's first temples." (William Cullen Bryant)

"It may be that our role on this planet is not to worship God, but to create him." (Arthur C. Clarke)

"Nature is the art of God." (Sir Thomas Browne)

"God is love." (New Testament)

"Is God willing to prevent evil but not able? Then he is not omnipotent. Is he able but not willing? Then he is malevolent. Is he both able and willing? Then whence cometh evil? Is he neither able nor willing? Then why call him God?" (Epicurus)

From the Rigveda:

Whence did this creation
Come into being?
Whether He supported it or He did not
The one who dwells in the highest region watches it,
He alone knows it,
Or perhaps He knows it not.

From the Bible:

The Lord is my shepherd;
I shall not want.

He maketh me to lie down in green pastures;
He leadeth me beside still waters.

He restoreth my soul:
He leadeth me in the paths of righteousness for his name's sake.

Yea, though I walk through the valley of the shadow of death,
I will fear no evil; for thou art with me;
Thy rod and thy staff, they comfort me.

Thou preparest a table before me in the presence of mine enemies:
Thou anointest my head with oil;
My cup runneth over.

Surely goodness and mercy shall follow me all the days of my life;
And I shall dwell in the house of the Lord for ever.

"We must question the story logic of having an all-knowing all-powerful God, who creates faulty Humans, then blames them for his own mistakes." (Gene Roddenberry)

From the Koran:

Praise be to God, Lord of the worlds!
The compassionate, the merciful!
King on the Day of reckoning!
Thee *only* do we worship, and to Thee do we cry for help.
Guide Thou us on the straight path.
The path of those to whom Thou has been gracious;—with
Whom Thou art not angry, and who go not astray.

The Upanishads (the ancient Hindu scriptures) teach that "Atman (individual soul) is Brahman (the supreme Godhead, beyond all distinctions or forms)."

The Bahá'í Scripture says: "Light is good in whatsoever lamp it is burning. A rose is beautiful in whatsoever garden it may bloom. A star has the same radiance if it shines from the east or the west. Be free of prejudice so that you will love the Sun of Truth from whatsoever point in the horizon it may arise."

"I believe in God, only I spell it Nature." (Frank Lloyd Wright)

How do the following words define a person's relationship to God? "Reason is like an officer when the king appears; the officer then loses his power and hides himself. Reason is God's shadow; God is the sun. What power has the shadow before the sun?" (Rumi)

"If there be gods we cannot help them, but we can assist our fellow-men. We cannot love the inconceivable, but we can love wife and child and friend. We can be as honest as we are ignorant. If we are, when asked what is beyond the horizon of the known, we must say that we do not know." (Robert Green Ingersoll)

H

Ham actor, Hamlet, Oscar Hammerstein II, ham radio enthusiast, the Hare Krishna movement, harlequin, Hassan and Hussein (descendants of the Prophet Mohammad and founders of two Islamic sects,) Hatfields and McCoys, Vaclav Havel, Lillian Hellman, Ernest Hemingway, Henry the Eighth's wives, Henry Higgins, "his and hers," Hitler as seen by a teenager, Ho Chi Minh, Billie Holiday, Sherlock Holmes, homebody, Captain Hook, Gerard Manley Hopkins, Julia Ward Howe, howitzer, Zora Neale Hurston

"Hell is other people." (Jean-Paul Sartre)

Give a deliberately stereotyped definition of a hero. To understand the stereotype is to understand, as well, what is not a stereotype.

Is the idea of the dying hero romantic or realistic?

After considering the following quotation from Ferdinand Foch, define the term *human soul:* "The most powerful weapon on earth is the human soul on fire."

Using definition, argue whether hypocrites know that they are hypocrites.

I

Iago, Henrik Ibsen, ideologue, St. Ignatius of Loyola, Incas, Indiana Hoosier, indispensable person, insider, intellectual, Inuit, Irish, Isaac, Ishmael, Ivy Leaguer

People once identified as Indians are now also known by such terms as first nations people, indigenous peoples, and Native Americans. What does each definition connote, especially as compared to "Indian"?

Define by comparison/contrast an Indian from India and an Indian from the United States or Canada.

What is an innocent? Is it the same in definition as an innocent person? How do we behave towards people who have been tried as criminals but have been found innocent?

A particular immigrant community.

Define a "wild Irish rose," comparing traditional and contemporary use of the phrase.

J

Jesse Jackson, Jazz musicians, Jelly Roll Morton, Jeremiah, Jesuit, JFK, jihad, Jim Crow laws, Jingoist, Mohammed Ali Jinnah, Joan of Arc, a "Job's comforter," Elton John, John Paul II, Magic Johnson, Jonah, Barbara Jordan, journalist, judge, junkie (choose a particular kind), Supreme Court Justice, Jute, juvenile

Someone wno's climbing Jacob's Ladder.

Jesse James was formerly the Treasurer of Texas, and he was replaced by someone who also had a famous name, Warren G. Harding. How might definition affect someone who has the same name made famous by someone else?

Define Justice _____, United States Supreme Court.

K

Franz Kafka, Helen Keller, Grace Kelly, Walt Kelly, Jomo Kenyatta, Jack Kerouac, the Kikuyu, Kilroy, Martin Luther King Jr., King Kong, knight in shining armor, Koko the gorilla, the Kurds

Distinguish, by definition, between the Kafir people of Africa and the Kafir people of Afghanistan.

Define *kaiser* by way of its etymology.

Define the kamikaze pilot in religious and patriotic terms, not just historically.

Define the Katzenjammer Kids of comic-strip fame.

In what sense can we consider Jacqueline Kennedy and Jacqueline Kennedy Onassis two different people?

The Kennedy dynasty

The Kennedy "legacy"

What is a kibitzer?

How does the popular perception of the king change, depending on what monarchy you're examining?

What, in *modern* terms, is a knave?

How does Kris Kringle differ, in definition, from Santa Claus?

L

Lao-tzu, layperson, left-handed person, Doris Lessing, David Letterman, libertine, Lilith, literati, loan shark, Lolita, lone wolf, look-alike, the Lost Generation, Low Churchman, Low German, Lucifer, Luke of the Bible, Luke Skywalker, Martin Luther of the Reformation

Define the current use of the term *Laodicean*, connecting the word to its origins.

"Lawyers talk, but it is their business to talk," said Thomas Jefferson. James Boswell said of the lawyer that he "has no business with the justice or injustice of the cause which he undertakes, unless his client ask his opinion, and then he is bound to give it honestly. The justice or injustice of the cause is to be decided by the judge." How do these statements define what a lawyer is in ways opposed to a stereotyped definition? How do you define a lawyer?

What does a liberal denounce about society? How does this denunciation define what a liberal is? What is an English liberal as opposed to an American liberal?

What does a libertarian believe?

Define *Lord Chancellor.*

Define *lord of misrule.*

What is your definition of a loser?

What would be a good example of a modern lotus-eater?

What would be a good example of a modern "Lot's Wife"?

Define *lowbrow.*

Define *lumpen* as a political term.

M

Yo-Yo Ma, Lady Macbeth, Machiavelli, Madonna, Mahavira, Miriam Makeba, Malvolio, Nelson Mandela, Imelda Marcos, mask (meaning *persona*), a human maverick, the Real McCoy, Golda Meir, mensch, Micawber, Mickey Mouse, Arthur Miller, minister's child, Minnesota Fats, misogynist, Martha Mitchell, a mod person, Marilyn Monroe, Monty Python, Thomas More as seen by his contemporary opposition, Toni Morrison, Moses, Grandma Moses, someone voted Most Likely to Succeed, mother, Mother Teresa, Iris Murdoch, mutual friend(s), someone morally myopic

What does it take to be in a marching band?

Define how Mr. Rogers's neighborhood is different from one that you know about.

Clothes make (or do not make) the person.

A newspaper item tells of a man who agreed to become another person to please passport officials who kept giving him a name other than his own.

"My favourite, I might say, my only study, is man." (George Borrow)

The term "man" is still sometimes used to refer, supposedly, to all humanity. What does this usage imply about women, or about the relationship between men and women?

Benjamin Franklin said of humanity that there are "those who are immovable; those who are movable; those who move."

Define who Mao's widow is, taking into account that she is known more as "Mao's widow" rather than by her name.

Define *media person.* Who are, or what are, the media?

A Bible verse says, "Blessed are the meek: for they shall inherit the earth" (Matthew 5:5). Who are the meek?

Give your own definition of *metaphysician* after noting the following: A metaphysician, said Charles, Baron Bowen, is "a blind man in a dark room—looking for a black hat—which isn't there."

Who are the mild?

What has come to be defined as "the model minority" in the United States? How might this definition be complicated?

The actor Ricardo Montalban insists on keeping his Latin accent so as to keep his dignity. How were earlier actors defined by their accents or their origins so that they became stereotyped?

Who is the "mother of all living"?

What is meant, in terms of definition, by someone's saying, "I'm not myself today"? Is there only one *myself* for each person? What are the differences in definition among the pronouns *me, myself,* and *I* as they refer to a single person? Is there any difference between *my self* and *myself?*

Give an elaborate definition of *mystagogue.*

Define someone who is said to be "a mystery."

Write an extended definition of a modern mystic.

Write about a mythical person as if he or she were defined by the real world.

Define *mythomaniac.*

N

Vladimir Nabokov, a human nag, the Nahua people, a naiad as a real person, a *naïf,* someone who is a namesake, a modern (and real) Narcissus, Gamel Abdul Nasser, Carry Nation, native, a "natural" for one pursuit or another, a literary naturalist, the Navajo Nation, Navy SEAL, Nazi, Neanderthal , Queen Nefertiti, Jawaharlal Nehru, neighbor, Willie Nelson, nemesis, neophyte, a modern (and real) Nestor, a neurotic, a "new face" or a "new kid on the block," news anchor, a 19th-century nihilist, ninny, a nit-picker, nitwit, Richard Nixon, a noble, the Noble Savage stereotype as defined in the eighteenth and nineteenth centuries, a nobody, Nobody (in a "Vote for Nobody" drive), a nonagenarian, a nondescript person, a nonesuch, the "Royal Nonesuch" of Mark Twain's *Huckleberry Finn,* the Normans, *nouveau riche,* someone who is just a number, Rudolph Nureyev

Define the New Yorker in a deliberately stereotyped way; then define a specific New Yorker.

Define *nonresident* better than the following definition (from a New York City document) does: "A non-resident individual means an individual who is not a resident."

After considering the following, discuss definition according to names and nicknames:

A newspaper item says that a man has 10-8 as his first name.

Will the real _____ stand up?

Are persons who change their names different persons?

How can our names sometimes wrongly define us?

Secret names are often used for protecting highly placed officials and those close to them.

Sometimes, two or more persons with the same name run for the same public office.

In Sweden, 40 percent of the population shares twenty names all of which end in -son.

What would you expect of someone named for, say, Watergate?

Who is No-Man? Who is Everyman? Who is Every-woman?

When names of certain streets named for certain persons are misspelled, what happens to definition?

Don Coryell May Become a Saint, says a headline, referring to the coach's possibly joining the New Orleans Saints, a professional football team.

Take into account how some names invite puns: Beane, Soldier, Tree, and so forth.

What is behind a certain nickname?

What's _not_ in a name? What's in a name?

Is it possible for someone to have the wrong name?

O

Oberon, Oceanus, a modern (and real) Odysseus, an Ojibway Indian, Oklahoma Sooner, oneself, an only child, Oprah (Winfrey), orator, a modern (and real) Orpheus, Ossian, Othello, outlaw, overachiever, an Oxbridge type, Oxonian, Ozymandias

In a cartoon, the old woman in a shoe gives an account of what her children, now grown, are doing. Define in your own terms what the "old woman who lived in a shoe" is like.

"You optimists are all alike," says a cartoon figure to a sign carrier whose sign reads: Doomsday Is Near. Define _optimist_.

Define _ordinary people._

What defines "the Orient"? What are old and new attitudes toward this term?

Define someone thought of as an "original."

What defines Orlando, the literary character, in Shakespeare's play or in Virginia Woolf's novel?

P

Pacifist, pagan, a modern and real Pan, a modern and real Pandora, Dr. Pangloss, a modern and real Pantagruel, Papa Doc Duvalier, paragon, Dorothy Parker, Parnassian of the second half of the 19th century, partisan, Dolly Parton, pastor, patriot, patron saint, a modern and real Pecksniff, Penelope, Peregrine Pickle, a peripatetic, the person inside, person of trust, person on the street, a whole person, _persona_, pessimist, philistine (in the modern sense),

Pict, a carnival pitcher, "plain folks," Pocahontas, James K. Polk, Jackson Pollock, an individual Polynesian, pooh-bah, President of the United States, prima donna, prince, Prince (the artist formerly known as The Artist Formerly Known as Prince), prison guard, prisoner, a modern and real Prometheus, Prufrock, psychotic, Puritan

Define _pandit_ (or _pundit_) in the traditional sense and in its current context.

What are the criteria for defining a great painter?

Have the words _patrician_ and _plebian_ changed in value?

What does it mean when someone is described as a Peter Pan?

What are the criteria for defining a great philanthropist?

What are the criteria for defining a great philosopher?

Can a philosopher be a philosopher without preaching philosophy?

What are the criteria for defining a great poet?

Define _poet_ as William Cullen Bryant does in saying "Every individual is more or less a poet."

Can a poet be a poet without writing poetry?

Who are "the poor"? Are there legal terms that, in the United States, define who the poor are and who the wealthy are? What does it mean that the poor, by definition, have to have money just to be poor?

President Ford could have named Vice-President Nelson Rockefeller as President in his last days in office. Are there other ways in which a President might be said to hold an ambiguous office?

What person is the most glorified professional person in the United States?

"A rottenness begins in the conduct of a man who casts his eye longingly on public office," said Thomas Jefferson. How do you define _public servant?_

Q

Quacksalver, quadrille dancer, Quaker, quarterback, Quasimodo, the Quechua people, queen, Queen Latifah, Quetzalcoatl, quibbler, quidditch-players (from J. K. Rowling's Harry Potter books), quintuplets, quisling, quitter, Quixote

R

Rabelais, ragamuffin, Bonnie Raitt, Raphael, Rasputin, Ronald Reagan, a literary realist, revivalist, Adrienne Rich, Renee Richards, a modern and real Rip Van Winkle, Jackie Robinson, Norman Rockwell, Eleanor Roosevelt, Roseanne, the Rosenbergs, Rumi, Salman Rushdie, the Russian people, Ruth

Can a raconteur be boring? When?

Describe a rebel without a cause.

Who is a modern-day Renaissance man or woman?

Define any robber baron, especially in terms of American history.

Define the characteristics of a particular music group.

Define *role player*. Is everyone a role player in some way?

S

Sacred cow, sad sack, Saddam (Hussein), sage, saint, Samaritan, Samson in the Bible, a sandman, the Biblical Sarah, Satan, scapegoat, schlemiel, Arnold Schwarzenegger, scoundrel, Seabee, second but not least, Section Eight (as defined to 1944 in the United States Army), self-image, self-made person, sepoy, Ravi Shankar, Shia Muslims/Sunni Muslims, Sikh, Bart Simpson, O. J. Simpson, sister, Sister, sitar player, skipper, slyboots, smart aleck, John Smith (of whom there are tens of thousands in the United States), Joseph Smith's wives, Snoopy, soldier, son, Steven Spielberg, spieler, Mr. Spock, a stage version of anyone (such as a hero, a villain, an Irishman, a drunkard), Stagedoor Johnny, Jimmy Stewart, Martha Stewart, Stradivarius, sultan, the Sultan of Swat (Babe Ruth), Billy Sunday, Superman or Supergirl, suzerain, swashbuckler

How might a child seeing a different Santa at every street corner define Santa Claus?

Is the term "senior citizen" insulting?

"She is the youngest of four brothers," says a newspaper item. Define the *she* of this quotation.

Define Siddhartha the man, Siddhartha the character in Hesse's novel *Siddhartha.*

"For she was the maker of the song she sang," wrote Wallace Stevens. How do you define *singer?* What makes a great singer?

Define *social climber.*

Define *sponge* in human terms.

Can a sport be a sport without participating in sports?

"I refuse to be data-processed," said a student, who was concerned about having to fill out so much computer information. How might a computer define a student?

Define *style-setter.*

T

the Tagalog people, tallyman, a modern and real Tarzan, Elizabeth Taylor, teacher, a television critic, a tenement dweller, terrorist, Texas Ranger, a thief who steals Bibles, a modern and real Thor, Jim Thorpe, tinker, titan, Tolstoy, top gun, tourist, trickster (as from fables and folklore), troubadour, troublemaker, troubleshooter, Sojourner Truth, Harriet Tubman, Desmond Tutu, Tweedledee and Tweedledum, twin, tycoon, type, tyrant, Mike Tyson

Is it true that the teacher who is defined as the "meanest" and most demanding of the students is the one who is the most respected?

What does it mean to be a teenager? Find a definition and say why it does or doesn't fit your experience.

It has been said, "There is no '*them,*' just lots of '*us.*'" How are *them, they,* and *us* defined?

Define a modern-day Thwackum, a glimpse of whom is seen in this quotation from Henry Fielding: "Thwackum was for doing justice, and leaving mercy to heaven."

Define *Transylvanian* as if you were an expert about, or an enthusiast for, horror tales.

U

Ugly duckling, a modern and real Ulysses as a compulsive wanderer, underachiever, undertaker, a universalist, Unknown Citizen, Unknown Soldier, upstanding citizen, upstart, Dickens's unctuous Uriah Heep, Uriah Heep the rock band, a user, a utilitarian

What distinguishes U2 from other rock groups? Why the choice of the name? Does it relate to the U2 incident of 1960?

A man who won an "Ugliest Man" contest says that he "looks forward to becoming still uglier." Discuss his statement in terms of definition.

Who is one of the "undecided" *after* an election is over?

Define someone who regularly uses understatement.

V

Vagabond, valedictorian, Valkyrie, Valley Girls, vamp, vampire, vassal, vaudevillian, veep, Vermeer, vernacular speakers, Vice President, viceroy, victim, a Victorian, Viking, villain, Dick Vitale, volunteer, vulgarian

What defines a venture capitalist?

Define Gore Vidal, taking into consideration the title of an article about him, "With Malice Towards Some and Charity for Few."

W

WAF, Wagnerian, waif, Mike Wallace "the jugular journalist," Walloon people, WAVE, Wednesday's child, Weird Sisters, Orson Welles, Westerner, Whig, whipping boy, Walt Whitman as Everyone, whiz, widow or widower, a "_____" widow, wimp, Walter Winchell, Winnie the Pooh, wizard, Wonder Woman, Bertie Wooster, wunderkind

XYZ

Xanthippe, X-Man (whether man or woman), Yahoo, Yankee, Yanqui, yes-man or yes-woman, yeti, yogi, you as seen by your best friend and then as seen by your enemy, *your self* as distinguished from *yourself,* youth, zealot, Zen Buddhist, Zionist, zombie, Zoot suiter, Zouave

"You are what you eat."

Human Conditions, Human Relations, Sociology

Achilles' heel, aging, alcoholism, alternative culture, American Indian Movement (AIM), angst, anti-establishment, Apocalypse, backlash, bandwagon, the Beatitudes, benign neglect, the big sleep, blackout (as used during World War II), blessing in disguise, bundling, caste, catbird seat, challenge, Christmas as a symbol of the American culture, circumspection, class; code-living, (skin) color, commencement ceremony (as a beginning), competition, conflict, consistency, contemplation, conventionalism, coordination, cost of war, counterculture, cult, the Cultural Revolution Decade (China), culture shock, death, delirium tremens, dog days, dot-coms, dyslexia, eclecticism (in a specific area, say religion), ecotactics, ecumenical movements, enrichment, environment, escapism, ethnic purity, etiquette (as opposed to "manners"), fad, failure (as defined by an American), *fatwah,* feedback, Fifth Column, *fin de siècle* mood, fixed idea, flag-waving, the Four Horsemen, generation gap, global village, gluttony, gossip, grass roots, gullibility, "hangin' out," hassle, heart, heartland, heredity, hiatus, high-tech, hip hop, hoarding (as in wartime), hoopla, human, human being, human condition, humanity, hypocrisy, idea, illumination, implication, incomplete investigation, inference, informality, innocence (as opposed to sophistication), introspection, involvement, jamboree, jealousy, jeopardy, judgment (not justice), justice, Kabuki, kibbutz, kindness, kismet, knowledge, kosher, life (including life after death and life after life), light as knowledge, light pollution, lingua franca, love, *machismo,* marriage-go-round, marriage of convenience, marriage to one's (job, motorcycle, pastime), meditation, meeting one's Waterloo, mellowness, Mexican *mordida,* middle-of-the-road, moderation as excess, moral cowardice, moratorium, nature/nurture, negligence, neutrality, new morality, new wave, noise pollution, notoriety/infamy, obedience, oblivion, old money/new money, over a barrel, oxymoron, pain, panhandling, panic, parasitism, paternalism, patriotism, pedantry, permissiveness, pilgrimage, prejudice, primogeniture, privacy, private Utopia, puberty, punk movement, pushiness, quintessence, raisin in the sun, ready for love/in love with love, recession, reclamation, relevance, responsibility, rumor, sacrifice, scandal, "semi-happiness," sense of place, sensibility, sentiment, sentimentality, September song, serendipity, the Shari'a (Islamic moral and legal code), showdown, sluggishness, success (as defined by an American), swan song, sweet sixteen, taboo, tact, carrying the torch/passing the torch, troubleshooting, the ultimate adventure, uncouthness, urban/rural, utilitarianism, vindication, Weltanschauung, Weltpolitik, Weltschmerz, wit/humor/sense of humor, women's liberation, wonder/awe/amazement, xenophobia, Zeno's nine paradoxes, the concept of zero, zero population growth

Draw subjects for definition from the following items about the human condition:

Augustine said that total abstinence is easier than perfect moderation.

"Anger is a short madness." (Horace)

Apartheid as it existed; as it exists now.

Back-to-school blues.

In *Dr. Faustus* by Christopher Marlowe, Helen of Troy is described thus: "Was this the face that launched a thousand ships?" How would you define beauty?

A particular kind of group behavior.

How does Emerson's phrase "the blowing clover, the falling rain" relate to the human condition?

"Boldness is a child of ignorance and baseness." (Sir Francis Bacon)

"Boldness is an ill keeper of promise." (Sir Francis Bacon)

Is there anyone or anything in the human condition that cannot be captured—that is, defined and understood—in a book?

"Being busy is a national excuse as well as a national passion." (Norman Cousins)

What is a "worthy cause" in these days when almost everything is said to be one?

"Character is destiny." (Novalis)

Define the "chasing-after-the-dream" syndrome.

"Give me chastity and continence," said St. Augustine, "but do not give it yet."

What does it mean to be "color blind"?

Common sense, someone has said, is uncommon sense.

"No true compassion without will, no true wit without compassion." (John Fowles)

"Conscience is a coward, and those faults it has not strength enough to prevent it seldom has justice enough to accuse." (Oliver Goldsmith)

What makes something or someone cool? You are cool if you _____.

"Courageous the pine that does not change its color under winter snow." (Hirohito)

What does it mean to dance with words?

What defines a particular kind of dance, old or new, e.g., ballet, break dancing, jitterbugging, swing, the twist, or any other of your choice. How does your choice of a particular dance define you?

"Dancing is just discovery, discovery, discovery" (Martha Graham). Define what you've discovered through a particular kind of dancing.

How is dating defined by your family? Your friends?

"Death is a continuation of my life without me." (Jean Paul-Sartre)

Find a definition for *dharma* as used in India. Now define your own *dharma.*

"Death, in itself, is nothing; but we fear, / To be we know not what, we know not where." (Dryden)

"Death is not extinguishing the light; it is putting out the lamp because the dawn has come." (Rabrindranath Tagore)

"Deeds, not words, shall speak me." (John Fletcher)

"You have delighted us long enough," says Mr. Bennett to his daughter, who is entertaining the company in Jane Austen's *Pride and Prejudice*.

"Desperate times call for desperate measures."

What in your opinion is the "whole duty" of a person?

Education is a "means of knowledge about ourselves. Therefore, after we have examined ourselves, we radiate outwards and discover peoples and worlds around us." (Ngugi Wa Thiong'o)

"To err is human, to forgive divine" (Alexander Pope). How would you define the key terms *err* and *forgive*?

"The Evil Empire." Take your pick and define.

How does a country's flag tell us about it?

"Rightly understood, freedom is the universal license to be good." (paraphrased from lines by Hartley Coleridge)

"Freedom is unbelievably precious." (Soviet seaman, now free in the United States, who once was captured by the Soviets when he tried to escape from them)

"To be furious / Is to be frightened out of fear." (Shakespeare, *Antony and Cleopatra*)

Define *future shock* as it relates to the human condition.

Define the Golden Rule as articulated in different faiths.

Define Graceland as depicted in Paul Simon's album by that name.

Define Hajj as a physical and spiritual experience.

"What is the worth of anything, / But for the happiness 'twill bring?" (Richard Cambridge)

Happiness is _____.

What is the first thing you think of when you hear the word "heart"? What are some other words with multiple definitions (literal, metaphoric)?

"Heredity," says a newspaper item, "is what you believe in when your child gets A's in school."

Hiroshima—what does it signify?

Define *Honi soit qui mal y pense* ("Shame be to he who thinks ill of it") as the statement relates to the human condition.

What is "honourable" as it is used in the title of John le Carré's novel *The Honourable Schoolboy*?

"Humanity is immense, and reality has a myriad of forms." (Henry James)

What is ethnic humor? (When is it offensive and when not? Who has the right to use it?)

How has the term "innocence" come to have negative connotations?

Can intelligence be defined as proportion?

Define the many faces of Islam.

Describe Jain beliefs about nonviolence and how they translate into everyday life.

Define what is meant by a jaundiced view of a particular thing.

"Justice was invented by criminals." (Dashiell Hammett)

Define the spiritual experience of kensho.

"Knowledge and experience bring contentment" (Bhagavad Gita). How do you define these key terms?

Define the four koans of the Zen tradition.

Define Krishna consciousness.

What are the different kinds of laughter?

Define the term *li* as it connects to Confucian philosophy.

"Whoever destroys a single life is as guilty as though he had destroyed the entire world; and whoever rescues a single life earns as much merit as though he had rescued the entire world." (Talmud)

"To live in hearts we leave behind is not to die." (Thomas Campbell)

What are different kinds of love?

An idea from Daniel Defoe is to love the subject for the sake of the teacher. Illustrate and define love put in a similar context.

"Love's tongue is in the eyes." (Phineas Fletcher)

"I loved not yet, yet I loved to love. . . . I sought what I might love, in love with loving." (St. Augustine)

How accurate is the definition of love in I Corinthians 13?

"Ever has it been that love is master where he will." (John Gower)

Define what is meant by Shakespeare's saying that one should "choose love by another's eye."

Mantra—the original definition and how the word is used now.

Karl Marx's definition and a current definition of Marxism.

What is a mystique? How can it be created and maintained?

Define different brands of nationalism—in the United States or around the world.

Define "Never-never land."

Define nonviolence viewed as an activist method.

Define *nirvana* as a metaphysical concept.

What does the syllable *om* signify?

John Keats believed that reading poetry should be like remembrance of something from your thoughts. Is that how you respond to poetry? How does it resonate with you?

"There is no crime as shameful as poverty." (paraphrase of a line by George Farquhar)

"Procrastination is the thief of time." (Edward Young)

"Prosperity is not without many fears and distastes; and adversity is not without comforts and hopes." (Sir Francis Bacon)

Describe a Pyrrhic victory you've encountered or experienced.

Define a quagmire as you have experienced it.

Define how one makes a quantum leap.

What kinds of quarantines are there?

Human beings have always gone on quests. Name one and define it. Or choose one you're on and define.

What is quid pro quo in a particular context?

How would you define a quirky sense of humor?

Define *quite nice* as used in New Zealand. How does it differ from your usage?

In which situations is a quorum necessary? Define your own.

Define a quota that could affect your life.

What would be a quotidian quiddity in your life at school?

Define the many things that a rainbow signifies.

Define how the Ramayana is a living epic.

Define rebellion, teenage style.

"Reputation is an idle and most false imposition, oft got without merit and lost without deserving." (Shakespeare)

Define the code of conduct presented in the Sermon on the Mount.

Define the Shinto belief system.

Define the significance of Mount Sinai in ancient Israel and present-day Israel.

The power of story as expressed here: "[O]nly the story . . . can continue beyond the war and the warrior. It is the story that outlives the sound of war-drums and the exploits of brave fighters. It is the story . . . that saves our progeny from blundering like blind beggars into the spikes of the cactus fence. The story is our escort; without it, we are blind. Does the blind man own his escort? No, neither do we the story; rather it is the story that owns us and directs us." (Chinua Achebe)

On seeing the Taj Mahal a poet wrote: "A mighty emperor, sustained by wealth, has made a mockery of us, the poor" (translated from Urdu by Zarina Hock). How would you define this monument?

"The strongest reason best." (Jean de La Fontaine)

"A tart temper never mellows with age, and a sharp tongue is the only edged tool that grows keener with constant use." (Washington Irving)

"Treason doth never prosper: What's the reason? / For if it prosper, none dare call it treason." (Sir John Harington)

"The tree will wither long before it fall." (Lord Byron)

"Truth cannot afford to be tolerant where it faces positive evil" (Rabindranath Tagore). Define a particular context in which you can apply this maxim.

"Truth is the daughter of Time."

Julius Caesar said, "Veni, vidi, vici" (I came, I saw, I conquered). Use this claim to define something you've experienced.

The term *Victorian* has changed in value many times since the reign of Queen Victoria of Great Britain.

Choose one value and develop the implications of your definition.

Western culture can mean several things. Pick one meaning and define in further detail.

Define a Zen belief system (choose one school of thought).

What defines a Zen garden?

What culturally distinguishes the Zoroastrian community?

Identity

What defines your identity? In other words, what makes you, you?

"If you come to fame not understanding who you are, it will define who you are" (Oprah Winfrey). Choose a famous person and show how his or her public image defined the person.

"When I discover who I am, I'll be free." (Ralph Ellison)

"It isn't where you came from, its where you're going that counts." (Ella Fitzgerald)

"Where your treasure is, there will be your heart also" (Gospel According to Matthew). How can your "treasure" define you?

Nonhuman Life/Creatures

aardvark, aardwolf, adder, Afghan hound, albatross, alpaca, amoeba, anaconda, ant bear, antelope, ape, armadillo, auk, baboon, bacterium, bee eater, beetle, bighorn, bison, black widow, blenny, brown recluse, buffalo, cat, chicken snake, cicada, clam, conch, crab, cygnet, dinosaur, dog-faced butterfly, a cross between a donkey jenny and a zebra stallion, dove, dragonfly, drake, duck, duck-billed platypus, elephant, fox, gander, heron, ibex, the mythical jabberwock, kite, kiwi, lizard, lobster, mealybug, mink, myna or mynah, nanny goat, okapi, prairie dog, puffin, quail, razorbill, sea horse, shark, springer spaniel, squab, staghound, tick, Galápagos turtle, the mythical unicorn, vulture, warthog, weevil, right whale, yellow jacket, zebra fish

Draw subjects for definition from the following items about creature life:

"Bull fighting is not a sport. It is a tragedy." (Ernest Hemingway)

Two headlines: Bulldogs Battle Demons Today *and* Scorpions Trounce the Eagles.

Are cats wrongly maligned?

What defines hunting dog behavior?

Do chimpanzees really talk, or do they merely imitate their human teachers?

Look over the first paragraph of Dickens's *Hard Times* for the stereotyped definition and the natural definition of a horse. Then write a stereotyped definition of any nonhuman creature, followed by an opposing, and natural, definition.

What is an animal emotion? (Is it the same as a human emotion?)

Define the process of metamorphosis.

How did the peacock gets its reputation?

Does a pet know its name?

Does a racehorse know it is a racehorse?

When is an animal "rare"?

What happens during hibernation?

What in elephant behavior indicates that they "never forget"?

Paradox

Is *young adult* a paradox?

Is it possible to be mildly fanatical?

How can fast food be so good and so bad for you?

An old hymn by Jane Taylor says that it is "quite a disgrace to be fine." How could this be?

Explore definitions involving paradox as prompted by the following quotations:

"In my beginning is my end." (T. S. Eliot)

From William Blake:

> To see a world in a grain of sand
> And a heaven in a wild flower,
> Hold infinity in the palm of your hand
> And eternity in an hour.

"There is a wisdom that is woe; but there is a woe that is madness." (Herman Melville)

"Every exit is an entry to somewhere else." (Tom Stoppard)

Define how the Internet broadens your universe and yet shrinks it.

"One should lift up the self by the self, And should not let the self down; For the self is the self's only friend, And the self is the self's only enemy." (Bhagavad Gita)

"He who loves his life loses it, and he who hates his life in this world will keep it for eternal life." (New Testament, Gospel According to John, 12:25)

"The way up and the way down are one and the same." (Heraclitus)

"If there is cause to hate someone, the cause to love has just begun." (Wolof proverb, Senegal)

"To be praised is to be lost." (Kikuyu proverb, Kenya)

"A joke's a very serious thing." (Charles Churchill)

"You can't win unless you learn how to lose." (Kareem Abdul-Jabbar)

"I believe that unarmed truth and unconditional love will have the final word in reality. This is why right, temporarily defeated, is stronger than evil triumphant." (Martin Luther King Jr.)

Psychology and the Mind, Emotions

"abnormality," after-vacation blues, anti-social, astro-soul, bipolar disorder, blood lust, blue Monday, brain waves, child's nightmares, compulsive behavior, conscience, depression, ego, "emotional cannibalism" (from Henry James), exploitation, fanaticism, fixation, *gestalt,* the green-eyed monster, guilty conscience, hijacker syndrome, hostage syndrome, id, insanity, instability, instinct, intelligence quotient, intuition, love/hate relationship, mania, manipulation, narcissism, neuroticism, normality, obsession, out-of-body experience, panic reaction, paranoia, passion, personality, perversion, psychiatry, psychology, psychopath, psychotherapy, "pushing the envelope," testing the limits, rebelliousness, sanity, schizophrenia, sense of the absurd, sixth sense, Skinner's "behaviorism," social friction, sour grapes, spring fever, superego, triskaidekaphobia, *Zeitgeist*

Ambiguity, Infinity, and the Kitchen Sink

Draw subjects for definition from the following terms and thoughts:

about/nearly/hardly, ambiguity, ambivalence, anachronism, black holes, Calvary, drop in the ocean, energy, euphemism, exoticism, fat/plump, forever, hard side/soft side, hypothesis, imagination, impossibility, infinity, insight, -ism, kaleidoscope, karma, less/few, malapropism, measurelessness, metaphysics, mirage sale, mutually exclusive, nomadic syntax (used by the journalist Tom Wicker to refer to Eisenhower's rambling public pronouncements), phenomenon, rare/unusual, reality, reasonable/unreasonable, semi-terrific, something that stays, sprezzatura, symbol, thief of time, to be or not to be, tomorrow/yesterday, ubiquity, unknown quality, unknown quantity, up/down, wacky names, want-ad terms, weather

A

Define what coming of age means to you in your everyday life. Are there any contradictions that you see?

Discuss the ambiguities in these defining parts: "used car" in "used car salesman"; "easy" in "easy chair"; "small animal" in "small animal hospital"; "match" in "match box"; "hot" in "hot cup of coffee"; "good" in "good and angry," "your universe in *the* universe."

Write of a characteristic problem arising from imprecise or ambiguous language in documents.

Illustrate the ambiguity in each of the following; then write a definition essay discussing ways to eliminate ambiguity where it is not intended:

> There wasn't a single man present.
> Visiting relatives can be dangerous.
> The chicken is ready to eat.
> I couldn't praise the candidate highly enough.
> Eye Drops Off Shelf (newspaper headline)
> Local High School Dropouts Cut in Half (newspaper headline)

She sold Mark Twain books.

Begin Conceding While Sadat Waits (newspaper headline)

What aspect of America does Muhammad Ali capture in this statement? "I am America. I am the part you won't recognize. But get used to me. Black, confident, cocky; my name, not yours; my religion, not yours; my goals, my own; get used to me."

What is the most coveted award?

B

Why are Darwin's definitions of beauty and love circular and therefore incomplete?

"Beauty is momentary in the mind— / The fitful tracing of a portal; / But in the flesh it is immortal." (Wallace Stevens)

"Beauty is in the eye of the beholder." (Margaret Hungerford)

"A thing of beauty is a joy forever." (John Keats)

Are the stars beautiful up close?

"Beauty is eternity gazing at itself in a mirror." (Khalil Gibran)

"Beauty is truth's smile when she beholds her own face in a perfect mirror." (Rabrindranath Tagore)

"No; we have been as usual asking the wrong question. It does not matter a hoot what the mockingbird on the chimney is singing. The real and proper question is: Why is it beautiful?" (Annie Dillard)

"Beauty is its own excuse for being." (Ralph Waldo Emerson)

When is big small? When is small big?

According to Montaigne, the thumb is the most important finger. Can the head commit a revolution against the body? Define the most important part of the body.

Show that "both sides" are not necessarily all sides.

"Brevity is the soul of wit" (Shakespeare). How would you define wit?

Why is Bugs Bunny an enduring part of American culture?

C

To card, according to the dictionary, means "to cleanse, disentangle, and collect together (as fibers) by the use of cards preparatory to spinning." What does *to card* or *to be carded* mean to you?

Note the definitions of these words, which either sound or look nearly alike: *ceras, cereous, ceres, Cereus, cerous, cerris, ceruse, cirrous, cirrus.* Can you offer some pairs of words to this collection, providing the definitions?

"When it is not necessary to change," said Viscount Falkland, "it is necessary not to change."

"What is character but the determination of incident? What is incident but the illustration of character?" (Henry James)

Discuss the change of definition of the word *chauvinism* since its origin.

"When I was a child, I spoke as a child, I understood as a child, I thought as a child: but when I became a man, I put away childish things" (New Testament, Paul's epistle to the Corinthians). What does it really and specifically mean to think as a child?

What logic do children use in choices of words—such as "snew" as the past tense of the verb "snow"?

How do children know when they are children? Does a "child" have to be a child?

What is the popular image or definition of Christ? Mohammad? Buddha?

Choosing paint (especially its colors) gets tougher all the time because of the great number of different shades and the names for them. Define some colors other than the primary ones.

An absent comma makes all the difference in this sentence from a newspaper account of a political barbecue: "It should be an interesting day to say the least." Define a punctuation mark by considering its importance.

In a letter to the House Committee on Un-American Activities, Lillian Hellman said, "I cannot and will not cut my conscience to fit this year's fashions." What metaphor was she employing? What is another way of expressing her idea?

D

Take certain terms and give them new definitions. Can you make these definitions seem to fit?

Does the number of words define the value of a document? There are 1,322 words in the Declaration of Independence, and there are 26,911 words in a certain government document regulating the sale of cabbages.

Define something that has at least two opposing names. "Stardust," for example, is also called "atmospheric contaminants."

Ask the question, "What's up with *that*?" about some important something that needs definition. Then write the definition that answers your question.

The power to define is the power to cure, says William Raspberry, syndicated columnist. He gives as examples: "school districts that cure the problem of non-learning not by improved teaching but by setting lower standards; social statisticians who cure poverty not by improving income but by reassessing the assets of those who are impoverished. . . . The prospects are endless. Robbers could be transmuted into income-transfer specialists. Joblessness could be redefined as full-time leisure. Racial animosity could be ethnotension. . . ."

Distinguish, by definition, between the terms "lower depths" and "the pits."

When she married again, Elizabeth Taylor sold the diamond Richard Burton had given her. This is an illustration of the fact that things have definitions of different kinds at different times and under different circumstances. What are some other examples?

"Diamonds are a girl's best friend." What definition of women is implied in this song? Why would it be considered offensive by many women?

Direction: Which way is east? west? north? south?

Franklin discovered, not invented, electricity. Write comparison/contrast definitions of *discovery* and *invention.*

How would you define distance in the context of outer space?

How might *divorce* be defined, as used in the headline Man Divorced from Army?

"Do one to others as you would have them do one to you," said an elementary student.

What could be defined as a case of "double reverse discrimination"?

How big, by definition, is a drop? How many droplets make a drop?

E

Does *egghead* imply the same thing *as intellectual*?

How is your e-mail persona different from your personality?

What defines empty? Are there empty spaces?

"Education's purpose is to replace an empty mind with an open one." (Malcolm S. Forbes)

To meditate you must empty your mind of clutter. How do you empty your mind?

According to Zen philosophy, "The everyday mind is the empty mind, . . . the mind which does not discriminate the self from the world." Define the everyday mind and the empty mind in this context.

The comic strip character Pogo said, "We have met the enemy and he is us." In what ways are we our own enemies?

Show by definition how contradictory and confusing the English language is. Some examples: *man's laughter* and *manslaughter* (pointed out by Mario Pei the linguist) and "It took a *month* of *fast talk* to convince them."

F

How would you define *fad?* How do fads define us?

The outstanding farmer of the year, according to a cartoon, is the one who had the lowest loss.

What's the distinction between farm subsidy and farm aid?

Define something by using the word *fradnip* to name it. (A *fradnip* is a term used as a substitute for any other term.)

"Our friends, the enemy." (Pierre-Jean de Béranger)

How would you define being a friend?

How would you define your expectations of a friend?

"The future becomes the present, the present the past, and the past turns into everlasting regret if you don't plan for it." (Tennessee Williams)

G

"The game is my wife. It demands loyalty and responsibility, and it gives me back fulfillment and peace." (Michael Jordan)

Nowadays, we avoid gender-specific references (*actor, poet,* rather than *actress, poetess*). How is this a consequence of a redefinition of gender?

What is the difference between *gentle* and *genteel*?

What were the "good old times"? Were they as good as people say they were?

A newspaper asks whether government is the incompetent's best friend.

What does this German saying mean, "At night, all cats are gray."

When everything is grotesque is nothing grotesque?

Below is one definition of growing up from Sara Teasdale. Can you offer an alternative definition?

When I can look Life in the eyes,
Grown calm and very coldly wise,
Life will have given me the Truth,
And taken in exchange—my youth.

H

"The hand that signed the paper felled a city," said Dylan Thomas. How do you define *hand* as it is used in this statement?

How do you think a woman's role is defined here: "The hand that rocks the cradle rules the world."

"Heaven lies about us in our infancy! Shades of the prison-house begin to close upon the growing boy" [or girl], says William Wordsworth. Define your experience of losing your carefree childhood as you grow up.

"O Lord, wandering with thee, even hell itself would be to me a heaven of bliss" (Ramayana). Define a situation that makes a heaven out of hell for you.

"History is a nightmare from which I am trying to awaken." (James Joyce)

"People are trapped in History, and History is trapped in them!" (James Baldwin)

"The world's history is the world's judgment." (Friedrich Schiller)

Your home is your castle. Is a king's castle his home?

Home is _____

Is "How much can I get for it?" a definition of "sentimental value"?

Give definitions of "How are you?" and "How do you do?"

I

"Ignorance is not innocence but sin," said Robert Browning.

What in your life has been an illusion? What happened when your illusion turned to reality, or when your reality turned out to be an illusion?

"Impression is nine-tenths of the law," says David Rife. What definitions are changed by this pun?

What is "in" this year? What is "out" or "not in" this year?

An Irish bar in Seattle is run by Japanese people; the original owner died fifty years ago.

Define an intangible something by using concrete terms or by giving it a concrete aspect.

Define an intangible of a concrete something.

Istanbul was Constantinople. What different connotations do different names for the same place create?

J

The name *Jack* appears frequently in nursery rhymes and fairytales. What qualities does a *Jack* have? When is a *John* not a *Jack* (and vice versa)?

"Jealousy is all the fun you think they had." (Erica Jong)

In the song title "June Is Bustin' Out All Over," what is implied about the month of June? Could some other month "bust out"?

One person's junk is another's treasure. Why?

How do you define *justice*?

K

Though Arthur, Henry VIII, and Edward VII were all kings of England, their roles as kings were very different. How has the definition of what it means to be king changed over the years?

What different meanings can a kiss have?

Write a comparison/contrast definition between an old airplane and a modern kite, in which the kite comes out the better of the two.

"Knowledge is the prime need of the hour" (Mary Macleod Bethune). How is this comment true today?

L

When, by definition, might a person be said to know two languages equally well, that is, be bilingual?

When is less more? When is more less?

"Lift not the painted veil which those who live call Life" (Percy Bysshe Shelley). How does the poet define life here?

Define the many ways in which you are literate.

If you lose a key, is the key itself lost? What defines being "lost"?

Intangible though it is, love can be measured and therefore defined. How?

M

"The map is not the territory it symbolizes." (Hayakawa)

"I hear that melting-pot stuff a lot, and all I can say is that we haven't melted." (Jesse Jackson)

The mind does not act separately from the body like a "ghost in the machine," said Gilbert Ryle.

"The mind is its own place, and in itself, can make a Heaven of Hell, and a Hell of Heaven." (John Milton)

There is only one witness to what goes on in the mind in thought or dream.

"It [the mind] has memory's ear that can hear without having to hear." (Marianne Moore)

Give an example that defines "mind over matter."

"In the old days," says a newspaper item, "if you saved money you were a miser; now you're a marvel."

February is the worst month of all, it is said, because it brings depression, boredom, and flu. What kind of month is April? What are April showers to different people of different ages? What is behind the quotation from T. S. Eliot's long poem "The Waste Land": "April is the cruellest month"? Write an extended definition for one of the months of the year.

How does Louis Armstrong's comment here apply to other things besides music? "We all do 'do, re, mi,' but you have got to find the other notes yourself."

N

How do our names help define us? What does it mean to say that someone doesn't "look like" his or her name?

Is there someone you could call your nemesis? Why?

Discuss the difference in definition between "Newfoundland" and "New Found Land."

Why do many Native Americans object to the term *New World*?

What are some "new words for old deceptions"?

"That noise scared my ears," said Alden Powell. What definition does this quotation give to the sense of hearing?

Define literally such nonliteral expressions as "Keep on your toes." Find other examples.

Write a definition essay showing that nothing is like anything else; that anything is unlike anything else.

Write a definition essay on *number(s)* after reading the following: "Round numbers are always false," said Samuel Johnson. "The half is greater than the whole," said Hesiod. A famous performer of mental arithmetic was asked, "How many bulls' tails to the moon?" to which he replied, "One, if it's long enough." Is it possible for something to add up to more than it is? Is it possible for something to add up to less than it is? Is it possible to count pearls and oysters together? Is it possible for the sum of parts of something to be less than the whole of that something?

O

What are onomatopoeic sounds really like? Define them as they should be.

What is Optimism as Voltaire has Pangloss define it?

Distinguish between optical illusion and other illusions.

P

"Paint what you know is there, not what you see," said Gertrude Stein in reference to cubism. Define what is meant by her statement.

Write a definition of what one might see in a particular photograph that is contrived to be confusing.

Write a definition showing that plain talk is the hardest kind of oral expression.

Write a definition of pleasure based on Aphra Behn's saying that "Variety is the soul of pleasure."

What does the pledge of allegiance mean? What do its individual words mean, especially the words *pledge, allegiance, flag, nation, indivisible, liberty, justice,* and *all?*

Everyone has a different definition for, or understanding of, the word *poetry.* There are as many different definitions for it as there are people. What is your definition of it?

Was all poetry, as the saying goes, written before time began?

A legislator said that he could get through legislation for teaching poetry in prison only if he did not call it poetry. What definition of poetry is so distrusted that legislators would not want it taught in prison?

Define a "portmanteau" word. Give some examples.

When is progress inhumane, or does progress always, by definition, help humanity?

What is the result of reversing the principal parts of a proverb? (Example: What goes down must come up.)

"A proverb is much matter decocted into few words," said Thomas Fuller.

R

A young boy is quoted in a newspaper item as saying that he likes radio more than television because he can "see the pictures better." What definition is at work in his seeing?

Define *reaction.* Remember that one person's reaction is not another's. There may even be many people whose knee reflexes are controlled, for example, by hitting their opposing knees.

Define *reductio ad absurdum* to illustrate that it is an ambiguous term.

Do children define what they draw? Do they draw to reproduce, or to represent? Write a comparison/ contrast definition of the terms *reproduction* and *representation.*

Show by comparison/contrast definition that *re-sign* and *resign* are opposites in meaning.

Show by comparison/contrast definition what a professor meant by saying that there was "entirely too much student rest" on campus.

Define *reverse discrimination.*

Show by definition that what is right or wrong to one person is not the same to another.

Define the "road-not-taken" syndrome.

What is a "roadrunner"? Is it, as Rod Powell says, a bird that is "still running" when some other creature might have stopped? Do definitions and names limit in this way the things they define or name?

S

Develop a definition of one of the seasons like this one from *Time* magazine: "Autumn: A Season for Hymning and Hawing."

What does it mean to be selfish in practice but not in principle?

What is the most important sense according to your definition?

"That kitten smells black," said Diane Ephthimiou. Are some things identifiable by similar ambivalence of the senses?

Illustrate unusual definitions of the senses, as in this quotation from Shakespeare: "The eye of man hath not heard, the ear of man hath not seen, man's hand is not able to taste, his tongue to conceive, nor his heart to report, what my dream was."

A cartoon asks, "Are you shocked at the things that don't shock you anymore?" What two definitions, at least, are there of *shock* in this quotation?

What is *future shock?*

What is *sticker shock?*

What activity do you consider to be "sick"?

A visitor to Northern Ireland was asked which side he was on in the conflict there, and he answered, "I am on the side that doesn't require that I have to be on a side." Is it possible, by definition, not to be on a side in some issue?

Sometimes the sign is not the real message, as when a welcome mat is put out just for convention or when a dictator says that he welcomes criticism. Define a sign that does not mean what it says.

Signs are read in a cultural context. Why might someone from another culture find these signs confusing. *Gone fishing. No strollers on escalators. No shoes, no shirt, no service. Toilet tissue—facial quality. Garage sale.* Can you think of other ambiguous or evocative signs?

What is a silver spoon? Is it necessarily a good thing?

Simple things are often the hardest to define. Illustrate the point by defining a door, a two-letter word, a color, or even the words *simple* and *simplicity.*

Is almost anything that is fun defined as a sin?

Define the expression, "since God knows when."

Define a human being as a social security number.

Show how spelling confuses definition, as in the following "One, two, three, Gough!"

Discuss by definition the fact of a statue's shaking its fist at a snowy sky.

What constitutes a stereotype? How is this different from recognizing difference?

Define an old stereotype, such as the one that said that a 50-50 sharing in the home was this: the wife cooked, the husband ate.

Does one have to be in prison to go "stir-crazy"?

"Style is whatever makes writing distinguishable even where it is not distinguished," said W. D. Powell. What is your definition of *style?*

Define someone so lacking in subtlety as to be like the mother, say, who sent her prisoner son a buzz-saw in a huge cake.

"There is a superstition in avoiding superstition," said Sir Francis Bacon. What is your definition of *superstition?*

Define, in your own way, what is meant by the song title, "Ah, Sweet Mystery of Life."

Does Swiss cheese have holes to help you recognize what it is? Which comes first in a definition, the thing defined—or merely our external impression of it?

T

What does "It takes two to tango" imply?

What is taste? What is good taste? What is bad taste?

What does it mean to be a team player?

Does teamwork mean team work?

Telephone books may be used not only for locating numbers but also for standing on. Does a momentary function of a thing change that thing's definition?

Do you define television as a literal, or a symbolic, medium?

Why, by definition, can there rarely be a television commercial that ends unhappily?

Show how the titles of certain television shows can be used interchangeably and with reasonable accuracy.

Someone accidentally defined television as an "escape goat." How accurate is this definition, whether or not it is an intended one?

Why is a television or a radio commercial referred to as a "message"?

How would you define "the thought of God"—meaning "God's thought"?

Can anyone—such as a timekeeper—"keep" time?

"The time is now . . ."—Is it possible by definition for time to be now?

"Scientists know no time," said da Vinci. Give a definition of time as he defined it, or understood it, in this statement.

"The time is now seventeen minutes before the hour," said the disc jockey, to which a listener responded, "What hour?" What two definitions of time are seen here?

What is the difference in definition between *time* and *eternity?*

How would a prisoner probably define *time?*

How do most Americans feel about time and distance? What definitions of each are implied in these feelings?

Define what Lord Byron meant by referring to Time as the "Avenger."

A prisoner is asked what comes after five and says "ten years to life." A time keeper might have said "5:01." A sophisticate might have said "cocktails." Consider different ways time is defined depending on the person defining it.

Is the term *totalitarianism* applied only to communism?

How is the tourist's view of a foreign locale defined?

Define *translation.* Myles NaGopaleen, the Irish journalist, said of it: "If I write in Irish what I conceive to be 'Last Tuesday was very wet,' I like to feel reasonably sure that what I've written does not in fact mean 'Mr. so-and-so is a thief and a drunkard.'"

Regarding translation of the Bible there is the contention of some that angels were symbolic of, rather than literal evocations of, messengers from God. How does definition affect translation?

What are the many ways that one can "travel light"?

"We forgive you for trespassing against us," says a church sign, "but you still will be towed away." What vastly different definitions are there of *trespassing?*

"He said true things, but called them by wrong names," said Robert Browning.

They really do say "All aboard!" What other truths are often defined almost as if they were clichés?

"Truth, when witty, is the wittiest of all things," said Julius and Augustus Hare.

U

How would you define what an "unaskable question" is?

"Unbelievable!" Define.

What does "understanding" mean when we understand people but not their handwriting?

How does William Butler Yeats define a unity of being in the following lines?

O chestnut-tree, great-rooted blossomer,
Are you the leaf, the blossom or the bole?
O body swayed to music, O brightening glance,
How can we know the dancer from the dance?

"The universe is neither hostile nor friendly; it is merely indifferent," said John Haynes Holmes. Do you define the universe, in part, that way?

Define what is meant by the unspeakable or the unthinkable.

V

Is an "upset victory" a victory that upsets the victor?

Some films get an "R" or "NC-17" rating because of the

violence that is portrayed. How much violence is too much? When does depiction of violence cross the line from acceptable to too graphic?

Who decides who is and who is not a VIP?

"One man's vulgarity is another man's lyric," a newspaper item said of the right of Nazis to march. Discuss this fact about definition.

W

Sports announcer Jack Whitaker said for a U.S. Open Tennis Championship, "I hope the weather stays well." Is it possible to define the weather as something measured in terms of its health?

Hilaire Belloc said: "Strong Brother in God, and last Companion: Wine." Define or explain his definition of wine.

"We thought that he was everything / To make us wish that we were in his place," said Edwin Arlington Robinson of Richard Cory. How is a wish a definition?

Writing to Santa Claus, Charlie Brown said, "'Tis the season to be wishy-washy." Define *wishy-washy* in this context.

Is a word a thought, or is it merely a reference point for one?

What are some words that can do quadruple duty?

"When I use a word," Humpty Dumpty said in a rather scornful tone, "it means just what I choose it to mean—neither more nor less" (Lewis Carroll). Name some words that you have redefined. Have they worked for you?

A Game of Fictionary

Without looking up the meanings of these words, define them, using your free association and imagination (fiction). Then check them in the dictionary*:

> aperient, babbitt, corm, devi, eelyadah, flageolet, galumph, hendiadys, intaglio, jipijapa, kiddush, loupe, moly, nisus, octroi, perestroika, quagga, rutilant, sampan, toff, ululate, viva voce, wergild, xenopus, yataghan, zenana

*You can play this game in a group, where each person makes up a definition designed to fool the others and writes it down. The definitions are collected and read out loud (they're anonymous, of course), including the correct one. Then you guess which one you think is correct!

10 RESEARCH AND REPORT

What Research-and-Report Writing Is

Research-and-report writing is nearly always formal and scholarly. Sources, both primary and secondary (from research in private papers, personal correspondence, verbal reminiscences, and so forth), are usually cited in footnotes and in a bibliography. In some cases strict formats are required. The mode of expression is basically expository, though other stylistic and rhetorical devices may certainly be used.

How to Write From Research

Effective research-and-report writing is almost impossible without clear and accurate notes. All sources should be investigated scrupulously, reported precisely, and interpreted judiciously. A disciplined effort should be made always to give credit where it is due and to see every idea, circumstance, and argument in the round. That kind of discipline is essential to good scholarship. This does not mean, however, that research-and-report writing has to be pedantic or dry. It can be as vigorous and imaginative and fulfilling as any other kind of writing. A scholarly exploration, for example, into the assassination of Becket might lead the researcher to wonder how the historical Thomas à Becket he or she discovers shapes up against the more literary Becket T. S. Eliot offers us, or Jean Anouilh. Using footnotes or not,

the scholar who is gripped by such a comparison is already breaking some fecund ground.

Locating Subjects for Research-and-Report Writing

As implied above, research-and-report writing may simply be an exposition of the information gathered on a certain subject, or it may seek to interrogate, interpret, or theorize upon that information. The subjects listed here are mostly of the information-gathering variety, but, as one can see from the example of Thomas à Becket, many students will be able to take flight from almost any one of them.

This section is readily informed, too, by ideas from other parts of this book. For example, one has barely to approach a random topic listed here, say, "Langston Hughes and the Harlem Renaissance," before one is into the area of definition. What did Harlem signify? What is a Renaissance? How did the literary movement connect with the music and other arts? What was the impact on the African American community and the wider culture? How did Langston Hughes enter this world? What was his role in shaping the Harlem Renaissance? Suddenly we are into argumentation. Before we know it we are using every stylistic device and discipline we can muster to explore the complexities of an unfolding topic.

Individual Personalities

Abdication of a Famous Royal Figure

Abigail Adams: Second First Lady

Abraham (what he stands for and his role in the scriptures of three major religions)

Chinua Achebe

John Adams and the Boston Massacre Trial

Jane Addams and Hull House

Adenauer's Stand Against Hitler

Adrian I and Charlemagne

Aesop: The Teller of Tales

Agassiz and Glaciation

Akbar the Great, the Enlightened Mogul Emperor

King Albert's Stand against the Germans (World War II)

Prince Albert: Consort of Queen Victoria

John Alden: Beyond the Legend

Alexander's Last Battle

Sherman Alexie

Ethan Allan

Amundsen: A Report of One of His Expeditions

Hans Christian Andersen: The Teller Not the Tales

Marian Anderson and Music

Maya Angelou

Kofi Annan (Secretary-General of the United Nations)

Susan B. Anthony and Suffrage

Gloria Anzaldúa's Experience of the Borderlands

Yasser Arafat

An Arctic or Antarctic Explorer

Neil Armstrong

Chester Alan Arthur: His Quarrel with President Hayes

The Real King Arthur

Ashoka, Emperor of India and Messenger of Peace

The First Astronomer

Attila the Hun

Crispus Attucks

John James Audubon

Aung Sang Suu Kyi, Nobel Peace Laureate

Marcus Aurelius

Jane Austen of the Small Town

Bach: His Occupation Not as a Composer

Francis Bacon's Legal Problems

Joan Baez—Activist and Singer

Balboa as Discoverer

James Baldwin

The Veep: Alben Barkley

P. T. Barnum as a Showman

Clara Barton and the Red Cross

Judge Roy Bean and "The Law West of the Pecos"

Becket's Assassination

Beethoven's Torments

Menachem Begin

Alexander Graham Bell as a Teacher

Bernadette of Lourdes

Bernhardt's First American Tour

Leonard Bernstein

Benazir Bhutto—Woman Leader of an Islamic State

Stephen Biko and the Anti-Apartheid Movement in South Africa

Bismarck's Unification of Germany

Elizabeth Blackwell, First Woman Doctor of the United States

Captain Bligh and the *Bounty*

Queen Anne Boleyn

Bolivar's Unsuccessful Beginnings

Boone and the Cumberland Gap

Lucrezia Borgia: All Evil?

Was There a *Good* Borgia?

Gutzon Borglum

Omar Bradley

Matthew Brady, Civil War Photographer

Willy Brandt: More Than a Mayor

Bertolt Brecht's Many Contributions to Music and Theater

Leonid Brezhnev and the Cold War

The Death of John Brown

Robert Bruce's Persistence

Martin Buber's Contribution to Jewish Philosophy

Gautama Buddha—His Life and His Name Change

Ralph Bunche and the United Nations

Edmund Burke in Support of Revolution

Ken Burns and Documentary Film

Aaron Burr and Alexander Hamilton

Byron's Last Days

Augustus Caesar

How Caligula Became Emperor

Julia Margaret Cameron

Stokely Carmichael and Black Power

Andrew Carnegie and Public Libraries

Jimmy Carter's Post-Presidential Career

George Washington Carver as a Scientist

Casement's Death, Burial, and Reburial

Johnny Cash

Castro as Revolutionary

Catherine the Great

William Caxton

The Fall of Neville Chamberlain

Neville Chamberlain's Treaty with Hitler

Charlie Chaplin

Cesar Chavez

Chiang Kai-shek and Formosa
Madame Chiang Kai-shek
How did Chiang Kai-shek Rise to Power?
Julia Child
Churchill's Loss of the Prime Ministership
Cicero as Orator
El Cid
Clemenceau as Peace Negotiator
Hillary Clinton
Bill Clinton's Failures as President
Bill Clinton's Successes as President
George M. Cohan, Showman
Christopher Columbus: Hero or Villain?
Sean "Puff Daddy/P. Diddy" Combs
Confucius's Real Message versus Commercial Distortions of His Teachings
Joseph Conrad's Self-Teaching
Coolidge and the Boston Police Strike
Copernicus and His Theory
Charlotte Corday
Cortez and Montezuma
Stephen Crane's Sea Rescue
A Great Criminal Reformer
The Fall of Richard Cromwell, Oliver's Son
Tom Cruise
Madame Curie before She Was Madame Curie
Currier and Ives
Dalai Lama
Salvador Dali's Art
The Public Personality of Salvador Dali
Richard Henry Dana and the Change of Naval Laws
David, King of the Israelites (before and after he became king)
Darwin and *The Beagle*
The Dauphin
Angela Davis
The Trial of Jefferson Davis
Charles Dickens and Prison
Diderot and the Encyclopedia
Babe Didrikson
Frederick Douglass
The Pardon of Dreyfus
Isadora Duncan
Amelia Earhart
Edward the Confessor in 1066
Will Eisner
Mary Ann Evans *alias* George Eliot
The First Queen Elizabeth
The Second Queen Elizabeth
Erasmus and Thomas More

The Empress Eugénie
Walker Evans and the Documentary Tradition in Photography
Guy Fawkes and the Gunpowder Plot
Dianne Feinstein
Edward Fitzgerald as Translator
Henry Ford and the Assembly Line
Bob Fosse's Dance Innovations
George Fox and the Quakers
Franco as a Soldier
Anne Frank and Her Diary
"Fulton's Folly"
Galen and Astronomy
Galileo's Troubles
Indira Gandhi and India's Rule of Emergency
Mahatma Gandhi and Pacifism
William Lloyd Garrison
Bill Gates and Microsoft
Artemisia Gentileschi
Geronimo in Old Age
Lillian and Dorothy Gish
Harold Godwin, 1066
Théo van Gogh and His Relationship with His Brother Vincent
Jane Goodall
Mikhail Gorbachev and Glasnost
Gordon at Khartoum
Katherine Graham
Grant and Lee at Appomattox
Grant's Troubles as President
The Nine-Day Reign of Lady Jane Grey
Zane Grey's Writing Success
D. W. Griffith and the Making of *The Birth of a Nation*
Günter Grass
Che Guevara
Alec Guinness
Haakon VII, King of Norway
Hadrian the Builder
Dag Hammarskjold
Hannibal and the Alps
Hawkins and the *Armada*
Hawthorne's Ancestor at Salem
Hemingway as a Young Journalist
Henry VIII's First Wife, Catherine of Aragon
O. Henry's Latin American Experience
A Medieval Heretic
Thor Heyerdahl and Kon-Tiki
Hindenburg and Hitler
Hippocrates
Hirohito: Merely a Figurehead?

Hiss and Whittaker Chambers
A Historian from Modern Times
Adolf Hitler as an All Too Human Being
The Hohenzollern Family
Hans Holbein
Oliver Wendell Holmes, Jr.
Who Was Homer?
Why Hoover Lost the Presidency
J. Edgar Hoover's Popularity Decline
Sam Houston as Governor
Howe's Patent Difficulties
Julia Ward Howe
W. D. Howells, "Father" of American Literary Realism
Charles Evans Hughes as a Presidential Candidate
Langston Hughes and the Harlem Renaissance
The Rediscovery of Zora Neale Hurston
Anne Hutchinson as a Religious Leader
The Huxleys
Ibsen and Censorship
Ivan the Terrible
Jesse Jackson
Stonewall Jackson before the American Civil War
Harriet Jacobs
King James I: Coming into Power
Thomas Jefferson as Inventor
Thomas Jefferson as Naturalist
Thomas Jefferson as Translator
Thomas Jefferson as Writer
Edward Jenner
Mohammad Ali Jinnah and the Creation of Pakistan
Joan of Arc in Battle
King John and the *Magna Carta*
Andrew Johnson's Stormy Presidency
Samuel Johnson's Dictionary
Joshua and the Battle of Jericho
Juarez, the Lincoln of Mexico
Judith and Holofernes
Keats in Italy
Helen Keller as a World Figure
John F. Kennedy
Robert Kennedy
Ted Kennedy
Jerome Kern
Khrushchev in America
Captain Kidd
Martin Luther King Jr.
Stephen King
Maxine Hong Kingston and Women Warriors
Jack Kirby and Marvel Comics
The Krupp Family

Winona LaDuke
"Fighting" Bob LaFollette
Mayor LaGuardia
Lao-Tse
Lenin's Tomb
Leonardo da Vinci
Lewis and Clark Expedition
Ben Lilly and Theodore Roosevelt
Charles Lindbergh
Lincoln as a Congressman
Livingstone's Contributions to Africa
Livingstone Viewed through Postcolonial Eyes
Louis XIV
Toussaint L'Ouverture
Clare Boothe Luce
Martin Luther
Madonna's Changing Public Image
Magellan's Circumnavigation
Maharishi Mahesh Yogi and Transcendental Meditation
Mahashweta Devi, Bengali Writer and Activist
Malcolm X
Mallarmé and the Symbolists
Sir Thomas Malory
Nelson Mandela from Political Prisoner to Politician
Horace Mann
How Did Mao Rise to Power?
Imelda Marcos
Queen Maria Theresa
Thurgood Marshall
The Marx Brothers
Margaret Mead
Golda Meir
Melville in Typee
Mesmer and Hypnotism
Mirabeau—A Nobleman for the People
An Authority on Molluska
Monet
James Monroe and the Era of Good Feeling
Toni Morrison
Zero Mostel
Mother Jones
Mother Teresa
A Movie "Dynasty" (e.g., the Fondas, the Redgraves)
A Figure behind the Scenes in the Movie World
The Childhood Genius of Mozart
James Murray and the Oxford English Dictionary
Ralph Nader
V. S. Naipaul—Literary Great or Colonial Messenger?
Napoleon as General
John Nash's Beautiful Mind—Fact and Fiction

Carry Nation's War Against Drink
Nefertiti, Egyptian Queen
Nero and the Burning of Rome
Ngugi Wa Thiong'o
Thich Nhat Hanh, Peace Activist
The Last Czar Nicholas
Florence Nightingale
Richard Nixon
Alfred Nobel and the Nobel Prizes
The O'Higgins Family of Chile
Jacqueline Kennedy Onassis
Paracelsus
Mungo Park, Explorer of the Niger
The Fall of Parnell
Pasteur before His Discoveries
Robert Peel and the Bobbies
Samuel Pepys and His Diary
Frances Perkins, First Woman Cabinet Member
Eva Peron as icon
Pershing and Pancho Villa
Petain in the Second World War
Peter the Great
Philip II of Macedon
King Philip of Spain
The Piccard Brothers and Underwater Exploration
Pickett's Charge
The Plantagenets
Poe at West Point
Polk: Why Is He Considered One of Our Great Presidents?
Polk's Acquisition of California
Marco Polo in China
Katherine Anne Porter in Mexico
Wiley Post
Chaim Potok, Rabbi and Writer
Colin Powell
Michael Powell and Emeric Pressburger
An Obscure President
_____ before the Presidency
_____ after the Presidency
Elvis Presley—Legend of the King
Sergei Prokofiev
Pythagoras
Ayn Rand
Rapp the Harmonist
Ronald Reagan as the Teflon President
Connie Douglas Reeves and the National Cowgirl Museum
Paul Robeson
Robespierre and the Reign of Terror
Will Rogers and Congress

Will Rogers and the Presidency
Eleanor Roosevelt as a Public Figure
Franklin Roosevelt's First Term
Teddy Roosevelt's Failed Campaign for the Presidency
Anwar Sadat
J. D. Salinger and Privacy
José San Martin's Last Revolution
Charles M. Schulz and the Popularity of *Peanuts*
Albert Schweitzer
Georges Seurat
Shackleton and the *Endurance*
Tupac Shakur
George Bernard Shaw's Alphabet
M. Night Shyamalan's Film Treatment of the Occult
Leslie Marmon Silko—Native American and Feminist
Sitting Bull
Death of Socrates
Stephen Sondheim and American Musical Theater
Art Spiegelman's *MAUS* (graphic novels about the Holocaust)
De-Stalinization of Russian History
Robert Louis Stevenson on Samoa
Martha Stewart as both Id and Superego of American Housekeeping Concerns
Harriet Beecher Stowe and the American Civil War
August Strindberg and Modern Drama
Amy Tan's Sense of Chinese American Identity
The Phenomenon of Shirley Temple
Margaret Thatcher's Political Career
Marshal Tito, President of the Former Yugoslavia
Arnold Toynbee
The Mystery of B. Traven, Author
Truman's First Weeks as President
Nat Turner
Queen Victoria's Diamond Jubilee
Booker T. Washington
Young George Washington's Military Defeats
Cornel West and *Race Matters*
George Westinghouse and Transportation
Elie Wiesel
Simon Wiesenthal: Hunter of Men
Oscar Wilde in America
The First King William of England
Wilson's Wife as Acting President
Oprah Winfrey
Women Nobel Peace Prize Winners (Aung Sang Suu Kyi, Rigoberta Menchu)
Frank Lloyd Wright
Zapata as a Revolutionary
Zola in Support of Dreyfus

Places, Events, Conditions

Aberdeen Shipping
Acapulco Tourism
Addis Ababa
Aegean Islands and Early Civilization
The Aegean Sea and Early Commerce
The History of Conflict in Afghanistan
The Purchase of Alaska
Alexandria, Egypt
Alsace-Lorraine and World War I
Recent Amazon Exploration
Travel on the Amazon
Andersonville Prison
The Central Andes
Peruvian Andes
The Temples of Ankor Vat
Human Life in Antarctica
Arden Forest
Atlantic City and Gambling
Atlantis: What Do We Know of It?
The Australian Outback
From Austria-Hungary to Austria and Hungary
The Government of Barbados
Basel as a 15th-Century Religious Center
Bath, England, during the 14th Century
The Belgian Congo
The Government of Belize
Bergen, Norway
Bhopal, India, and the Union Carbide Catastrophe
The "Black Hole" of Calcutta
Branson, Missouri
Brasilia: The Foundation
Britain as It Appeared to the Roman Conquerors
Buckingham Palace
The Island of Capri
Chesapeake Bay
Chinatown in a Major U.S. City
The Congo and Colonialism
Constantinople to Istanbul
Political History of Costa Rica
Cypress
From Czechoslovakia to Czech Republic and Slovakia
Darjeeling—Land of Mists and Tea Plantations
Devil's Island
The Kingdom of East Anglia
Easter Island: Its Care and Operation
El Salvador Population Problem
The Equator of Ecuador
The Faeroe Islands

The Falkland Islands: The Quarrel Over Their Ownership
Fiji Islands and Progress
The Government of Finland
Flanders and the Flemish Language
Florida Keys
The Government of French Guiana
The French Quarter in New Orleans
Mt. Fujiyama and Religion
The Gadsden Purchase
Administering the Galápagos Islands
Giant's Causeway
Granada as a Separate Country in Spain
The Grand Canyon
The Great Divide
Great Lakes Shipping
Great Salt Lake
The History behind the Great Wall of China
Guadalajara Architecture
Guam and the Military
Gulf War
The Government of the Hague
The Unity of Hawaii
Hawaii and the Pineapple Industry
The Hebrides
Helsinki
The Heptarchy of England
The Himalayas
Hollywood
Indigenous Honduras
Hong Kong
Volcanoes of Iceland
The Intracoastal Waterway of the Atlantic Coast
Volcán Irazú
Isle of Man
Tourism and the Local Economy in Jamaica
Japanese Economy
Japanese Government during American Occupation
Game parks in Kenya
Klondike
Krakatoa
The Political Status of Labrador
Lhasa—City on "the Roof of the World"
Liechtenstein
Lithuania and Relations with Russia
Battle of Little Big Horn
London and Taxation
Londonderry
Machu Picchu
Mammoth Cave of Kentucky
The Mississippi River during the Civil War

Montreal and Its Two Major Languages

Exploration of the Moon

Mount Rainier as a Training Center

Mount St. Helens National Volcanic Monument

Mumbai and Commerce

Nepal as Tourist Attraction

Makeup of the Netherlands

Nevada: Not Just Divorce and Gambling

New York City's "Ground Zero"

New Zealand Government

Indigenous Peoples of New Zealand

New Zealand's Topography

Niagara Falls

Nicaragua and Earthquake Recovery

Nicaragua's Politics

Northwest Territories and the Royal Canadian Mounted Police

Norway and Neutrality

Inhabitants of Nova Scotia

Habitat of Okefenokee Swamp

The Founding of "Old Town" in _____

U.S. Invasion of Panama

Panama Canal

The Papal States

The (Disappearing) Petrified Forest of Arizona

Philippine Government Since World War II

Poland as a Satellite

Prince William Sound, before and after the Exxon Valdez Spill

Puerto Rico: What Is Its Political Status?

Puget Sound: Steps toward Ecological Control

Quito, Ecuador: Two Cities in One

The Mystery of Roanoke Island

South Africa before and after Apartheid

Sumatra

Switzerland and the European Union

The Republic of Texas

U.S. Involvement in the Vietnam War

Wales: Its Origins

The West Bank

Yellowstone National Park—Threatened by Development?

Yosemite National Park

The Former Yugoslavia

The Yukon and Adventure

Government of Zaire

Zululand's Birding Routes

Zurich as Center of the Reformation

World Peoples, Ancient and Modern

The Acadian People

The Aleuts

The Amish and Their Way of Life

Apaches in the Nineteenth Century

The Arabian Nomads

The Armenian Genocide

The Basques: A People Apart

The Bedouin

The Celts

Central American Indians

The Civilization at Chichen-itzá

The Druids and Sun Worship

Early Humans in the Bering Strait

Ebla People, 2400–2250 BC

The Last of the Etruscans

A European People in Argentina

The Hittites

The Hopi Indians

Huns

Hutus vs. Tutsis

The Iberi People

The Incas

Who Were the Indo-Europeans?

The Israeli-Palestinian Conflict

Mayan Civilization

Mediterranean Cultures and What They Share

The Pennsylvania Dutch

Pueblo Indians

The Roma People—Their Origins and Migrations

The Serbs

Stonehenge

The Tarahumaras

The Tasaday Indians: Then as Now

What Civilization Was at Tikal?

The Visigoths

The Walloons

War, Political Strife, Wartime Conditions and Operations

The Admiralty of Great Britain during World War II

The Battle of Agincourt

The "Alabama Claims"

After the Famous Battle of the Alamo

American Expeditionary Force

American Neutrality in World War II

Angola's Civil War
The Battle of Antietam
Bacon's Rebellion
Barcelona and the Spanish Civil War
Anti-Aircraft Defense during the Battle of Britain
Bikini Atoll
Blackouts during World War II
A Famous Blockade
The Boer War
War in Bosnia
The Boxer Rebellion
Burma Death March
Cambodian Blood Purges, 1970s
Cavalry of the Middle Ages
The Cheyenne Wars
The CIA: Its Early Operation
Conflicts in Chile
Civil War in _____
Coxey's Army
Dachau during World War II
Delaware during the Civil War
The First Democratic Struggle
Desertion during Wartime
Dunkirk (Dunquerque) during World War II
Espionage
Occupation of Ethiopia by Italy
"Fifty-Four Forty or Fight"
The French and Indian War
French Revolution: The Bastille
Galveston in War Defense
What Happened at Guernica?
Gulf War Syndrome
Battle of Hastings
Hiroshima
Holy Alliance
The Hundred Years' War
Hungarian Revolution, 1956
British Intelligence Operations during World War I
Ireland: The Easter Uprising
War of Jenkins's Ear
Battle of Jutland
Kashmir—Paradise Torn by War
A Famous Liberation Struggle
The *Lusitania*
The Mercenary Soldier of Early Times
The Mexican War
Neo-Nazi Movements

The October Revolution
The Office of Price Administration
Paraguay and the Gran Chaco
The United States Patriot Act
Pearl Harbor: What Did the Americans Know Before?
Potsdam Agreement
Prisoner-of-War Agreements
Sarajevo
September 11, 2001, and the War on Terrorism
The Six-Day War
The Soccer War
Soldiers as Viewed by Walter Bagehot
Taiwan and Mainland China
Andrew Jackson and the Trail of Tears
Post-Vietnam Stress Syndrome
Radio and World War II
Yalta: What Happened There?
Yokohama

Philosophical, Political, and Religious Groups or Movements

AIM (American Indian Movement)
The Anabaptists
Anthroposophy and Its Connection to Fascism
The Baptists
The John Birch Society: Where and How Is It Now?
What Was Bolshevism?
The Brook Farm Experiment
Christianity Comes to (Ireland, England, or the United States)
Christianity 100 AD
Civil Rights Movement
Where Does the Idea of a Constitution Originate?
The Counter Reformation
The Greek Origin of Democracy
Ecumenical Government
An Evangelical Movement
Early Feminism
The Decline of Feudalism
The Geneva Convention
The Greenback Party
Islamic Fundamentalism
Early References to Jesus, Mohammad, and Buddha Not in Religious Books
Is the Concept of Liberty New?
The MacDowell Colony
Mahayana Buddhism

Marriage and Courtship in _____
Mayan beliefs
Monogamy and Polygamy in Religious Groups
The Mormons
The NAACP
Old-Time Religion, BC
Polygamy
The Protestant Reformation
Quakers
The Shia Sect of Islam
Early Sikh Settlements in the Pacific Northwest
The Sunni Sect of Islam
The Supreme Court and FDR
Theosophy and Its Connections to Eastern Religions
The Underground Railroad
UNESCO
Wicca

Nonhuman Creature Life

Aardvark/Aardwolf
Albatross
An Amphibious Creature
Anaconda
Ant Colony
Appaloosa
Baboon
The Badger in Defense
Barracuda
The Bear in Hibernation
The Beaver's Engineering Skills
Killer Bees
Beetle Invasions
Bird Migration
A Bird Type
Boar
The Boll Weevil and Cotton
The Bumblebee—How Does It Fly?
Canadian Wild Goose
Chachalaca Bird
Cobra—"King" of Snakes
Creatures of the Deep
The Dingo of Australia
Dinosaurs
Dogs with Herding Instincts
Dolphins and Intelligence
Dung Beetle
The Exciting Life of the Earthworm
Everglades Bird Life
Firefly

Flamingo
The Frog—Prince/Princess of Amphibians
The Guidance System of _____ (a certain insect, bird, or reptile)
Hornbill
Hummingbird
Insect Colonies
Kangaroo
King Snake
Locusts
Magpies
Meerkat
Minnows as Mosquito Controls
The Migration and Survival of the Mysterious Monarch Butterfly
Mongoose
Monkeys—Almost Human
Mosquitoes and the Spread of Diseases
The Nest of the _____
The Behavior of Opossums
Oyster Beds
Parrots
Pigs—Brainiacs of the Barnyard
Piranha
Praying Mantis
Pterodactyl
Raven—Genius among Birds
"Roadkill"
Salamander
Scorpion
The Truth about Sharks
The Shrike
Spring Peeper
Squids
Stick Insects
The Virginia White-Tailed Deer
Eating Habits of the Whale
The Wolverine—Does It Kill for "Fun"?

Language-Related Subjects

African American Vernacular English
Origin of Anglo-Saxon
Borrowings in English from Other Languages
"Code Switching"
How the Computer Has Changed Our Vocabulary
How the Connotation and Value of Certain Words Has Expanded or Narrowed (e.g., _rainbow, gay, cool_)
Creole
Origin of the English Alphabet

A Study of a Single Letter in the English Alphabet

The Major Periods of English Language Change

Esperanto, World Language

On "Passing Away," "Expectorating," and "Issuing Forth"—A Study of Victorian Euphemisms

The Gullah Language

The Language of Hawaii

Icelandic Language

Indo-European Language

The Internet and Its Effect on Language

Jargon: Its Uses and Abuses

The Language of Wider Communication (aka Standard English)

Code Languages

Computer Language

Constructed Languages

Dead Languages

Endangered Languages

Language on the Isle of Skye

A New Language in the Old

Any Language Family and Its Offspring, e.g., Afro-Asiatic, Indo-European, Iroquoian, Niger-Congo, Sino-Tibetan, Uto-Aztec

The State of the Language at the Time of the American Revolution

Programming Computers to Understand Human Language

Current Slang

Slang of Past Generations

Varieties (or Dialects) of a Particular Language

Medical Subjects

Acupuncture

Addiction and Recovery

AIDS

Alchemy

Allergies

Alzheimer's

The First Anesthetic

Angioplasty

Anthrax Contamination

Arthroscopic Surgery

The Artificial Heart

Aspirin

Attention Deficit Hyperactivity Disorder (ADHD)

Autism

Cause of the Black Death

Botox Treatments

Cancer Treatments

Carpel Tunnel Syndrome

Cloning Technology

The Common Cold—Comforts and Cures

Computer Technology to Assist People with Disabilities

Contamination

Crohn's Disease

Danger Symptoms of _____

Depression and Its Treatment

Dermatology

Down Syndrome

Eating Disorders

E. Coli Infections

Epstein-Barr Virus

Euthanasia

Extraterrestrial Biology

Fertility Drugs and Multiple Births

General Health

Genetic Research

Grafting as a Medical Technique

Heart Disease(s)

Successful Heart Transplanting

Hemophilia

The Unknown in Human Behavior

Hypnotism

Hypochondria

Inoculation

Legionnaire's Disease

Liposuction

Mad Cow Disease

Magnetic Resonance Imaging

Mental Illness

Obesity in Americans

Obsessive-Compulsive Disorder

Osteoporosis

Out-of-Body Experiences

Prosthetics

Pulsed Electro-Magnetic Technology

Quack Medicine

Revascularization

Rcynaud's Condition

Schizophrenia

Self-Injury (Cutting)

Sickle Cell Anemia

Sleep Disorders

Sleepwalking

Sports Injuries

Trepanning

Ultrasound Imaging

Water Therapy

West Nile Virus

X-Ray Dangers

Inventions, Devices, Operations

Abacus
Agricultural Machinery
Air Bags
Air Conditioning
Air Vessels Before the Plane
The First Automobile
The First Bathysphere
Automobile Brakes
Computer Technology
The Cosmotron
Electric Car
The Elevator
Flat-Screen Technology
The Flywheel
The Gutenberg Press
Sikorsky's Helicopter
The *Hindenburg* Airship
Laser Technology
Motion Detectors
Paper Shredders
The Pinhole Camera
Pneumatic Tools
Refrigerators
Rocket Launching
Seat Belts
Self-Stick Notes
Solar Power
Sound Systems
Submarines
Synthesizers
Synthetic Dyes
The Toilet
The Ultimate Weapon
Wind Power
Use of X-Rays in the Oil Industry

Natural Phenomena

Canyons
The Dead Sea
Earthquakes
Eclipses
The Results of Glaciation
Global Warming (Natural or Unnatural)
Gravity: What It Is, How It Works
The Gulf Stream
Holes in Space
Eye of the Hurricane
Icebergs

Magnetism
Migration
Moon Mysteries
El Niño
Outerspace Life
Plate Tectonics
Sand Dunes
Saturn
Seasons
The Truth about Snowflakes
Sunspots
Waterfalls
Winds
Zephyr

Written Media, Special Books

Early Egyptian Almanacs
Astrology Books
Audiobooks
Publishing: The Creation of Bestsellers
Book Design
Electronic Books
The First Book
The Change of the Calendar to Its Present Form
The Egyptian Calendar
The Roman Calendar
Consumer Complaints through Newspaper Columns
The Dead Sea Scrolls
A particular epic
Hornbook
Illuminated Manuscripts
Library of Congress
Poor Richard's Almanack
Pulitzer Prizes: Origin and Definition
Sacred Texts of (a particular culture)
Translation(s) of the New Testament

Education

Adjunct Faculty and Gender
Teaching in the Alaskan Wilderness
Bilingual Education Programs
Boarding Schools
Chautauqua and Early Education
Cherokee Education
Culinary Institutes
Curriculum Content Decisions
John Dewey's Theories of Education
Distance Learning

The Entertainer as Educator: Medieval Minstrels, Scops, and Troubadours

Paolo Freire and the Cultures of Silence

The GED (General Educational Development) Diploma as an Option

Home Schooling

Educational Institutions in Ancient Cultures

Correctional Systems for Juvenile Offenders

Knighthood Training

Learning as Critical Thinking

Learning as Transmitted Wisdom in Traditional Cultures

Literacy and Its Many Interpretations

Medieval Monks and Education

The Montessori Method

Multicultural Education

John Henry Cardinal Newman's Opinion about the Purpose of the University

The One-Room Schoolhouse

Education through the Oral Tradition in a Particular Culture

Oxford or Cambridge—The College System

Plato's School

Public School Funding

Theories on the Purpose of Education

Segregation: Reappearing in U.S. Schools?

High-Stakes Standardized Testing

Substitute Teachers—Expectations and Performance

Teacher Certification Requirements

Teaching for the Twenty-First Century

Textbook Selection Processes

The Founding of the First American University

Recruiting of University Athletes

Urban Education—a New Emphasis

The Founding of West Point

Professions, Occupations, Employment

Air Traffic Control

"Big Blue"—the IBM Image

The Boat People of Asia

Book Editor

Canadian Fishers

The Canadian Mounted Police

Carpet Weavers in India

Chinese Workers as Producers of U.S. Consumer Goods

Chiropractic Care

Civilian Conservation Corps

Corporate Espionage

Equal Opportunity Employment

Firefighting

The Glass Ceiling

Hiring Practices and the Americans with Disabilities Act

Hmong Settlement in the Upper Midwest

The Industrial and Professional Role of Women during World War II

Internet-Related Jobs

Labor Unions

"The Man in the Gray Flannel Suit"—a Changing Image

Market Week in _____

Midwives

Mining in Chile

The Operation of an Ocean Liner

Peonage

Pirates

Quacks

Right-to-Work Laws

School Board Member

School Counselor

School Social Worker

Seafolk of the Sub-Arctic

American Seaman/Seawoman Occupations

Siberian Occupations

Silk Industry in China

Snake-Oil Salespeople

The State with the Best Unemployment Benefits

The U.S. Mint System

Unemployment in History

The WPA

Human-Made Constructions and Designs

Any abandoned city (e.g., Bagan, Fatehpur Sikri, Machu Picchu, Mesa Verde, Pompeii, Tiahuanaco, Vijayanagar)—reasons for the abandonment

The Ajanta Cave Temples

The Alcan Highway

The Building of the Alhambra

Teatro Amazonas

The First American East-West Trains

Angkor Vat

Pressed-Metal Ornamentation in Architecture

The Atlantic Cable

The Great Aztec Temple

The Tower of Babel

The Battle Helmet in _____

The Bayeaux Tapestry

Bell Founding

The Borobudur Temple

Bridge Building

Testing Bridge Strengths

Canal Building
Notre Dame Cathedral
Cathedrals of Sir Christopher Wren
Covered Wagon
The Crystal Palace of Queen Victoria
Deep Sea Submersible Vehicles
Construction of the Eiffel Tower
Brunelleschi and Florence's Duomo
Egyptian Obelisks (e.g., Cleopatra's Needle)
Elgin Marbles
The Empire State Building
Erie Canal
Buckminster Fuller's Geodesic Dome
The Gold Museum of Bogotá
The Golden Gate
The Great Hedge of India
The Great Wall of China
The Guggenheim Museum in Bilbao
The Hanging Gardens of Babylon
Hollywood Bowl
Making of Hoover Dam
Houston Ship Channel
The International Space Station
The Interstate Highway System
The Leaning Tower of Pisa
Mount Rushmore
New Mexico Fort of the 19th Century
The Orient Express
The Panama Canal Locks
The Parthenon
The Pentagon
The Petronas Towers
Philae
The Original Puppets
Pyramid Construction
Early Railroad Building
Jungle Railroads: Costa Rica or Panama
The Richest Street in the World
Robots and the History of Robotics
Showboats
The Sphinx
The Statue of Liberty
Stonehenge
Stradivarius Violins
The Taj Mahal
Tikal Pyramids: How They Are Uncovered
Trails at the Grand Canyon
The Trans-Canada Railroad
The London Underground

A Viking Boat
The Washington Monument
The Construction (or Reconstruction) of Westminster Abbey
The World Trade Center Towers
World's Fair in Chicago, 1893
The Dam of the Zuider Zee

Sports, Entertainments, Recognitions

The First Automobile Race
Women's Baseball
Boogie Woogie
Break Dancing
The Circus
Classical Dance from a Particular Culture
English Channel Swims
ESPN
Figure Skating
The Baseball Hall of Fame: Its Operation
Hockey
Ice Skating—Venue for Grace and Fury
The Kentucky Derby
Kung Fu
The Olympic Games
Rap Music
Taekwando
Tai Chi
Teenage Dancing
The Triple Crown
Women Breaking the Barriers into the Sports World
The X Games
Yacht Racing

Sciences, Studies, Skills, Inquiries, Observations of the Universe

Acoustics
Aerial Photography
Determining the Age of the Earth
Anthropology: One Way of Studying the History of Humanity
Timing the Ages of Humanity by Archaeology
Archimedes' Principle
Artificial Intelligence
The Use of Astronomy to Measure Time
Black Holes and Beyond
Carbon Dating
Chaos Theory
Research in Egyptology
Extrasensory Perception

Fingerprinting
Futuristics
Tracing Genealogy
Stephen Hawking's History of Time
Hieroglyphics
Hymnology
Number Theory and Ramanujan
Oceanography
Theories of the Origin of the Universe
Paleontology
Psychology
Einstein's Relativity Theory
Telepathy
Heisenberg's Uncertainty Principle
Worship of the Heavens
Yoga

Flora and Derivatives

Banyan Tree
The Big Thicket of Texas
The Black Forest
Cocoa
Cotton History
Cranberries
Dandelions
Deforestation
Ethanol
Giant Ragweed
Gingko
Ginseng
Kudzu
Marijuana
Poppies
Preserving the Rain Forests
Protection of Crops without Insecticides
Reforestation
Soybean Oil as a Processed Food Ingredient

Media and Media Events

The Abbey Theatre of Dublin
The Academy Awards
Early Advertising Slogans That Have Survived
The First Advertising
The Alternative Press
Amateur Filmmaking
The Appeal of Radio Shows, Past and Present
Beauty Pageants
Cannes Film Festival
Confessional TV Shows

CNN
How the Comics Began
Dramatic Film Critiques of War
Game Shows
The Evolution of Headlines in Newspapers
Famous Hoaxes
Life Magazine and Photography
Media Conglomerates: Deciding What the News Is
Napster
Newscasters and Anchorpersons—Their Personalities
   and Persona
The Persian Gulf War and CNN
The First Photography
Political Conventions as Media Events
The History of Public Television
Quiz Show Scandals
The Origin of Radio Broadcasting in the United States
Early Radio Technique
Reality TV
The O. J. Simpson Trial
Subliminal Advertising
The Sundance Film Festival
Tabloids—Their Content and Their Appeal
Great Television Debates
The Origin of Television News in the United States
How War Can Become a Media Event
The Watergate Hearings
Orson Welles's Report of an "Invasion," October 30,
   1938
The Woodstock Festival, 1969
Yellow Journalism

Miscellaneous

The Aa River
Absorption and Osmosis
Adenoids
The Complexity of Adoption Procedures
The Albany Congress
The Alien and Sedition Laws
Chronological History of Integration in America
How to Become an American Citizen
Theories about the Anasazi
Annexation of Territory
April Fools' Day
"Arctic Hysteria"
Arlington Cemetery
Auctions of Famous Peoples' Belongings
Aztec Priests
The Case That Ended "Blacklisting" on Television
Carpetbaggers

Cave Paintings of Vallon Pont d'Arc

Caviar

Chaco Canyon—Record of Lost History?

A Cheese Type

Chic Europe: Mainly American?

Collectibles—Fads and Obsessions and What People Do to Acquire Their Collectibles

Is There Consciousness before Birth?

Ancient Cosmetics

Criminal Reform

The Deirdre Legend

Can You Spare a Dime?—The Conditions of the Average Citizen during the Depression

Divorce among Royal Members

The Welsh *Eisteddfod*

Emancipation Proclamation

The Last Emperor of China

The "Eternal" City

The Belief in the "Evil Eye"

Expeditions

The Fair Deal

Farm Aid

History of Fasting

Fata Morgana

Ancient Financial Credit

The First Labor Union

Get-Rich Quick Schemes

Great Lakes

Hairstyles Past and Present—Different Aesthetics

Hairstyles Past and Present—Different Cultural Interpretations

Hairstyles Past and Present—What Kinds of Statements They Make

The Origin of Halloween

Heraldry

The Holy City of Banaras

The Holy City of Mecca

The Holy City of _____

Holy Roman Empire

House of Commons, House of Lords

The Huguenots

The Ice Age

The Industrial Revolution

Inheritance Taxes

The Iron Age

The Italian Renaissance

Juvenile Court

The Real King of Siam (as opposed to the one in *Anna and the King of Siam*)

Law Enforcement

A Legal System in Elizabethan Times for Protecting the Writer

Marriage-Ceremony Traditions

May Day

The "Miss Saigon" Controversy

The New Copyright Laws

The New Deal

Nuremberg Trials

The Historical Limits of America's Open Door Policy

Care of Orphaned Children

What We Know about Ourselves

What We Don't See in Ourselves until Others Tell Us

Paintings as History

The Canadian Parliament

The Parliament of India

Popular Songs during the Civil War

Culture during the Restoration Period

Riverboat Journeys

How Do/Did Members of the Royalty View Commoners?

Runaways

Salem Witchcraft Trials

Seven: The Magic Number of the Ancients

Small States—Israel, Athens, Florence, Elizabethan England—as Great Influences

Snake Worship

The Spanish Inquisition

The State Lottery

The Stonewall Riots

U.S. Aid to Other Countries

Voodoo in Haiti

Voting Rights of Blacks in the Post–Civil War South

Women's Suffrage Fights in Great Britain

World Trade

Yugoslavia during and after the Reign of Slobodan Milosevic

The Ancient Yule

The Zambezi River

Zanzibar—Best-Kept Tourist Secret

An Aspect of Zuni Culture

11 CREATIVE WRITING

What Creative Writing Is

Creative writing is essentially imaginative. It most often takes the form of drama, fiction, or poetry (including songs). But given that imaginative reach, along with the language tools and techniques needed to realize it, keep in mind that any form of writing discussed in this book can become creative. In fact, a piece of simple exposition or an essay on cause and effect may be greatly enriched by creative examples, analogies, or brief accounts of personal experience that bring the topic to life.

For example, in *My Family and Other Animals* (Viking Press, 1956), Gerald Durrell, the British naturalist and zoologist, writes about his childhood years on the Greek island of Corfu, recreating not only the vibrant natural life of the island, but also the eccentricities of his family, including his famous novelist brother Lawrence Durrell. Appealing to readers of all ages, this memoir captures the world as seen through a young boy's eyes—his wide-eyed delight in nature, his hilarious observations of his eccentric family, and his instinctive love of the local culture. Although not a work of fiction, drama, or poetry, the book lays claim to all these modes, serving as a felicitous example of creative writing.

In this chapter, however, the focus is on the imaginative. One might call this type of writing *full-blooded*—nourished, as it must be, with an abundance of heart.

How to Write Creatively

In creative writing, following a format can cramp a writer's style. At bottom, there is no way one can tell another person *how* to write creatively. Probably no teacher can do much more than inspire students with high-quality rhetorical tools, an open atmosphere, a love of language, and a sense of possibility, then let the newborn beast have its head and hope for the best.

The natural element of creative writing is freedom. This is the place to let go, to let the student *be.* Of course that does not mean that the teacher abandons any new writer to a miasma of self-indulgence. Rather, the student should be guided and encouraged through the certain failures, through try after try and endless errors and those very few quiet triumphs, until he or she begins to realize that dreams can indeed come alive, take shape and grow, stand full and real as any creature of bone, flesh, blood.

Here again is where we call up every writing mode and device we can think of—not only the modes touched upon in this book, but other more literary devices as well. We bring to bear the full force of metaphor, alliteration, repetition, rhyme, rhythm, meter, and so on—with the understanding that nothing is sacred if it holds the student back from creative expression. It can be instructive and fun simply to experiment with such devices. But in the end they will probably be used less for their own sake than because they are evoked, called up out of the material itself, whatever it may be.

So it is indeed clear that this is not the time to worry too much about sentence fragments, erratic punctuation, or many of the other grammatical elements that must necessarily concern us in more formal types of composition. There is at least one handy rule-of-thumb for creative writing: If it works, use it.

Locating Subjects for Creative Writing

The subjects listed in this section do not pretend to be anything more than suggestions, ideas for approaching various forms of creative writing. They could inspire almost anything—a play, a story, a poem or song, a character sketch, a writing experiment. It hardly matters. More important than the image or idea is the imagination it fires.

It is in many ways apparent from the above that any section in this book may be used to fire that creative imagination. Special attention might well be paid, though, to the chapters on narrative and description. Some narrative element is often important, even essential, in creative writing. Crafting more or less footloose material to the demands of a narrative line, making it fit, making it belong, can lift a common piece of descriptive or expository writing towards something larger, give it form, harmony—turn it, that is to say, towards art.

Brainstorming Fictional Themes

saved by the bell
the computer and me
memories in smoke
one more, too many
due unto others
eating around a campfire
homeless people eating around a barrel fire
smashing taboos
barbarians at the gates
deprivation of the mind
knowing how to keep company away from the door
living on borrowed time
moving in reverse into the future
vowing a new fight
toughest break
expectations fulfilled/unfulfilled
a decent interval
mislaid values
tar-and-feathering
losing battle(s)
still not enough
daring/not daring to do
second chance
on solid ground
duplication(s)
at the corner store
something due
expecting the unexpected
almost famous
unexpected celebrity
a short, sharp shock
marking the spot
a tinkling cymbal
the forgotten year/hour/day
the day everything changed
prisoner at home
any reasonable offer
suspension/suspense
new world
a goodbye to _____
final questions of commencement
seizing the day
open to suggestions
trying to hold on
not able to face it
carrying on
impetuosity
repeating history

"Oh, the places you'll go!" (Dr. Seuss)
in the interim
hocus pocus
head over heels
bankruptcy
life in TV commercials
frustration(s) of the final hour
being tempted to do something one doesn't want to do
expression of love
dehumanization of sex
searching for Atlantis
the kindness of strangers
holocaust
promise, no delivery
born every minute
repository of records found 1,000 years from now
never made public until now
the perfect arrangement
best in the West
acquiring a new name
an old (or ancient) mystery solved
unrecognized, unrewarded
short reflection(s), long ideas
private hall of fame of local characters
"Et tu, Brute?"
surprising discoveries about one's ancestry
genetic destiny
the death or decline of _____
walking away from the impossible
out o' sight
a historian of the _____ building
the last challenge
admitting the truth at last
seeing the light
my own crystal ball
third chance
three wishes
witness to _____
making history
monkey business
tourist trap
walking tall/walking short
slinking away
crawling back
individualism as defined in the future
being told to leave home
whitewashing
backfire of ploy
lights, camera, action
beyond the limits

the dignity of independence

recognition at last

switching over

challenge of the spirit

unauthorized biography

oversympathetic, considering what happened

the real beginnings of humanity

not by choice

the white(d) sepulcher

early responsibilities

bitter truth(s)

just between friends

a house divided

mission/vision accomplished

brief encounter(s)

a voice still heard

controlling destiny

cabbages and kings

memoirs

easy way out

the price of glory

best rival, best friend

last refuge

too awed to do anything about it

long-distance dating

giving away secrets

keeping secrets

those forgotten by time

afraid to let go/afraid not to let go

still at large

born exile

all shook up

darkness, my old friend

behind the wheel/behind the eight ball

shadow-boxing

my doppelganger

armed and dangerous

history as it happens

heaven-sent

no closed doors

unwanted

curiosity about _____

the wrong person

secret life/double life/secret lives

war between _____ and _____

rescue squad

_____'s mad idea

my Oedipus complex

a report from _____

the last hurrah

the last fling

looking backward and forward

the secret word

discovery of the first wheel

discovery of fire

discovery of speech

stay of execution

forgone but not forgotten

before I was five

due to circumstances beyond our control

conversation about a movie, a book, a show on television

going forward

disowned, disinherited

disappearing ships, planes, persons

when I was old

surrendering

on a quest

hunkering down

turning the tables

bystander

returning

king of the hill

short but glorious career

hair on end

but waking up

sour grapes

lifeline

the flesh and the spirit

long journey, bad roads

marked man/woman

unsigned

riders to the sea

witch watch

parents and children

seeking a long-lost relative

first sighting

tracking someone, as in a spy movie

the three strangers

if I were not alive

a thousand miles of mountain road, a thousand miles of desert sand

"Look on my works, ye mighty, and despair." (Shelley)

conversation between clerks in a department store

going backward

taking the plunge

doing what is expected of you, not doing what is expected of you

covering an escape

letting off steam

the beginning of consciousness

the learning tree
captive of time
bull ring
the search for a missing letter, notebook, diary, etc.
for auld lang syne
the wrong connection
a moment's surrender
cross-conversation confusing the main point
family reunion requiring introductions
Melchior's telling about following the star
words, thoughts, and feelings of the first people on earth
ancient astronauts
the road to _____
morally right, legally wrong
night in a _____
not even for money
outlaw with a cause
rebel without a clue
conversation in a barber shop or a beauty shop
for whom the bell gongs
one day late
a tortoise that lost the race
desire or will power that goes beyond death
the incredible journey
the ringing phone
overnight
returning home after many generations away
first theme
a rock speaking of its history
a homeless person insulted by someone for his or her
    dress, manner, or mere presence
prehistoric hunt
consequence of someone's not reading a letter in time
a dream of someone who helps carry the crucifixion
    crosses up a hill only to find that he is among those
    to be crucified
Socratic dialogue in a fictional piece
appointment/date/liaison
account by a prisoner of the last day in a concentration
    camp, after the Germans had fled
conditions of an island prison
having a party of one
paradise lost/regained
a criminal sentenced to be someone's butler
a friendly relationship between a millionaire and his/her
    chauffeur
gold fever
invisible people
trouble between the weatherperson and the movie critic
    on the TV news
money in the mattress

sibling against sibling
a "now" story
coming back to life
coming back as another person or thing
the crazy mirror (title of a children's book)
getting through somehow
something to win over
birds of a feather
a fascination for the abominable
the switch/the sting
a child's trip unaccompanied by adults
a thousand years, a thousand days
falling in love against one's will
awake in the dark
prolonged attack(s)
without benefit of clergy
the seasons of _____
deadlines
leave cancelled
getting out after a long time
together again
going home
the first meeting in the Garden of Eden
asking the unaskable
parent talking to child
rematch
once upon a time
guests of the _____
things that set off memories
the world according to _____
someone at the door
as up they grew
long, dark night
an experience remembered more often than any other
    one
any way the wind blows
rites of passage—birth, first love, maturity, death
carnival of souls
a reprieve after many years of being wronged
surprise ending
rewriting a narrative poem as narrative prose
a tent meeting
a medicine show
facing a hard race
from the files
if I should die before I wake . . .
a kind of glory
futureworld
instant fame
a thankless child, as in Shakespeare's *King Lear*

snowstorm

dialogue including a portrait of someone who makes a threat to leave someone else

making the first phone call

special cruise

eternity versus the moment

out of time

omen

preaching fire and brimstone

forbidden alliance

the source of a proverb

the Mexican legend of "La Llorona"

the relationship between good fortune and ignorance

a talk with someone who has lived the history

cameo

the reader over your shoulder

the star in a grain of dust

scenes from next (week's/month's/year's) (book/movie/ TV show)

diving for treasure, real or metaphorical

a peculiar case

maze(s)

coming in, going out

coming out

the missing piece of the jigsaw puzzle

someone in a story absorbed by a mirror, a book, or a piece of music

a single subject treated in various ways and for different purposes

same story, different points of view

a day, a dog, an argument, and a reunion

writing a story from the theme of a poem

close to, but not a part of, nature

out of season

short stay in _____

the mind's eye

the mind's I

inside the universe of a snowflake

behind the sealed (tomb, door, passage)

#309

ghost story

a fable/parable for our time

a touch of class

rooms without floors

in touch with the sublime

hunting with a camera instead of a rifle

refusing to leave the solitary places

something seen in early England by one of Caesar's legions

the Ouija board

the Will of the Wind

out past curfew

costly encounter

police officer taking a report from a witness and from the accused

never giving up

getting to know the world by walking

making a deal

link with eternity

wandering all our ways (phrase from Sir Walter Raleigh)

just an act, not the real thing

a proverb refuted

unraveling lies

foundling at the doorstep

legend of the Blarney Stone

no room at the inn

a feeling of place

the pattern in the mosaic

friendship between human and animal

looking at what _____ has done/is doing

something seen on the road

standing on the head

interest in the news

local witches

born into the same life again

misunderstanding causing humorous results in a foreign country

first day of school

first day at a new school

last day of school

the hour that stretches

forgiveness

breaking away

setting forth

coming back

"How could you?!"

three's a crowd

any day now

keepin' on keepin' on

deer in the headlights

finding strength

reason to believe

a hard-earned day

with or without you

the great divide

bridging the gap

only connecting

a conversation that changed everything

if I'd lived in the _____ century

if I lived in _____ (another country)

atonement

losing my religion
overheard
drive on
ain't no stoppin'
same as it ever was
new day dawning
when the going gets tough
meeting the day
overcome by events
blind spot
here and now
undelivered letter
busted!
wrongly accused
"Guilty, Your Honor"
keeping up appearances
telling it like it is
in the nick of time
outside looking in
inside looking out
reaching out
reaching in
story in real-time
any objections?
honest I do
beast of burden
blood, sweat, and tears
like a butterfly
coming to blows
cleaning up the mess
at last
behind bars
working it out
walking the walk
peace is every step
keepin' the faith
ships passing in the night
close encounters
on the brink
The End Zone is Near!
The End Times Are Near!
Step right over here, folks!
Do Not Disturb
It started with . . .
The door swung open . . . .
Hear That Lonesome Whistle Blow
It Happened One Night
"The Road Not Taken" (Robert Frost)
The Way It Should Have Been
A Long Way from Home

"Here Lies the World: RIP"
out-of-body experience
"heaven lies about us" (William Wordsworth)
some enchanted evening
leaving "Footprints in the sands of time" (Longfellow)
Time Stands Still
Five Ways to Simplify Your Life
meeting on the Net
trucking on
the good soldier
rock on
Stepping into the Time Machine
I was there when _____ happened and this is what I saw (e.g., at the Great Chicago Fire, the Great Plague in London, the Allied landing in Normandy).
When I was born as _____ . . .
our eyes met across a crowded room
if only . . . .
in the shadow of _____
waiting in vain
riding on the subway
a funny thing happened
"Cast your bread upon the waters." (Bible)
a "magnificent obsession"

Questions, Titles, Assignments, and Brainstormers for the Short Story, Novel, Novella, and Fiction Sketch

Write as if you were someone else, e.g., someone who has had an experience in a prisoner-of-war camp.

Such love, so well-expressed, is rather unusual in these times.

_____ is paradise enough.

Fictionalize an event as seen by different eyes' views, for example, by a detective, a small child, a judge, a newspaper reporter.

Begin a story with the picture of a family walking along the dusty road during the Depression. The mother and father have a pole which they are carrying mounted on their shoulders; on the pole their clothes and the clothes of their four children are drying in the sun. Take the story wherever it goes.

How useful is a hunch?

The more problems you have, the more alive you are, it has been said.

Imagine where humanity can go after our current evolution.

No one escapes feeling guilty about something.

Space explorers may not find the earth inhabited on their return.

What would a space visitor to the earth most want to talk about? What would we most want to ask him/her/it?

The journey is more important than the destination.

"It is better to remain silent and appear dumb than to speak and remove all doubt."—popular proverb

"I do not believe in using women in combat, because females are too fierce."—Margaret Mead

"An event has happened, upon which it is difficult to speak, and impossible to be silent."—Edmund Burke

What will it be like if/when you graduate/join the Peace Corps/enlist in the military/get married/make a million dollars?

What would you have done if you had been a young adult during World War II?

"O holy simplicity!" said John Huss the martyr while at the stake.

"We are always the same age inside."—Gertrude Stein

"You can't be brave if you've only had wonderful things happen to you."—Mary Tyler Moore

"War is the unfolding of miscalculations."—Barbara Tuchman

What will be found in the time capsule for the year 2788?

How would you live if you had great personal wealth?

What did you miss out on when you were young?

"When I am an old woman I shall wear purple" says writer Jenny Joseph. What will you do?

"Phenomenal Woman, / That's me" (Maya Angelou). Write about yourself as a phenomenal person.

Is all well that ends well?

She was so confused she didn't know if she was going to bed or getting up.

Seeing _____ again brought back the memory of _____.

Whatever happened to _____?

Write about someone who has developed a self-image that clashes with his or her hometown.

"Hometown boy [or girl] makes good." Write about a celebrity returning home.

Write a story about the Clementine of the song.

Write a narrative of someone happy with natural learning rather than formal learning.

Write a fictional narrative about a young person having a first experience of doubt.

Write a fictional account of a young person covering up what he or she really feels.

Write about a fearful moment, such as a close call or a brush with death.

Write a tall story intended to sound convincing.

Show fictionally how a common danger brings people together.

"Where the arrow falls, bury me."—Robin Hood

"You can't rob me," said the grocer to the young man with the gun held shakily in his hand. "Your buddy there with you robbed me two hours ago."

Waving at the train was one of the delights of my childhood.

Trace the history of someone found alone and injured at the side of the road.

The hotel Maid squinted against the coarse daylight, and, shading her eyes with a white hand spotted with huge, burnt-brown freckles, said, "Sorry, no strangers allowed here."

"It was the best of times; it was the worst of times." (Charles Dickens)

"Call me Ishmael" (Herman Melville). Choose any mythic figure and write creatively about that person.

Falling asleep for five years and waking up to find _____.

I (would, would not) like to look into the future.

Dip into a dictionary of folklore and write a story suggested by one of the motifs you find there.

Many things might happen between now and then.

Write a fictional narrative developed by dialogue that reveals cause and effect.

"My life's an open book. Time and again I have had things happen to me that belong in the pages of a best-selling novel. I will tell you about one of these earth-shaking incidents." (The writer may want to entitle this story or novel with the title of a famous book or movie. The possibilities of writing with comic irony—that is, saying humorously precisely the opposite of what is meant—should be explored.)

Not being there—that was the story of my life at the moment.

"What happens to a dream deferred? Does it dry up like a raisin in the sun?" (Langston Hughes). Write a story of a dream deferred.

Write a progression, outline, or frame for a long narrative.

Where would you like to explore?

Find an appropriate news story in a newspaper or magazine and rewrite it as a first-person narrative.

Take the title of a song and use it as the title of a story having the same theme. Examples: "All Apologies," "Spirits in the Material World," "My Baby Just Cares for Me," "Delia's Gone," "Harvest Moon," "Man on the Corner," "Me and Bobby McGee," "Yesterday," "When I'm Sixty-Four," "Starry, Starry Night," "Lift Every Voice and Sing."

The man at the table in the corner began to answer his own question.

Every day is (opening day/the first day/the last day).

He hesitated, then said, "No sir."

Write a story in which the sequence of events is critically important. Possible subjects: a student demonstration, a certain process in which you participated, or an important cultural or historical event.

The truest kind of courage comes from defeating a mountainous fear.

I find happiness in the simplest things.

Put together with other writers—each one taking a certain part—a novel on a certain historical incident.

"I want what I want when I want it."—Henry Blossom

There I was, right in the middle of _____.

Then I got to thinking, and I decided that maybe he was right after all.

There wasn't a thing I could do about it . . .

No way was I going to let this happen . . .

Then, in my peripheral vision, I saw it, and things would never be the same again.

It was too late—you can't unfire a gun.

Prom night wasn't the best or worst night of my life. But it gave me this story that I will never stop telling . . .

It was the first time I'd talked to my father that way in months, maybe longer.

I would have told my mother, but I thought she would never understand. Now I see it a little differently.

I guess fenccs don't always make good neighbors, after all.

I always knew there was something about her.

I never would have guessed he would do something like that.

An urgent knock startled me from my newspaper. When I opened the door, I could hardly believe my eyes.

You wouldn't have known it from looking at us, or listening to us, but we were brothers, and that meant I had to do something to help.

I could feel it in the air that night.

At the time, it seemed like the right thing to do.

My advice to you: Never win the lottery.

I had never been outside my own country. I was scared, but I told myself I'd meet the challenge. I turned to face my hosts . . .

Each decision had been logical, justified. And yet the whole thing had ended in disaster. Why?

There's no single day on which I "grew up." But that Saturday was a definite step in the process.

It's never too late.

I was standing on a street corner in Budapest; I didn't know the language and I'd just lost my Hungarian-English dictionary.

"The rebels are attacking," someone shouted.

"I could have sworn the gas station was here."

Human Beings and Types for Creative Writing Subjects

fictional self-portrait

a born eccentric

someone quaint

the class clown

narrative of Thomas Jefferson's trying to decide on the wording of the Declaration of Independence

caricature of a character out of a famous movie or book

interview with the president (when he/she is ten years old)

narrative about someone who garners automatic respect from individuals and groups

the hunter

Coleridge's Kubla Khan, the person (not the poem)

tomorrow's (hero/friend/enemy/stranger)

duel between Hamilton and Burr

stranger in a strange land

show-off

merchant

out-of-towner

God in the process of Creation—God as living character, perhaps an artist, who needs to create for fulfillment

someone who knows only penitentiary life

"I regained my freedom with a sigh" (Byron). Write about someone adjusting to life outside prison.

someone who is lucky, told about so as to suggest that more than luck is involved

someone who unknowingly reveals oneself while telling someone else's story

someone brought to life by way of a secret diary

a character from an ad

a remarkable person

a modern-day Icarus

the death of Socrates

a person feeling compelled to tell his or her story

a human being's first meeting with another human being

my roots

buccaneer

shadow-seeker(s)

practical joker

Lord Randall, the figure in the ballad

an animal-like person

a person-like animal

a novelistic character transplanted from the novel to a story by you

someone, real or imaginary, that the world ought to know about

someone who becomes associated both in name and behavior with what he/she does

a character from literature placed in an uncustomary context: Humpty Dumpty as a decathlon hero, for example

the widow(er) of _____

the leader of the expedition

your life as a movie (perhaps with you watching it)

keeper(s) of the flame

martyr

dual role/multiple masks

a mother or father, presented as a character in a story

a legacy from _____

someone of your invention who is involved in public life, whether in politics, entertainment, military, sports, or teaching—told about in a long comic history beginning, "The truth about _____ has yet to be told."

characters having dialogue drawn from their separate books

a well-known person, in a story having nothing to do with what he or she is famous for

your best friend

the person you like least, in a story sympathetic to him or her

your sibling

a favorite uncle or aunt

your favorite grandparent

your most difficult relative

a young adult who is dying

a young adult who has narrowly averted a tragic death

a high school student who has just become a parent

a student who abstains from sex before or outside of marriage

a curious child

a curious grandmother or grandfather

a courageous parent

a police officer

a teacher

a social worker in a troubled part of town

a student whose family has fallen on hard times

a rich boy or girl

a student whose family has known nothing but hard times

your boyfriend or girlfriend

your parent(s)

a school principal

your family's plumber

how Dave Barry might describe a family gathering

Creative Language

advertising voice of a person not seen

a letter from jail, camp, college, the army

a prize-winning essay with nothing but clichés

hackneyed proverbs rewritten with fresh language and depth

pastoral(s)

book epigraph or dedication

the dozens

signifying

talking and testifying

"leaning and depending"

The Play (on Words) is the Thing

winged words

singing telegram

stand-up comedian

TV theme song

scene from your life rendered in Shakespearean dialogue

scene from your life rendered in rap

conversation(s) in the closet

famous people arguing with one another from their quotations on a certain issue

a parody of a superintendent telling what *curriculum* means

spoonerism(s)

witty words

deliberate gobbledygook or double-talk

rap song (or parody of the genre)

country song (or parody of the genre)

punk rock song (or parody of the genre)

operatic aria (or parody of the genre)

children's song (or parody of the genre)

note found in a bottle

note found in the trash

satire on sightings of UFO's or Bigfoot

a letter to a newspaper thanking someone for helping you in your campaign

a parody of a scandal sheet

an exam spoof

infomercial spoof (selling something most people already own)

"Think before you hit send": Story of an E-mail Indiscretion

parody of an e-mail exchange between friends with emotions running high

the discrepancies between movie subtitles and sound tracks

useless words passed off as useful ones

writ of "habeas escapus" as if written by fleeing inmate

a letter to the editor about being ripped-off

speeches each consisting of one long sentence

a narrative constructed as a series of images presented in haiku form

a narrative in which pseudo-learning shows itself by pseudo-language

a parody of self-conscious purple prose

a parody imitating the language and mannerisms suggested by popular self-help psychology books

a parody using advertising language to sell Zen, pragmatism, Christianity, or another tradition . . .

a parody of "Rime of the Ancient Mariner"

a pompous speech by a politician, a school superintendent, a head of a fraternal organization, or a business executive a report of an incident in various modes: in the style of newspaper journalism, in elaborate diction, in oversimplified expression

a parody of psychoanalytical language explaining body language

a parody of language that says nothing, used for writing a book report or book review for a book you have not read

a story, poem, or song using an invented vocabulary of nouns, verbs, adverbs, and adjectives

Write a comic-satiric advertisement for someone who sells term papers over the Internet.

Describe a non-Biblical scene with Biblical language.

Parody of a product recall letter intended to fulfill the company's legal obligation to notify customers of a dangerous defect without actually worrying them or even letting them understand clearly what you are saying.

Offer proof of Santa Claus in extremely scientific jargon.

Write a sketch showing the language of righteous indignation—especially to show how impressive, and therefore effective, such language can be.

Read a certain notable style of writing and parody it. You might, to begin, want to read James Thurber's parody of Henry James— "The Beast in the Dingle"— and write your own parody of James.

Choose a common subject for parody and parody some famous lines from various poets.

Read passages from several authors—e.g., George Orwell, J. D. Salinger, Gwendolyn Brooks, Ernest Hemingway, Emily Dickinson, William Faulkner, or Sandra Cisneros—and imitate them in their methods of moving along in their narrative writing.

Rework a number of proverbs around a certain theme. The following example is a reworking of one of the most familiar proverbs: "You can send a student to school, but you can't make him or her learn."

Song and Poetry

Spoon River epitaph

Untitled

a song of myself

a song of butterflies

a song using the theme from a folktale or an old religious book

a translation of a poem into English from a second language you know

haiku

a ballad

An Ode to My Shoestrings

a ballad of "La Belle Dame Sans Merci" (John Keats) using personal experience

a song of everyone

a song about a song

a song using the music of an old hymn

a song about not singing anymore

a poem about a poem that tells of something you might have thought of yourself

A New Song

a song about singing

a song with new verses consistent with the theme and form of an old ballad

a poem *not* about love/hate/beauty

a song of pride in _____

a song to mourn the passing of something

a commemorative poem

a song of the open road

a song about the call of the faraway hills

a comic song about what's at the end of the rainbow

Creative Writing for a Children's Audience

Your version of a story from *The Jungle Book.*

children and the stars

Circus at Dawn

Day of the Rotten Tomatoes

Runaway!

Run Away!

rectangles and circles

an oversized mole residence for human beings

There's Nothing Under the Bed After All

There *Is* Something Under the Bed, and It's Really Cool!

a trickster story in which the trickster is tricked

a story or poem about what happens when one enters a fairy tale

a story that responds to the question, "What do you like stories to be about?"

The Orange Eggplant

The Day the Number 3 Went Missing

The Private Kingdom

The Enchanted Forest

A Dog's Devotion

In the Cloud(s)

The Woman or Man in the Moon

A Living Camera

a view of what happened when the world began

an experience of *déjà vu*

a story of a dollar

an independent excursion

moving to the city

moving to the country

moving to a new country

a glove as a character

a mischievous turtle

a monster's story (titled "Monstory") told by the monster

a fantasy in which concrete details are used

a story about a hat that has feelings and does not want to be discarded

The Big Bad Bully Learns a Lesson

Keshia Goes to Kindergarten

Nasser's Nightmares

Henry's First Haircut

a story about a dream house (into which one goes in order to have dreams)

a poem that responds to the question, "What do you like poems to be about?"

In the Sky

a story or poem telling how a certain person got his name/her name

a view of what happens when the world ends

a story or poem answering the question, "Where were you the year before you were born?"

a story or poem affirming there were, and are, unicorns

variation on a nursery rhyme

a haircut misadventure

trouble with pinking shears

Saturday cartoon(s)

baskets as characters

a story about the king of the barnyard

a story about a dream into which one can enter at will

a story or poem about a comic-strip character

a cat is lost, then found

A Hairy, Scary Hallowe'en

The Unwise Owl

a pet's life story in a story or poem

a day when the little things made all the difference

a day when something big didn't make a difference after all

Life of a Tumbleweed

A Legend Relived

an unconventional letter to Santa Claus

fair-minded letter from Santa Claus to a child who has behaved very badly

a story or poem putting fairy tale or folktale characters in unfamiliar roles

new ending, old story

unfinished story to be completed

a collaboration in which you and a fellow student (or several) each write a segment of the story

The Little Engine That Couldn't

The Little Engine Whose Friends Helped Out

The Little Engine That Could But Chose Not To

The House That Went to Sea

a stowaway on a ship

The Dog on the Airplane

And then, guess what happened?

The mouse peeped out of the cupboard . . .

Adapt a children's story from another culture to your context.

Take a fairy tale and give it a twist, e.g., the story of Cinder Fella.

Other Creative Exercises

Write spontaneously and without direction on one of these: dog, brick, tree, mountain stream.

See how many words you can write—without stopping, without thinking of order, without worrying about a grade—in fifteen minutes.

Write a fictional piece or a poem that severely cuts out details but still evokes a purpose.

Write a character sketch using understatement or overstatement.

Write about the process of writing a short story—the original impression, inspiration, and thought, the talking to the mirror or computer to push you along, and so forth.

Live what you write about (but in writing). That is, become the person you write about or re-create; this, as better to understand her/him as a character or a subject.

Write a new proverb (one that is suggested by an old one) and accompany it with an explanation of its origin and meaning.

For various basic techniques of creative writing, study and imitate one or more of the following: Chinua Achebe, Lord Byron, Miguel de Cervantes, Anton Chekhov, Stephen Crane, Hector St. John de Crèvecoeur, Jonathan Edwards, T. S. Eliot, , Thomas Hardy, Nathaniel Hawthorne, Langston Hughes, Barbara Kingsolver, Doris Lessing, Toni Morrison, Flannery O'Connor, Edgar Allan Poe, Katherine Anne Porter, William Shakespeare, Salman Rushdie, Aleksandr Solzhenitsyn, Leo Tolstoy, Mark Twain, Eudora Welty, Walt Whitman, Virginia Woolf.

Write an annoyingly happy stream of consciousness.

Write a heartbreaking stream of consciousness.

Write an angst-filled stream of consciousness.

Write a stream of consciousness that is confident without being boastful.

Write a highly dramatic and self-consciously profound discussion of a very ordinary item or event—for example, the existence of facial tissue, the placing of a letter in a mailbox, or a dog scratching its ear.

Write an egregiously understated account of a truly dramatic event.

Write a profile of the person whom you imagine created this book of topics.

Write a press release announcing a new television program (sitcom, drama, or reality show) based on your daily life.

Fun with the Bulwer-Lytton Fiction Contest

When writing creative fiction, watch out for opening lines that are melodramatic or overblown. A classic example of this is the famous (or infamous) "It was a dark and stormy night." This line has in fact inspired a fiction contest on the subject—just how dreadful can an opening line be? See the Bulwer-Lytton Fiction Contest <http://www.bulwer-lytton.com/>*, and just for fun, try writing your own preposterous opening line for your turbid novel, effulgent with purple prose. Doing so will help you to reflect critically on your choice of words and on writing creatively.

* Web sites are likely to change or disappear. If you cannot find the contest at this URL, a name search will help you locate it. Otherwise, hard copy versions may be available through your local library.

12 CRITICAL WRITING

What Critical Writing Is

Generally, critical writing sets out to evaluate or to analyze a work of art. This analysis may be attempted in any number of ways, but for our purposes here we will divide critical writing into its two basic types—the theoretical and the practical. The theoretical concerns itself with general notions about the value of art as a whole (see Aristotle's *Poetics,* to cite one classic example), while the practical evaluates particular works, writers, styles, and so forth, in terms of whatever aesthetic theory the critic may hold.

Critical writing and theories of criticism have been articulated in many different ways by many civilizations. In English studies, literary theory in the last century alone has undergone radical transformations, resulting in a whole spectrum of approaches that range from the textual and structural to those grounded in culture, gender, or political ideology. In fact, the whole notion of what constitutes literature or a text has come into question, so that, as literary critic Terry Eagleton says, "literary theory can handle Bob Dylan just as well as John Milton" (*Literary Theory: An Introduction*).

Teachers are encouraged to suggest different approaches to their students when they analyze a text. As Deborah Appleman puts it, "literary theories can sharpen one's vision and provide alternative ways of seeing"; indeed, "these multiple ways of seeing have become vital skills in our increasingly diverse classrooms as we explore the differences between and among us, what separates us and what binds us together" (*Critical Encounters in High School English: Teaching Literary Theory to Adolescents*).

How to Write Criticism

It will be evident from the preceding discussion that critical writing is yet another mode that is complex because of the many approaches it opens up to the writer. Probably the beginning critic should settle for a simple analysis of the content and form of a given piece of writing and an evaluation of how the form and content work, or fail to work, together to achieve the desired effect. He or she would do well to stick close to the work at hand and to document rigorously from that text any criticisms made. This disciplined approach should eventually make for concrete, vigorously thought out, and fully felt critical writing, and it proves valuable for other types of writing as well.

It might also be wise to let the specific critical approach—or combination of approaches—be dictated in part by the work itself. For an obviously autobiographical novel, e.g., James Joyce's *A Portrait of the Artist as a Young Man,* a biographical tack might be of some value. On the other hand, Kate Chopin's novel *The Awakening* would call for a feminist reading. And studying Toni Morrison's novels would demand a consideration of race and identity.

Locating Subjects for Critical Writing

The topics in this section were listed primarily with literary criticism in mind. However, many of them may be applied to criticism in other disciplines—music, painting, film, architecture, photography, almost anything. Indeed, such works can be viewed as "texts" of their own sort which can be approached through the same kinds of critical lenses (to use Appleman's metaphor) that one might use to explore a work of literature. The themes presented here generally lend themselves to practical criticism rather than to the theoretical. This is the type of criticism most students are called upon to write and also the type they are most likely to come upon in newspapers and magazines.

We have seen many times over how thoroughly the kinds of writing outlined in this book are related. This is especially true of critical writing. Surprisingly, even research-and-report writing assumes an important place here—a survey of almost any library's collection of critical works will reveal that some of the most exacting and often vitally written criticism has been scholarly. Process, classification/division, exposition, argumentation, definition, creative writing—any one of these is of rudimentary value in writing criticism. In fact, critical writing seems an appropriate place to end this book. A working familiarity with the kinds of writing dealt with before will cement a reliable foundation on which to write critically—not, one would hope, to mock and tear, but to carry forward for us all the wonder and love of language, and to enable students to look critically at the world they live in and to be constructively engaged with that world.

Common Themes in Literature for Critical Analysis

adventure

adversity

aging and the aged

alcoholism

alienation

ambiguity/ambivalence

ambition

angst

animals

appearance versus reality

aristocracy

art and artists

beauty

beliefs and customs

betrayal

Biblical types

birth, fertility, and rebirth

borders and border crossings (cultural, physical, political, psychological, social)

boredom and malaise

bribery

bureaucracy

capital punishment

change and progress

chaos

charity

childlikeness, childishness, and immaturity

children

choice and decision

Christ, Christ complex, Christianity, and martyr complex

civilization

class conflict, class relations

clergy

collectivity

colonialism

colonization

coming of age

common destiny

communication (or lack of it)

community (or lack of it)

complacency

comprehensiveness and infinity

confession

conflict

conscience

conservatism

consolation

convention

conversion

counterparts and counterpoints

country versus city

courage and cowardice

crime and punishment

cruelty and violence

cultural concerns (traditions, differences, relations)

cultural politics

curse

dance

danger

death

deconstruction

deduction

defeat and failure

demons and devils

dependence

depression, despair, discontent, and disillusionment

despair

destruction and destructiveness

determinism, chance, fortune, fate, and indifferent universe

devotion

difference

discovery, including self-discovery

diversity

divorce

domination, enslavement, and suppression

double-character, analogue, and reflection of self in others

dreaming, dreams, imaginings, and fancies

drug addiction

duty

emotional disturbance

empowerment

emptiness

endurance

enlightenment

ennui

entitlement

envy

epiphany

escape

essentialism

ethnic identity

ethos

evil eye

the examined (or the unexamined) life

exile

existential angst
expediency
exploitation
faith and loss of faith
falsity, pretense, and artificiality
fame
family, fatherhood, and motherhood
fanaticism
farming
Faust(ianism)
fear and terror
feminism
folly
forgiveness
freedom
free will and willpower
Freudianism
friendship
frugality
fulfillment
gambling
games, contests, sports, competition, and trickery
gender (individual identity, limitations of social concep-
    tions of gender)
God and creation
God and Humanity
Godliness
good and evil
government
greed
grief and remorse
grotesquerie
group behavior
guilt
happiness
heaven, including paradise on earth
hell
helplessness
heroes, heroines, and leaders
holiday
home
hope
hospitality as a social custom
hubris
human and animal
the human condition
human frailty
humanity and human understanding
human limitation/human potential
hunting

hypnotism
hypocrisy and duplicity
ideality, perfection, and exemplariness
identity
identity politics
illusion and innocence
immorality
imperialism
imprisonment
independence
individuality
initiation, experience, manhood, and womanhood
innocence; the loss of innocence
instinct versus reason and heart versus reason
jealousy
journey, travel, excursion, and voyage, including
    psychological journey
joy
justice
killing
law
learning, schooling, and knowledge
leave-taking
liberation
life, *joie de vivre,* and life spirit
life (the meaning of)
loneliness and aloneness
loss
love and affection
loyalty
luck
machine versus humanity
macrocosm
manhood
marginalization
marriage
master/servant and employer/employee
materialism
maturation
memory
mercy
metaphysical experience
militarism and military life
mind and matter
miracle
mischief
mob psychology
moral code
mortality
multiculturalism

music and song

the mysterious stranger

mystery

mystical experience

natural force and natural disaster

nature and humanity

obsession, monomania, compulsion, and habit

oppression

optimism

origins of the world, universe

pacifism

parent/child relationship, adult/child relationship

past, present, future

patriotism

persistence and perseverance

pessimism

playing God

pleasure

politics

postcolonialism

postmodernism

poverty

power relationships

prejudice

pride

primitivism

profession

promise

prophecy

prostitution

quest

race and racial attitudes

reality and realness

rebellion

redemption

reincarnation and immortality

relativism

religion

repentance

rescue

resistance, rebellion, and revolution

resolution

respectability

responsibility

return

revenge and retribution

revising history

revolution

ritual

rivalry

sacrifice

sadism/masochism

sanity, insanity, and senility

scapegoat and victim

science as savior or downfall

seafaring

search

secrecy and secret world

self-assertion

self-awareness

self-deception

self-empowerment

selfishness

sexuality and sexual conquest

sickness

silence

social criticism

social status

societal or cultural differences

societal pressures

society in change

sophistication

soul and soul mate

spiritual crisis

stoicism

suffering

suicide

supernatural, magic, fairies, and ghosts

survival

suspicion

technology's benefits and limitations

theft and ransom

time and circumstances, timelessness, eternity, time and space

tolerance

tradition and insularity

understanding

uniqueness

unity and human solidarity

universality and microcosm

value/value system

verbal traditions of specific communities/cultures

visions

voice in the wilderness

voice(s) of the self

war

the wasted life, the empty life

wealth and the wealthy

womanhood, feminism, and the rights of women

youth

This book was typeset in Gill Sans, Gill Sans Extra Bold, and
Times New Roman by Tom Jaczak.

Typefaces used on the cover were Arial, Arial Rounded MT Bold,
and Gill Sans Extra Bold.

The book was printed on 50-lb. Husky Offset by
IPC Communication Services.